Winchcombe

A history of the Cotswold borough

Winchcombe

A history of the Cotswold borough

D. N. Donaldson

'Winchelcombe is set in the roots of Cotiswolde'

JOHN LELAND, 'ITINERARY'

THE WYCHWOOD PRESS

Our books may be ordered from bookshops or (post free) from
The Wychwood Press, Alder House, Market Street, Charlbury, OX7 3PH
01608 811969

Credit card orders should be phoned or faxed to 01689 870437 or
01608 811969

Please send for our free catalogue

First published in 2001 by
The Wychwood Press
an imprint of Jon Carpenter Publishing
Alder House, Market Street, Charlbury, Oxfordshire OX7 3PH

e-mail: wychwood@joncarpenter.co.uk

ISBN 1 902279 12 3

Printed in England by J. W. Arrowsmith Ltd., Bristol

CONTENTS

This book is dedicated to the memory of my mother and father

LIST OF PLATES

Plate 1: Hailes Street, Winchcombe (c. 1900): 'king John's houses' have front-facing gables on right, half way along

Plate 2: a horse fair in North Street (c. 1910)

Plate 3: house supposedly built on abbot Richard Kidderminster's instructions (c. 1500-1520)

Plate 4: old house owned by John Oakey's father, North Street

Plate 5: parish church's interior (facing chancel) before 1872

Plate 6: parish church's interior (facing tower arch) before 1872

Plate 7: parish church's exterior before 1872

Plate 8: The Grape Vine inn, North Street (c. 1874)

Plate 9: Emma Dent inaugurates Winchcombe's piped water supply, 1887

Plate 10: Marquis of Granby inn, North Street – a Victorian jubilee

Plate 11: The Presbytery, Chandos Street (formerly Chandos grammar school)

Plate 12: Thomas C. Webb and pupils at Chandos grammar school

Plate 13: William Smith's infants' school, Abbey Terrace (c. 1860)

Plate 14: Three Gables, Gloucester Street, before 1882 rebuilding

Plate 15: Emma Dent in the library, Sudeley castle

Plate 16: G. W. R. motorised bus at Winchcombe station, 1905

Plate 17: the grotesques, Winchcombe parish church

Plate 18: North Street, looking north (c. 1922)

Plate 19: Winchcombe flour mill – the buildings

Plate 20: Winchcombe flour mill – the mill race

LIST OF PLANS

Plan 1: the kingdom of the Hwicce (Alecto Historical Editions)

Plan 2: hundreds of Greston and Holford at Domesday (John S. Moore)

Plan 3: Winchcombe's market area, 1066-1100 (John S. Moore)

Plan 4: late medieval Winchcombe (Dr. S. R. Bassett)

Plan 5: street plan of Winchcombe in about 1500 (D. N. Donaldson)

Plan 6: creation of Abbey Terrace in 1835 (Winchcombe highway surveyors)

ACKNOWLEDGEMENTS

T
he amateur local historian could not produce any worthwhile account of Winchcombe's past without help and advice from many people. These acknowledgements gratefully recognise the help I have received and, in some cases, permission to refer to published works or information in privately owned sources.

My greatest debt is to Dr. Steven Bassett, senior lecturer in the Department of Medieval History, University of Birmingham, who generously read and commented on draft chapters 3 to 11, and thus enabled me to improve greatly on the finalised account of Winchcombe's Anglo-Saxon and medieval history. Additionally, Dr. Bassett's numerous learned articles and contributions to books illuminating Anglo-Saxon and medieval history have helped me immeasurably in understanding the town's past.

I owe a posthumous debt to four authors. The first is the Rev. David Royce, vicar of Nether Swell parish from 1850 until his death in 1902, who undertook the herculean task of editing the cartulary (land charters and other legal documents) of Winchcombe abbey and arranging for its publication in two volumes entitled '*Landboc sive Registrum Monasterii de Winchelcumba*'. The numerous footnote references to '*Landboc*' indicate how greatly I have relied on this work. Secondly, Emma Dent's antiquarian interests led her to produce the one-volume '*Annals of Winchcombe and Sudeley*' in 1877, which can still be profitably read. Her inspiration in starting '*The Winchcombe and Sudeley Record*' in January 1890 also ensured that much detailed information about Winchcombe's past was permanently preserved. Thirdly, Eleanor Adlard's '*Winchcombe Cavalcade*' and '*A Short History of the Postlip Mill, Winchcombe*' help to illuminate local topography and customs. Fourthly, '*The History of Winchcombe Abbey*' by the Rev. Gordon Haigh, curate of the parish church of St Peter, Winchcombe, for four years during the 1930s, helps in understanding the abbey's influence on the borough.

Especial thanks are due to the staff of Gloucestershire libraries for their unfailing help. This includes the staff of the County Record Office in Gloucester for the production of numerous documents for research purposes; and Barbara Herod and her colleagues in Winchcombe library for obtaining books and maintaining much useful research material. I also gratefully acknowledge the County Archivist's permission to refer to, and quote from, documents archived in the Record Office, as indicated in footnotes with the prefix 'GRO'.

Staff in Evesham library have been most helpful in providing access to the microfilmed record of '*The Evesham Journal and Four Shires Advertiser*' (to give the newspaper's full title); and I gratefully acknowledge the authority of '*The Journal's*' editor to use extracts from this valuable archive.

No historian in Gloucestershire could fail to recognise the continuing achievement of the Bristol and Gloucestershire Archaeological Society. I am particularly grateful for the Society's permission to quote from articles in the annually published Transactions (cited in footnotes as 'Trans. BGAS') and other publications. I am also glad to acknowledge help from the Society's honorary librarian, Steve Bailey.

In Winchcombe, I have been immensely helped by Barbara Edward, as honorary curator of Winchcombe folk and police museum, kept in the town hall's first-floor rooms, who has transformed this collection into a well-organised display and historical archive. I also gratefully acknowledge the museum's trustees' permission to quote from, and refer to, documents and photographs in their keeping.

Philip Wilkinson, author of '*What The Romans Did For Us*', kindly read the draft chapter on the Roman influence in the Winchcombe district and commented helpfully on it. I am also grateful to the Sudeley Castle Estate Limited for permitting me to see the report entitled '*An Archaeological Evaluation at Almsbury Farm, Winchcombe*', by John Samuels Archaeological Consultants; and to Dr. John Samuels for authorising a reference to the report.

Dr. Ann Williams, editor-in-chief of '*The Gloucestershire Domesday*' (published by Alecto Historical Editions in 1989) has kindly authorised me to refer to material in that work; and I gratefully acknowledge permission from Alecto Historical Editions to reproduce from that volume the plan of the kingdom of the Hwicce.

John S. Moore, lecturer in economic history in the Department of Historical Studies, University of Bristol, has permitted me to refer to his extremely valuable discussion of Winchcombe at the time of the Domesday Survey entitled '*The Sudeley and Toddington Area in Domesday Book*' which appears in '*The Sudeleys – Lords of Toddington*', proceedings edited by Lord Sudeley. I am also grateful to John Moore and The Manorial Society of Great Britain for permission to reproduce from that volume the two plans of the Winchcombe district at Domesday. Additionally, John Moore's exposition of Winchcombe at Domesday in his translation of Domesday Book for Gloucestershire has been immensely valuable.

I gratefully acknowledge the permission of the Society of Antiquaries of London to reproduce the plan of late-medieval Winchcombe from Dr. Steven Bassett's article entitled '*A probable Mercian royal mausoleum at Winchcombe, Gloucestershire*' (page 83 of The Antiquaries Journal, 1985, volume LXV).

The early history of Winchcombe's first school was thoroughly researched in the 1960s by Nicholas Orme, now Professor of History in the University of Exeter. His work has been used in compiling the account, in chapter 13, of this school's early years. I am extremely grateful to him for elucidating a subject which is still quite widely misunderstood.

Frank C. Adey, formerly circuit archivist to the Cheltenham Methodist circuit, has generously permitted me to refer to information about Methodism in Winchcombe contained in his booklet entitled '*A Cotswold Methodist Heritage*', published in 1979.

Jean Bray, authoress of '*The Lady of Sudeley*' (the biography of Emma Dent) has helped by providing factual information from the Sudeley castle archive about some of the expenditure by the Dent family on buildings and institutions in Winchcombe.

I have benefited from correspondence with Rob White, a member of the Gloucester Street History Group, about the town's street layout in medieval and later times.

Mrs. Dorothy Le Bourgeois (maiden name Dorothy Shekell) has very generously permitted me to refer to factual information in the private memoirs of her late father, Arthur Shekell, well-known as the proprietor of West End Stores, in Gloucester Street, for many years until 1980.

Rex Butler has kindly discussed his clear recollections of his boyhood and youth in Winchcombe, during the Second World War and afterwards, when great change was being experienced.

John Crawforth's numerous line drawings help to bring the subject alive and his cartographic skill was used to produce the plan of Winchcombe's main streets in about 1500.

I am most grateful to Dawn Mountain for coping so efficiently with the daunting task of converting my manuscript into a faultless text, ready for publication.

Finally, but most importantly, I am extremely grateful to Jon Carpenter, proprietor of The Wychwood Press, for his willingness to undertake the task of publication which others had refused.

Whether this generously given help has been used to good purpose is for the reader to judge. The author alone is responsible for any shortcomings, whether they be factual errors, misinterpretation or too self-opinionated views.

D N Donaldson
Postlip, Winchcombe, Gloucestershire
New Year's Day, 2001

INTRODUCTION

The close of western Christendom's conventionally calculated second millennium is an apt moment to reflect on Winchcombe's past. To study the town's history may not help to shape its future; but it should enable the student to understand some of the geological, economic, cultural and social influences that have formed today's Winchcombe.

Any student of Winchcombe's history is immediately aware of two insuperable difficulties. First, a reliable account of the past relies heavily on archaeological evidence. There has been remarkably little investigation by archaeologists, for the obvious practical reason that the town's most interesting sites are beneath existing shops, houses and other buildings, or below gardens and paddocks whose owners do not want them excavated. While serious archaeological investigation continues to be impracticable, it will be impossible to gain a historically complete understanding of the town's past. Secondly, despite the scarcity of archaeological data, there is an immense volume of historical information about Winchcombe. To say that it would require a lifetime's study to evaluate the available information and present it digestibly is probably not an exaggeration. The necessarily brief and selective account given in this book can only hope to scratch the past's surface.

The book's main purpose is to make a historically reliable account of Winchcombe's past available to the general reader interested in it. The academic historian who wishes to trace such facets as the descent of the manorial lordship, or the frequency of meetings of the court leet, will be disappointed. Instead, because Winchcombe remains today a town with recognisably medieval origins, the book concentrates on topographical, social and cultural factors which have shaped its development. Above all, the account attempts to show how important the influence of particular individuals has been.

The method of presentation is mainly chronological, apart from specific digressions to deal with largely self-contained topics, such as formal education. But each chapter can be regarded, if the reader prefers, as an essay in its own right. This results in some minor repetition, to avoid the need to cross-refer to information in another chapter. And for those who find footnotes at the bottom of a page distracting, the references in the footnotes are grouped together at each chapter's end.

One feature of the presentation perhaps needs particular explanation. The narrative relies on numerous verbatim extracts from original documents, personal observations and contemporary reports of events. The justification for this approach was explained by the Rev. Samuel Seyer, in the preface to his 'Memoirs, historical and topographical, of Bristol and its neighbourhood', published in the 1820s, as follows:

'It may be observed, perhaps, as a peculiarity in some part of these Memoirs, that much of it consists of quotations. I have not done this without due consideration, ... the words of the original writer carry you back into the manners and language and sentiments and party-spirit of the age in which he wrote.'

In short, to paraphrase or summarise the words originally used is to risk a loss of historical authenticity and to put a gloss on them which may be entirely mistaken.

Some thirty years ago, local historical research in Winchcombe was a largely solitary pursuit. Happily, this is no longer so. The Gloucester Street History Group in the town, established in 1990, has accomplished much useful work, especially in census analysis and the history of property ownership. And the Winchcombe museum's welcome revival in the 1990s now provides an archive where vital historical information about the town can be kept where it should be. This book is intended to complement those efforts and, perhaps, stimulate some further historical research which will help towards a better understanding of the town's past.

CHAPTER 1

THE PREHISTORIC ERA

Reliable documentary evidence for the Winchcombe area is not available until about the end of the eighth century. Nevertheless, other evidence shows that human activity had shaped the landscape and established early patterns of settlement during at least the previous four thousand years. As this evidence relies mainly on archaeological interpretation of known sites, it must be approached cautiously, acknowledging that some sites may have been destroyed by later settlement and farming activity and others may yet be discovered.

Among the earliest evidence of human settlement in the Winchcombe neighbourhood is the late-Neolithic long barrow known as Belas Knap (meaning beacon hill, from the Old English words 'bel', a beacon, and 'cnaepp', a hill top[1]). This chambered tomb stands high above the present town, at more than 950 feet above sea level, on the brow of the lovely wooded escarpment over Humblebee How plantation. It is scheduled as an ancient monument in the care of English Heritage.

Belas Knap is one of a group of some eighty-five Neolithic tombs in the Cotswold-Severn area which form one of the most important concentrations of such monuments in Britain. It is impossible to say exactly when the original monument was built. Informed estimates range from about 3000 B.C.[2] to perhaps not earlier than 2000 B.C.[3] The most recent estimate is that the whole period of building long barrows in the Cotswolds spanned the years 3800 B.C. to 3000 B.C.[4]

However, there is no doubt that the purpose of a long barrow was to provide a monumental burial chamber. There are two types of barrow found in the Cotswolds, of which Belas Knap is in the form of a lengthy, but comparatively low, mound with

lateral chambers entered from the side. It measures about 178 feet long, 60 feet at its maximum width and about 13 feet 6 inches high. Although somewhat crude excavation and restoration of the monument occurred between 1863 and 1865, the main archaeological excavation and restoration did not take place until 1928 to 1931 by, respectively, W. J. Hemp and Sir James Berry (the investigation) and Dr. C. A. R. Radford (the restoration), who carefully recorded their work.[5]

What can reliably be conjectured about the people who lived in this area of the north Cotswolds some five thousand years ago and were capable of organising and carrying out such a substantial engineering project as Belas Knap represents? As has been pointed out elsewhere, the dry stonewalls forming the portal at the north end of Belas Knap use the same building methods as today's Cotswold stone-wallers, except that the stones are thinner and very carefully chosen.[6] Thus they can properly be regarded as the forerunners of a building tradition with a quite extraordinary longevity and utility. The Neolithic people who settled in the Cotswolds probably originated from Mediterranean Europe and crossed what is now the English Channel in groups from about 4000 B.C. onwards. Unlike the earlier population of hunter-gatherers, these people were farmers, bringing with them domesticated animals and seed corn, so that they naturally sought places of permanent settlement. They would have felled some of the native woodland to establish sites for their settlements and to provide materials for primitive domestic structures, probably comprised mainly of wood, wattle and thatch. The oolitic limestone in the area would have been regarded as a precious material, probably reserved for ceremonial building purposes.

The daily life of these Neolithic people would have been essentially pastoral, centred on rearing domestic animals in the relative safety of the upland slopes and supplementing their food by hunting animals in the woodland valleys. As they became permanently established, tribal or social structures would be developed which are perhaps exemplified by the enterprise of building the long barrows.

How and why these major building works were constructed must be largely conjectural. One possibility is that they were intended as the mausoleum or burial mound of a local chieftain and his extended family. Alternatively, because the burial chambers formed a comparatively small proportion (perhaps as little as 5%) of the entire structure, perhaps the long barrow also represented a territorial statement by which a particular grouping or community indicated their permanent presence in a locality to their neighbours. A hilltop beacon would seem an especially appropriate way of conveying a message to other tribes or groupings in the area. In either event, the importance of the long barrows can be measured by the effort and quantity of materials used in building them. One estimate puts the amount of labour required to construct a long barrow at 5,000 man-hours, using enough stone to build a parish church.[7] Whether this work was carried out by the community itself, or perhaps by an itinerant labour force using their own primitive tools and equipment, the degree of social organisation which produced such an elaborate structure as Belas Knap confirms that these Neolithic farmers possessed remarkable co-operative enterprise and a readiness, enforced or otherwise, to devote considerable resources to lasting monuments.

The Neolithic Age was followed by the Bronze Age, dating from about 2400 B.C. and lasting about 1,600 years. This saw successive invasions from the European mainland of people with the knowledge to use metals, which enabled them to shape their environment more effectively. But it seems unlikely that the Bronze Age landscape differed markedly from Neolithic farming patterns. During the Bronze Age the transport of tin from mines in Cornwall and of copper from Ireland made it necessary to improve communications along prehistoric track-ways, used intermittently by traders in metals. One of these routes was the Jurassic Way, running from the Bristol Avon to the river Humber, which crossed the river Coln near Andoversford and the river Windrush near Naunton. As this route was within five miles of Winchcombe, it may have enabled Bronze Age settlers in this area to obtain improved tools and equipment, thus helping them to work the land more productively.

The succeeding Iron Age, beginning in about 800 B.C., was a period when invading groups of Celts from the European mainland compelled the already settled populations of the Cotswolds to defend themselves by building and occupying, first, hill-top enclosures and, later, hill-forts. Although Nottingham hill is not within the present parish of Winchcombe, it is a good example of an extensive hilltop enclosure, comprising about 120 acres of flat promontory defended by a pair of banks and ditches. This must have represented an immense building operation for the people who occupied it. Presumably, their main purpose was defensive; but its considerable extent suggests that it may also have been used for safeguarding livestock and some cultivation.

It seems likely that, by the turn of the first millennium (B.C. to A.D.), the north Cotswolds was an area of quite dense agricultural settlement, with the population living in farmsteads or small hamlets and cultivating the land, using a variety of flint, bronze and iron tools. There may also have been a few independent craftsmen whose skill enabled them to make some of the domestic equipment used by their neighbours. And, although communications beyond the distance of other settlements in the locality must have been difficult, there may well have been some inward trade in commodities such as high quality pottery and wine from as far away as Gaul and the Mediterranean.

1   A. H. Smith: 'The Place-Names of Gloucestershire', EPNS, Volume xxxix, Part Two, The North and West Cotswolds, Cambridge University Press, 1964, page 5

2   L. V. Grinsell: 'Belas Knap Long Barrow', Department of the Environment (Ancient Monuments and Historic Buildings) pamphlet, HMSO, 1966

3   Nicholas Thomas: 'A Guide to Prehistoric England', 1960, pages 114-115

4   Timothy Darvill: 'The Cotswolds in Prehistory' in 'The Buildings of England – Gloucestershire I : The Cotswolds' by David Verey and Alan Brooks, Penguin Books, extensively revised 1999

5   Sir James Berry: 'Belas Knap Long Barrow', Trans BGAS, 1929, Volume 51, pages 273-304; Volume 52, 1930, pages 123-150; C. A. R. Radford: 'Belas Knap Long Barrow', Trans BGAS, 1930, Volume 52, pages 295-299

6   H. P. R. Finberg: 'The Gloucestershire Landscape', Hodder & Stoughton, 1975, page 33

7   O.G.S. Crawford: 'The Long Barrows of the Cotswolds', John Bellows, 1925

CHAPTER 2

THE ROMAN INFLUENCE

Lowland Britain was divided into tribal kingdoms when the Romans launched their invasion of what they called Britannia, in A.D. 43, under the command of Aulus Plautius, with four legions and auxiliary forces. The area now comprising Gloucestershire was within the kingdom of the tribe known to Ptolemy, the Roman geographer of the second century A.D. who described the invasion, as the Dobunni. To the east of this tribal kingdom was the kingdom of the Catuvellauni; and the Silures controlled the land to the west in what is now South Wales. Within about four years the Roman forces had secured control of most of the area to the south and east of a line drawn from the river Severn to the river Humber, including the kingdom of the Dobunni.

Archaeological evidence appears to suggest that the main administrative centre of the Dobunni was established at Bagendon, north of Cirencester, possibly known to the tribe as Corinion. There may also have been a separate centre of population at Minchinhampton where earthworks provide evidence of a substantial settlement. The chieftain of the northern part of the kingdom at Bagendon was known as Boduocus, while a chieftain whose full name is unknown, but is abbreviated as Corio, led the southern part.

The tribal kingdoms of lowland Britain relied mainly on agriculture, which was sufficiently prosperous to enable exports to Gaul of corn, cattle and animal products, such as hides. There was also some trade in iron and precious metals. The Roman invaders wished to exploit this prosperity, rather than destroy it: their approach was therefore to adapt existing tribal forms of government to conform to Roman political and institutional arrangements.

In the northern area of the kingdom of the Dobunni the second governor of the province of Britain, Publius Ostorius Scapula, appears to have reached an agreement with Boduocus which enabled Roman forces to advance across this territory and establish the important military base at Corinium (Cirencester), possibly as early as A.D. 45. He was later able to launch a campaign against the Silures, to the west of the Severn, from a fortified base at Glevum (Gloucester). The significance of the agreement between Boduocus and Ostorius Scapula was that comparatively soon after the second Roman invasion, possibly as early as A.D. 60, the former tribal kingdom of the Dobunni became the 'civitas Dobunnorum', with the important Roman centre of Corinium as its capital.

The Roman road system radiated outwards from Corinium, from which Ermin Street led north-westwards to Glevum; and the Fosse Way took a north-eastwards course towards what is now Bourton-on-the-Water. An important secondary route branched off the Fosse Way to the east of Chedworth, crossed the river Coln near Withington, served the villa estate at Compton Abdale and came into the vale where Winchcombe now is before continuing northwards beyond Didbrook. This was not a Roman road constructed for the quick and efficient movement of the invasion forces and their equipment: rather, it was an ancient trackway along the Cotswold ridge which the Romans and their client tribe successfully adapted to provide better communication between Corinium and the rich agricultural area of the north Cotswolds. This ancient ridgeway is nowadays identifiable as the White Way: it is called Salter's Lane (because it was much later used to transport salt through the Cotswolds to the river Thames at Lechlade) where it climbs Hailes hill to pass Little Farmcote; and the Salt Way where it forms the eastern boundary of the Sudeley estate and continues to Roel Gate and beyond.

The extent of Roman influence in and around Winchcombe is problematic. Eleanor Adlard mentions what she describes as 'Roman remains and black pottery' found under the parish church of St Peter during the major refurbishment of the building in 1872.[1] However, apart from the very limited archaeological investigations referred to later in this chapter, there is insufficient evidence to establish whether the present core area of the town was a site for Roman, or Romano-British, settlement. At a short distance from the town the sites of two Roman villas provide conclusive evidence of Romano-British settlement in this wider area. Despite their present dilapidated state, they merit detailed study as examples of the pattern of Romano-British life between about A.D. 100 and 400.

Roman villas in the Winchcombe area

The settled system of government and improved road communication resulting from Roman dominion produced an economic and social climate in which a highly civilised and Romanised way of life could flourish in the north Cotswolds. One result of this improved standard of living was the establishment of Roman villas at various sites on the Cotswold plateau, typified by Chedworth and Woodchester. Use of the description 'Roman villa' may create a misleading impression of a substantial residence, built to pattern-book external design. In practice, the term was simply used to describe a house in the country, broadly of two main types. The 'villa urbana' was a country house whose owner aspired to dignified living; whereas the 'villa rustica' fulfilled a strictly utilitarian purpose, perhaps best described as a farmstead.[2]

The secluded valleys of the river Isbourne and the Beesmoor Brook evidently provided suitable locations for villas, as well as being within easy reach of the important highway to Corinium. It is now impossible to say how many villas existed in the Winchcombe area between the second and the end of the fourth century. There were certainly villas at Wadfield and Spoonley Wood. Although no archaeological evidence supports it, the possibility that villas existed at Millhampost and in

Stancombe Wood should not be excluded. Mrs. Emma Dent claimed that a site awaited excavation in Stancombe Wood since what she believed to be the monumental stone of a Roman soldier, illustrated in her book, was found there.[3] More recently, Martin Henig has suggested that this figure depicts a local hunter god.[4]

Wadfield villa

The site of Wadfield villa is just to the north of Humblebee cottages, about 675 feet above sea level, facing east and overlooking the valley of the Beesmoor Brook. The spring line is a short distance behind the site, to the west; and the villa dwellers may have obtained their water supply from the spring known locally as Puck's Well. Mrs. Dent described how the site was discovered in 1863 in this account:

'As usual, this was brought to light through the instrumentality of the plough, which struck against a stone. Upon the removal of this and other stones which were then found, a Roman villa was discovered beneath the surface of the soil, the plan of which was in a perfect state of preservation. It was of the usual form, and, in addition to the reception rooms, with hypocaust or bath. The average dimensions of the rooms were about 15 feet square, and they apparently must have been occupied by some individual holding a high military appointment. The tessellated pavement was as perfect as if just completed by the workmen; but its speedy removal was found to be absolutely necessary in order to preserve it from the Winchcombe public, who in the space of one Sunday afternoon carried off a large portion, in small pieces, as souvenirs.'

What then happened to the Wadfield villa site is unclear. However, it seems likely that Mrs. Dent arranged for it to be filled in and covered over as a safeguard against vandalism. It was not until 1894 that she was able to commission some archaeological investigation by E. P. Loftus Brock, Honorary Treasurer of the Society of Antiquaries, who reported his findings in a paper read to the British Archaeological Association on 3 April 1895 and published in *The Winchcombe and Sudeley Record*.[5]

On his first visit to the site in 1894 Loftus Brock found what he described as traces of pottery and Roman brick scattered here and there over the surface of the ploughed field. This description suggests that, unlike the pasture sometimes surrounding the villa site, it was then cultivated as arable land, so that damage might already have resulted from regular ploughing. When Loftus Brock and his team of local workmen dug deeper they found that the villa had consisted of a central building with two wings, enclosing a courtyard 34 feet wide. One of the two main rooms in the central building had neatly laid red tesserae (or small cubic stones) as floor covering; and the other had a fine mosaic pavement, which appeared to have been only half finished. There were also traces of the type of internal heating system known as a hypocaust. Away from the main villa Loftus Brock found the remains of what he described as massive but very irregular walls which had been demolished to their foundations and apparently removed, presumably for use elsewhere as building materials.

In December 1968 the laying of a natural gas pipeline close to the Wadfield villa site enabled Bernard Rawes to carry out a small rescue excavation on a building uncovered by the contractors.[6] The outbuilding, measuring about 29 feet by 40 feet and consisting of rectangular-faced blocks of oolitic freestone, was situated some 50 yards south of the main villa buildings. Although no archaeological evidence enabled the outbuilding's purpose to be reliably established, it seems reasonable to speculate, from its situation and substantial construction, that it originally served some agricultural purpose, such as a storage barn.

Spoonley villa

The villa in Spoonley Wood was not discovered until March 1882. Subsequently, Mrs. Dent arranged for it to be thoroughly excavated under the supervision of the Rev. William Bazeley, then Honorary Secretary of the Bristol and Gloucestershire Archaeological Society. The result of this investigation was briefly described by Professor J. H. Middleton in a paper given to the Society of Antiquaries.[7]

Professor Middleton found Spoonley villa similar to other Roman houses in Gloucestershire. The entire space occupied by the villa, including its central courtyard bounded by buildings on three sides and a precinct wall on the fourth side, was about 170 feet by 190 feet. A stream ran close beside it on the north-western side, bringing a water supply from a spring on the hill behind it. Professor Middleton's plan shows a central courtyard with substantial buildings comprising living quarters, fronted on each of the three sides by a verandah. The house was approached through a door in the centre of the precinct wall and by a roughly paved path leading across the courtyard, under the verandah, into the main public room (known as the 'tablinum'). There appear to have been three furnaces, used to provide warm air for the hypocaust system and to heat water for the three bathrooms. A number of the rooms had elaborate mosaic floors, which may have been designed and laid by the school of mosaicists working in Corinium who gained renown during the first half of the fourth century.[8] In the south-east corner of the building a room which was thought to have been a kitchen contained a stone-lined well which is reported to have supplied water shortly after the accumulated rubbish of the intervening centuries had been removed.[9] Typically diamond-shaped limestone slates showed that the villa had been roofed with what would later be known as Stonesfield slates: they were recorded as measuring 17 inches long by 18.5 inches wide, fixed with long iron nails. The villa was clearly built to withstand the worst features of the British climate.

About 60 feet away from the villa to the north-west a separate stone-built structure was discovered, measuring about 54 feet by 35 feet, with its remaining side walls about 2 feet high. In Professor Middleton's opinion this building would have served the villa-owners as a barn or granary.

Although largely conjectural, reliable conclusions about the villa owners' way of life may perhaps be drawn from the more numerous artefacts found at Spoonley, in comparison with Wadfield villa. Among the finds were metal knives, spoons, tools and door hinges, together with what Professor Middleton describes as 'a very pretty little bronze bowl plated with silver, like a mirror'. Roman forms of pottery were discovered, along with many pieces of window glass and a fragment of a shallow glass dish on which a simple pattern had been cut.

We can now add to this evidence Dr. Jocelyn Toynbee's account of the find, in a field near the villa, of an intact marble statuette of Bacchus which had been placed at the feet of a skeleton in a grave.[10] Dr. Toynbee postulates that the grave could have belonged to the villa owner, or to some member of his family, who regarded Bacchus as an other-worldly saviour god. Martin Henig suggests that this sculpted marble may initially have been intended as a work of decorative art before eventually being devoted to the religious purpose of protecting its owner in his grave.[11]

A further discovery occurred in 1948, at Cole's Hill, about half a mile south of Spoonley villa, where the torso of a stone-made eagle was ploughed out. This figure was made from the local oolitic limestone in somewhat coarse modelling, with diagonal and criss-cross incised lines to indicate feathers on the breast and wings. The Royal Commission on Historical Monuments describes this site as a probable Romano-British shrine.[12]

Altogether, the finds in and around Spoonley villa appear to suggest that the villa owners enjoyed a remarkably sophisticated standard of living, perhaps lasting throughout the period from about 150 to 400. They may have been wealthy Romano-British landowners, or possibly municipal administrators from Corinium, who chose to live in the manner of independent farmers with domestic servants and agricultural workers quartered around them in less comfortable accommodation. Their prosperity was probably based on agriculture, which would have involved a mixture of livestock and arable. If the outbuildings discovered at Wadfield and Spoonley were indeed storage barns or granaries, the area of arable cultivation is likely to have been substantial. In addition to what the villa owners produced for their own needs, there would almost certainly have been imports of luxury items, such as high quality pottery and ornaments, jewellery and wine, from Gaul or the Mediterranean.

The finding of artefacts of ritual significance in the vicinity of Spoonley villa suggests that, although under the emperor Constantine and the 'Peace of the Church' in 313 the Christian religion was legal throughout the Roman empire, the villa owners may have continued to follow pagan cults. In much the same way as the senatorial class in Rome remained largely pagan in outlook, some of the villa owners may have been reluctant to follow the Christian way favoured by the imperial house and its supporters.

A Romano-British presence in the area of the present town?

While much of the detail of the villa owners' way of life remains conjectural, whether there was any Romano-British presence within what is now Winchcombe's central core borders on guesswork. This is because there has been so little opportunity for archaeological investigation by modern methods. However, settlement in the fertile valley of the river Isbourne may not have been confined to the villa dwellers. There might also have been some form of village settlement within the area of the present town, where village dwellers may possibly have lived in timber-framed structures and cultivated small fields around the settlement as subsistence farmers.

The best evidence of possible Romano-British settlement within the town's core is provided by the archaeological investigation carried out in the spring of 1977, in association with building works to extend the back of the premises comprising the Co-Op retail store at 12 North Street into what was then a largely overgrown garden area. This investigation concluded that the finding of a small quantity of Romano-British pottery indicated human activity on or near the site in the second to third centuries and possibly into the fourth century.[13] Other investigations, between 1962 and 1972, of sites at Back Lane (the former Junior School) and Cowl Lane produced a quantity of pottery and building material, in residual contexts, which appeared to confirm that there was a Romano-British presence within this central area of the later town.[14]

Most recently, the proposed development of the buildings comprising Almsbury Farm on the Sudeley estate provided the opportunity for a preliminary archaeological investigation in this area, during the spring and summer of 2000. The most significant discovery was made in the field to the south-west of Almsbury Farm where trial investigations established the probable existence of a Roman farmstead, including at least one stone-built structure. The discovery included two fragments of wall plaster and a quantity of tile which led the investigators to conclude that the building had been relatively substantial and finished to a comparatively high standard, perhaps reflecting the status of its original occupier.[15] If the Sudeley estate commissions further archaeological investigation of this site, which is effectively part of the town, it may provide persuasive evidence of substantial Romano-British settlement in the Isbourne valley; and, possibly, of such a presence within the existing core area of Winchcombe.

Historians' opinions vary on the long-term effect of the Roman occupation of Britain. But, in the north Cotswolds, there can be little doubt that two factors were of lasting significance. First, improved communication had opened the area to incomers who introduced new ideas and higher living standards. Secondly, Roman municipal government's civilising influence provided the ordered basis on which a comparatively prosperous and well-settled agricultural economy could thrive.

1   Eleanor Adlard: 'Winchcombe Cavalcade', E. J. Burrow & Co Ltd, 1939, page 34

2   A fuller account of a Roman villa is given by Peter Salway: 'Roman Britain', The Oxford History of England, 1981, pages 608-611

3   Mrs. Emma Dent: 'Annals of Winchcombe and Sudeley', John Murray, 1877, page 15

4   Martin Henig: 'Roman Sculpture from the Cotswold Region', British Academy (Oxford University Press), 1993, page 37

5   The Winchcombe and Sudeley Record, Volume 7, No. 84, December 1896, pages 438-443

6   The excavation is reported in Bernard Rawes: 'An Outbuilding at Wadfield Roman Villa', Trans BGAS, 1971, Volume XC, pages 124-128

7   Paper published in 'Archaeologia', Volume LII

8   P. Salway, op cit, pages 656-657

9   G.B. Witts: 'Archaeological Handbook of Gloucestershire, 1883, pages 70-71

10   J. M. C. Toynbee: 'Roman Sculpture in Gloucestershire', published in 'Essays in

Bristol and Gloucestershire History', edited by P. McGrath and J. Cannon, BGAS, 1976, pages 79-80

11   M. Henig, op cit, page xx

12   Royal Commission on Historical Monuments: 'Iron Age and Romano-British Monuments in the Gloucestershire Cotswolds', HMSO, 1976

13   Alan Saville: 'Salvage recording of 'Romano-British, Saxon, Medieval, and Post-Medieval remains at North Street, Winchcombe, Gloucestershire', Trans BGAS, 1985, Volume 103, pages 101-139

14   Peter Ellis: 'Excavations in Winchcombe, Gloucestershire, 1962-1972: a report on excavation and fieldwork by B.K. Davison and J. Hinchliffe at Cowl Lane and Back Lane', Trans BGAS, 1986, Volume 104, pages 95-138

15   John Samuels Archaeological Consultants: 'An Archaeological Evaluation at Almsbury Farm, Winchcombe, Gloucestershire', report submitted to Sudeley Castle Estate Ltd, February 2000.

CHAPTER 3

THE MERCIAN FOUNDATION OF WINCHCOMBE

After the Roman garrisons were finally withdrawn from Britain, in 410, to support the imperial government's defence against invading barbarians, forms of Romanised government in the region of Corinium probably declined quite quickly. No evidence suggests that the inhabitants of Wadfield and Spoonley villas ended their lives violently. More probably, they experienced a gradual decline in prosperity and eventually accepted that an agricultural enterprise on the scale of the villa-estate was no longer sustainable. Perhaps they then withdrew to whatever settlement may have remained at Corinium, abandoning their land to other local inhabitants who perhaps subsisted in and around the former estates as peasant farmers.

In the post-Roman era, the invading Saxons probably saw the north Cotswolds area as a rich agricultural domain to be wrested from the chieftains of the occupying Britons. Saxon ambitions resulted in two important battles. In 577 Saxon forces led by Cuthwine and Ceawlin of Wessex defeated the three British princes of kingdoms based on Bath, Cirencester and Gloucester at the battle of Dyrham (about four miles south of Chipping Sodbury), enabling Saxon overlords to extend their influence north-wards from the Bristol Avon to the Warwickshire Avon.

The Hwiccian principality

The battle of Dyrham did not result in lasting peace in the north Cotswolds because the influence of Wessex in this area was contested by the Anglo-Saxon mixed tribe known collectively as the Mercians, who sought to extend their reach south-west-wards from their main area of occupation in the Trent valley. Mercian ambitions culminated, in 628, in the battle of Cirencester where Penda, a member of the Mercian royal house and subsequently Mercian king, defeated Cynegils who was Ceawlin's successor as ruler of Wessex. Dr. Steven Bassett has persuasively suggested that Penda's victory hastened the process by which smaller Anglo-Saxon kingdoms were already being brought under one ruler of a territory centred on Winchcombe, whose people were called the Hwicce. It was in Penda's interest to have an ally on Mercia's south-western boundary which could eventually be absorbed as a Mercian sub-kingdom.[1]

The Hwicce were a mixed population of Angles, Saxons and some native Britons.

They occupied territory now comprising the counties of Worcestershire, Gloucestershire east of the Severn, and the western third of Warwickshire. By the later seventh century, the Hwicce had become Christian and this territory approximated closely to the area of the medieval diocese of Worcester, as illustrated in Plan 1, showing the kingdom of the Hwicce.[2] The ecclesiastical centre of the Hwiccian kingdom appears to have been in Worcester, where a bishopric was created in 679 or 680; and Osric, king of the Hwicce, founded a monastery dedicated to St Peter in Gloucester at about the same time. Although the kingdom was subsequently absorbed into Mercia, this area continued to be known as the Hwiccian province until the tenth century.

The Hwiccian principality's significance for Winchcombe is that the settlement (whatever its extent may have been) occupied a strategic position in the valley of the river Isbourne from which the way into the north Cotswold sheepwalks could be controlled. The importance of sheep-rearing as early as the seventh and eighth centuries can be gathered from a letter, in 796, from the Frankish king Charlemagne to king Offa of Mercia, mentioning the export of woollen cloaks or blankets to the Continent as part of a thriving woollen industry in Anglo-Saxon times.[3]

The rulers of the Hwicce founded churches in their province from about 670 onwards. Apart from a possible convent of nuns, there is no documentary record of a 'monasterium', or minster church, founded by the Hwicce in Winchcombe. However, Dr. Steven Bassett, who has published several papers on Anglo-Saxon Winchcombe, considers that such an important place as the town then was would almost certainly have had a church by the end of the eighth century.[4]

The nature and location of this church in Winchcombe are unknown. A Saxon minster was usually a community of secular priests, or a double house of men and women, whose responsibility was the spiritual care of the population within the founder's settlement area. This may possibly have been the pattern for Winchcombe. There is a persistent local tradition that a Saxon church of St Nicholas was situated at the junction of Bull Lane and Chandos Street (which is believed to have been known previously as St Nicholas Street) and that the building was only demolished in the latter part of the nineteenth century, when it was being used as a cart shed.[5] However, despite the fact that the present Roman Catholic church in Chandos Street is dedicated to St Nicholas, there is no reliable evidence to support the tradition of such a Saxon foundation. It is particularly significant that the numerous documents preserved in Winchcombe abbey's cartulary do not mention any Saxon church somewhere else in the town. In Chapter 6 some explanation for the basis of this tradition is attempted.

The founding of Winchcombe abbey

When the Mercian ascendancy peaked during king Offa's reign, from 757 to 796, the Hwiccian principality had been fully absorbed into Mercia, so that Winchcombe was an important outpost on the southern boundary of the Mercian kingdom. There is some evidence that Offa established a convent of nuns at Winchcombe in 787 and his successor, king Coenwulf (Kenulf) added a monastery of monks in 798, when the foundation became a double monastery.[6] However, Dr. Steven Bassett, relying on Sir Frank

Stenton's doubts about whether any religious houses were founded for women alone during this period, suggests that any convent of nuns which may have been founded at Winchcombe was almost certainly an enlargement of an already existing house.[7]

Whatever the constitution of this earliest Mercian religious foundation may have been, two factors are important for later developments. First, as with some other Mercian houses, it seems that the initial dedication of the monastery at Winchcombe was to St Peter.[8] Secondly, king Coenwulf's daughter, Cwoenthryth (Quendryth), was apparently appointed abbess of the convent at Winchcombe, although she subsequently (in 824) also held the post of abbess of Southminster, near Thanet in Kent.

According to the almost certainly forged annals of Winchcombe abbey, king Coenwulf gave instructions for the building of an abbey to start in 798 and Wulfred, archbishop of Canterbury, dedicated the completed abbey church on 9 November 811. The kings of East Anglia and Kent, ten ealdormen and twelve other bishops were said to have attended the dedication, which was also marked by Coenwulf's release from captivity of another Kentish ruler, Pren, who had been taken in 796 during a battle with Mercian forces. The royal foundation provided for a community of 300 monks who were to be maintained from the income derived from property totalling about 13,080 acres. However, it seems doubtful whether the community ever amounted to 300 members, even though the earliest followers of the monastic life adopted the most frugal habits.[9] The foundation charter was subsequently confirmed by Pope Leo III in 811, and Pope Paschal in 818, respectively exempting the monastery from the liability for secular service and granting legal title to the possessions owned by all the monasteries Coenwulf had founded.

Part of king Coenwulf's purpose in founding a monastic establishment at Winchcombe was to provide a suitable place of burial for the Mercian royal family. Accordingly, when Coenwulf himself died in 821, he was buried in the abbey's church, presumably with the splendour and reverence appropriate to a Mercian king's departure.

The legend of St Kenelm

The final years of Coenwulf's reign were a time of Mercian stability and prosperity; but they may have been clouded for Coenwulf himself by the comparatively early death of his son Cynhelm (Kenelm). The facts of Cynhelm's life are hard to establish. It seems that, as a young Mercian prince, he witnessed charters granted between 803 and 811; but his death preceded that of his father in 821. Cynhelm may have been in his mid-twenties when he died: as a member of the Mercian royal house, his body would have been buried in the monastic church his father had founded at Winchcombe.[10]

From the life of this Mercian prince the 'Kenelm legend' grew and later became vital to the standing of Winchcombe abbey as a place of pilgrimage. The essential elements of the legend are that Kenelm was believed to have been murdered by his guardian or tutor (Askebert), at the instigation of his older sister (Quendryth), when he was only seven years old and had succeeded to his father's throne for five months. Kenelm's body was then buried secretly under a thorn bush at Clent, near Hagley in Worcestershire, where the little church of St Kenelm was built on the site of his supposed murder; news of the crime was later revealed to Pope Sylvester by the dropping of a parchment message from the beak of a white dove above the altar of St Peter's in Rome; and Kenelm's body was recovered from its burial place at Clent, on the Pope's instructions that it should be re-buried beside that of his father, king Coenwulf, in Winchcombe abbey.

Further elaboration of the legend maintained that, at each stopping place of the monks who carried Kenelm's body from Clent to Winchcombe, a spring of water miraculously appeared.[11] The last of these springs, situated on the Sudeley estate, is still known as St Kenelm's well. A chapel dedicated to St Kenelm stood for many years near this spot but was demolished in 1830. As with some other historic buildings in Winchcombe, the chapel was recorded in a drawing by Edmund Thomas Browne (antiquarian and high bailiff of Winchcombe in the mid-nineteenth century) before its demolition.[12]

When Winchcombe abbey was being revived in the latter part of the tenth century, the name of the boy-martyr had already begun to appear in liturgical works used by monks, including a sacramentary which may have been produced at Ramsey abbey for the community at Winchcombe and was later presented to the French monastery of Fleury.[13] The legend was embellished in the work of later chroniclers, including the monk Florence of Worcester, writing towards the end of the eleventh or beginning of the twelfth century; William of Malmesbury, a few years later; Matthew Paris, a

monk of St Alban's, towards the beginning of the thirteenth century; and Richard of Cirencester in the later fourteenth century.

In 1916 the President of the Bristol and Gloucestershire Archaeological Society, Sidney Hartland, analysed the Kenelm legend in detail. He claimed that this Mercian prince was not less than fourteen years of age in 811 (and was thus not aged seven at the time of his death, whenever it actually occurred); his sister, the maligned Quendryth, was a highly competent abbess of Southminster and in 824 was engaged in a long-running legal dispute with Wulfred, archbishop of Canterbury, about land ownership; and later chroniclers had invented the substance of the legend.[14]

However, despite its obvious fabrication, the Kenelm legend was vitally important for the future prosperity of Winchcombe abbey, and the town of which it was the centre piece, because the monks were able to establish a holy shrine dedicated to the boy-saint which became a popular destination for pilgrims throughout the medieval period, ending only with the abbey's dissolution in 1539. The festival of St Kenelm was held on 17 July and William of Malmesbury recorded that

Kenelmus

'The little saint's body is solemnly revered, and hardly anywhere else in England is venerated by a greater throng of people attending a festival'. The story was so well known that Geoffrey Chaucer mentions it in the recital of the Nun's Priest's Tale, in his 'Canterbury Tales', of which a modern translation is as follows:

'Now take St Kenelm's life which I've been reading;
He was Kenulphus' son, the noble King
Of Mercia. Now, St Kenelm dreamt a thing
Shortly before they murdered him one day.
He saw his murder in a dream, I say.
His nurse expounded it and gave her reason
On every point and warned him against treason.
But as the saint was only seven years old
All that she said about it left him cold.
He was so holy how could visions hurt?'[15]

Despite the subsequent discrediting of the Kenelm legend, one curious factor is worth recalling. The abbey site was extensively searched for any materials of value in about 1815. The result of the excavation was recorded by Edmund Thomas Browne, who was present along with the antiquarian, the Reverend Thomas Fosbroke. Part of the record is as follows:

'The deep and massive foundations of the church were clearly traced, and several ponderous stone coffins, containing remains of human skeletons, were then discovered; but the circumstance which attracted most particular attention arose from the examination of a small stone coffin, which was found at the east end of the interior of the church, close by the side of another, of the usual size. Upon the removal of the flag-stones which covered it (and which took place in the presence of the writer of this article) there appeared a skull, with a few of the other larger bones, and a very long-bladed knife, which had become a mass of rust, and fell to pieces on being handled. The bones also vanished, like a vision from their sight, immediately they were exposed to the air ... This circumstance, therefore, combined with that of the knife, which it is possible the murderer left with the body, and which might have been removed and deposited with it, induces a celebrated antiquary [namely, the Rev. Thomas Fosbroke] to form the conclusion that the largest coffin was Kenulph's and the smaller Kenelm's.'[16]

After passing through a number of private hands, these two coffins were eventually presented to the parish church of St Peter, where they can still be seen on either side of the west end. But the presence of the coffins on the abbey site in 1815 and their macabre contents prompt the question: were the monks of Winchcombe abbey so keen to demonstrate the authenticity of the Kenelm legend that they arranged for a child's embalmed body to be placed in this small stone coffin, along with the supposed murder weapon?

The condition of Winchcombe during Mercian rule

The founding of Winchcombe abbey confirmed the political stability and comparative security the town's inhabitants experienced during the Mercian ascendancy. There is insufficient archaeological and documentary evidence to provide a reliable account of the town's layout and its main buildings in the late eighth and early ninth centuries. However, it is likely that the Mercian rulers constructed some perimeter defences; and whatever fortification existed may well have included, on the northern side of the settlement, the earth mound which now stretches in an approximately east to west line, parallel to Back Lane, in the School playing field. Excavations carried out in this area between 1962 and 1972 appeared to justify the conclusion that a defensive ditch and bank existed along this line by the ninth century; and it was later the basis for improved fortifications.[17] As to the site of the earliest monastic buildings, they were probably in the approximate position of the later abbey buildings immediately to the east of the existing parish church of St Peter, but probably not further east than the present line of Cowl Lane.

In view of the town's importance as a centre of Mercian royal estate management at the beginning of the ninth century, it is also likely that the Mercian kings would have established a building they could use as a royal household and court at Winchcombe. The Ordnance Survey sheets for central Winchcombe published in 1884 and 1923 indicate the site at the east end of Abbey Terrace (now occupied by Lloyds-TSB bank) as 'supposed site of King Kenulph's palace'; although no archaeological or documentary evidence is available to support this supposition. But Edmund Thomas Browne, writing in 1857 about the supposed palace, reported the following hearsay:

'Nothing beyond what rests merely on oral tradition as to its site, can now be told. This is said to have been on the south side of the top of the present High Street, and some of the aged inhabitants who were living within the last twenty years could remember there the remains of an apparently very ancient pile, which they saw demolished to make room for the present large brick residence [this is the building then occupied by Dr. Newman and now by Lloyds-TSB bank]. These they described as consisting of arches and oddly-shaped architectural masses; and affirmed that their forefathers had been accustomed to point to the spot and observe that "there stood King Kenulph's Palace".'[18]

As the town was so important in Anglo-Saxon times, it is appropriate that the Saxon description of its geographical situation is still used today (with some minor adaptation) to name it. The most authoritative opinion is that the town's name derives from a union of the Old English words 'wincel' (meaning a corner or bend) and 'cumb' (meaning a valley).[19] The splendid westward view from the top of the parish church's tower confirms Winchcombe's location in the valley with a bend in it. Similarly, two Old English words unite to provide the name of the river Isbourne. The words are the personal name 'Esa' and 'burna' (meaning a stream), so that Isbourne signifies Esa's stream, or the stream of Esa's people.[20]

A further sign of Winchcombe's importance to the Mercian royal family at the beginning of the ninth century is provided by Dr. Steven Bassett's suggestion that there was a free-standing royal mausoleum in the town where the bodies of Cynhelm, and perhaps of his father king Coenwulf, were first entombed, prior to their subsequent re-burial in the re-founded abbey church. The precise site of this royal mausoleum cannot now be reliably established. But Dr. Bassett presents compelling documentary and topographical evidence to support his opinion that it was a chapel, dedicated to the boy-martyr St Pancras, which stood between the abbey church and the present parish church. In his view, the most likely site for this structure was just to the east of the present parish church of St Peter.[21]

Without extensive archaeological investigation, the existence and whereabouts of a Mercian royal burial place in Winchcombe must remain uncertain. But, while the physical layout and extent of the town are largely speculative, there is no doubt about Winchcombe's importance as a Mercian administrative centre and religious foundation during the eighth and ninth centuries.

1   Dr. S. R. Bassett: 'In search of the origins of Anglo-Saxon Kingdoms' in 'The Origins of Anglo-Saxon Kingdoms,' edited by Steven Bassett, Leicester University Press, 1989, pages 6-17

2   This plan is reproduced, with permission, from 'The Gloucestershire Domesday' by Ann Williams, editor-in-chief, Alecto Historical Editions, London, 1989, page 10

3   cited in H. P. R. Finberg: 'The Formation of England, 550-1042', Paladin edition, 1976, page 76

4   Dr. S. R. Bassett: 'A Probable Mercian Royal Mausoleum at Winchcombe, Gloucestershire', in The Antiquaries Journal 1985, Volume LXV, Part I, pages 82-100

5   Eleanor Adlard: 'Winchcombe Cavalcade', E. J. Burrow & Co Ltd, 1939, page 34
6   Wilhelm Levison: 'England and the Continent in the Eighth Century' (Ford Lectures at Oxford University, Hilary Term, 1943), Oxford University Press, 1946, pages 31 and 257-259
7   S. R. Bassett, op cit, page 85
8   W. Levison, op cit, page 31
9   Gordon Haigh: 'The History of Winchcombe Abbey', Skeffington & Son Ltd, 1947, page 18
10   S. R. Bassett, op cit, page 85
11   R. C. S. Walters: 'The Holy Wells of Gloucestershire', pages 7-14
12   Emma Dent: 'Annals of Winchcombe and Sudeley', John Murray, 1877, page 53
13   Alice Corrêa: 'Liturgical manuscripts of Oswald's houses' in 'St Oswald of Worcester, Life and Influence', edited by Nicholas Brooks and Catherine Cubitt, Leicester University Press, 1996, pages 296-299
14   E. S. Hartland: 'The Legend of St Kenelm', Trans BGAS, 1916, Volume 39, pages 13-65
15   Geoffrey Chaucer: 'The Canterbury Tales', translation by Nevill Coghill, Penguin Classics, 1951, page 246
16   E. Dent, op cit, page 150
17   Peter Ellis: 'Excavations in Winchcombe, Gloucestershire, 1962-1972: a report on excavation and fieldwork by B. K. Davison and J. Hinchliffe at Cowl Lane and Back Lane', Trans BGAS, 1986, Volume 104, pages 95-138
18   E. Dent, op cit, page 151
19   A. H. Smith: 'The Place-Names of Gloucestershire', EPNS, Volume xxxix, Part Two, The North and West Cotswolds, Cambridge University Press, 1964, page 30
20   E. Ekwall: 'Concise Oxford Dictionary of English Place-Names', Oxford University Press, 1960, page 266
21   S. R. Bassett, op cit, pages 89-94

CHAPTER 4

THE SHIRE OF WINCHCOMBE

Mercian power and influence steadily declined after king Coenwulf's death. The decline was hastened by successive waves of Danish invasion, firstly of eastern England, later of central and south-western areas. Although there is no evidence that Viking forces reached Winchcombe, they were as near as Gloucester in 877 and Cirencester in 879.

With the Mercian decline and the ever-present threat of Danish invasion, monastic life and influence collapsed. In Winchcombe, the result appears to have been that the monks in the abbey were replaced by secular clerks.[1] Some of these men may well have been the sons of noble families, so that the abbey's property effectively passed into the hands of laymen who were able to use it for their own purposes and leave it to their descendants.

The abbey's revival in the latter part of the tenth century was strongly influenced by the French monastic regime. The abbey of Cluny had been founded in 910, where the rule of St Benedict was strictly observed; and in 930 the already ancient monastery at Fleury became subject to control from Cluny. In England king Edgar was determined to revive monastic life and he chose Dunstan (later to be sanctified) for this task. When Dunstan was translated from the bishopric of Worcester to the archbishopric of Canterbury in 959, his friend Oswald (who had just spent five years at Fleury) succeeded him at Worcester. Through Oswald's influence another monk from Fleury, Germanus of Winchester, was recruited to found a monastery at Westbury-on-Trym which became a centre of Benedictine revival. Germanus was appointed prior of Ramsey in 971, but Oswald appears to have been responsible for his appointment as abbot of the re-founded Benedictine house at Winchcombe in the following year.[2]

There was inevitable friction between the newly arrived monks and the secular clerks who had gained possession of the abbey. Oswald may have permitted the clerks either to leave or take holy orders. In any event, king Edgar's support seems to have ensured that the abbey regained most of its former landed possessions of some 13,000 acres.[3] The abbey church was re-dedicated to the Blessed Mary, but the child saint Kenelm was now added to the dedication. Although king Edgar's death in 975 resulted in the monks' expulsion from the abbey by Aelfhere (whom Edgar had appointed to administer the Severn area), Aelfhere's own death in 983 meant that the monks were able to return and, eventually, to consolidate their position during the first half of the eleventh century.

After the death in 918 of Aethelflaed, the 'Lady of the Mercians' and the last effective Mercian ruler, Mercia was absorbed into the West Saxon kingdom. Some historians previously considered that this absorption resulted in the introduction into the West Midlands of the West Saxon unit of defence, and eventually local government, known as the shire. However, Dr. Steven Bassett has persuasively shown that the West Midland shires derived from the five provinces of Mercia, each of which corresponded to the area of a diocese. Winchcombe was then in the diocese of Worcester. From the mid-eighth century Mercian kings had established fortified towns, each at the centre of a rural area supplying the necessary manpower. Gradually, these areas acquired the functions previously carried out by the provinces, and in some cases considerably altered in their geographical area, so that the West Saxon kings were able conveniently to adapt them to a shire system of local government.[4]

Each of these areas looked to its fortified town as a 'burh' (borough) which would have provided the local population with a defensive garrison at times when invasion threatened. There is no doubt that Winchcombe was one of these burhs, although the first documentary reference to its borough status is not found until Domesday Book (1086). There is also evidence that the town was at the centre of an administrative area known as Winchcombeshire, although that status may have been relatively brief. Research by C. S. Taylor suggests that none of the Mercian shires bore that title before 1000; and the Midlands area in the former kingdom of the Hwicce, with the fortified towns as focal points, had been divided with shire boundaries on the West Saxon model by about 1016.[5]

Archaeological investigation in the Back Lane and Cowl Lane areas between 1962 and 1972 produced evidence of a possibly defensive ditch and a possible bank, both of pre-tenth- century construction, and similar to the defences of other Mercian burhs. Subsequently, by about 970, the re-founded abbey was bounded by a ditch and bank on the line of the present Cowl Lane; and the defensive rampart running in parallel to Back Lane was renewed with a stone front in about 1000. There was also evidence that the town was mainly established to the east of the abbey precinct. The investigators concluded that the circuit of the town would have been some 1,800 metres (1,950 yards) in length, of which the Back Lane rampart comprised about 500 metres (540 yards). The town's defences would have enclosed a diamond-shaped area extending to 17 hectares, within which a street grid would have been laid out.[6]

Whatever its origins, Winchcombeshire was an extensive area in north-east Gloucestershire (as we now know it), comprising twelve separate administrative units known as 'hundreds'. The evidence that this shire title was short-lived is provided by a monk in Worcester, known as Hemming, writing in the latter part of the eleventh century, as follows:

'Eadric, whose cognomen was Streona [that is, the acquisitive], first under King Aethelred, and afterwards for a while under Cnut, was set over the whole realm of the English and held dominion over it like an under-king, insomuch that he joined townships to townships and shires to shires at his will; he even amalgamated the hitherto independent county of Winchcombe with the county of Gloucester.'[7]

Eadric Streona was a powerful ealdorman during the reign of Edmund and Cnut, with strong personal ambitions which compelled him to unscrupulous actions, fairly described as a turncoat. He was suspected of plotting against Cnut in 1017; and, when invited to a royal council in Gloucester at Christmas of that year, he and three others were executed for suspected treason. Thus, if Eadric ordered that Winchcombeshire be amalgamated with Gloucestershire, the union cannot have occurred later than 1017.

Further evidence of Winchcombe's importance at this time is provided by the existence of a mint in the town, apparently operated by a coin-maker or moneyer working on his own. It has been shown that throughout the period from the beginning of the reign of king Edgar (959-975) to the end of William I's reign (1066-1087) a moneyer was producing coins in Winchcombe.[8] The moneyer known as Goldwine may have been responsible for producing coinage for more than forty years between 1042 and 1087. Examples of his coins can be seen in Gloucester Museum. Although the Winchcombe mint appears to have closed by about 1087, its traditional site is still remembered by the name of The Old Mint House at 8 Hailes Street.

To attempt a detailed description of the borough of Winchcombe in the early eleventh century would be over-ambitious. But it seems reasonable to suppose that it was well-established as an important centre of local administration and trade. It would have been adequately fortified, although the fortifications on the southern edge of the town may have consisted largely of palisaded earthworks alongside the river bank, rather than the stone-faced rampart on the northern boundary. Although perhaps not yet stone-built, the abbey church, with living and working accommodation being gradually added to it, dominated the town's centre, where the Mercian kings' former palace was probably already in disrepair. The street pattern would have been laid out in much of the town, with individual land ownerships legally recognised; but it is doubtful whether any domestic buildings would have consisted of more substantial materials than wattle and daub, attached to a wooden frame, with a thatched roof.

1   G. Haigh: 'The History of Winchcombe Abbey', Skeffington and Son Ltd, 1947, pages 23-24

2   G. Haigh, op cit, pages 24-25

3   Landboc, Volume II, pages xiv-xv

4   Dr. S. R. Bassett: 'The administrative landscape of the diocese of Worcester in the tenth century' in 'St Oswald of Worcester, Life and Influence', edited by Nicholas Brooks and Catherine Cubitt, Leicester University Press, 1996, pages 147-173

5   C. S. Taylor: 'The Origin of the Mercian Shires' in H. P. R. Finberg: 'Gloucestershire Studies', 1957, Leicester University Press, pages 17-51

6   Peter Ellis: 'Excavations in Winchcombe, Gloucestershire, 1962-72: a report on excavation and fieldwork by B. K. Davison and J. Hinchliffe at Cowl Lane and Back Lane', Trans BGAS, 1986, Volume 104, pages 95-138

7   quoted in Julian Whybra: 'A Lost English County: Winchcombeshire in the 10th and 11th Centuries', 1990, The Boydell Press, page 6

8   L. V. Grinsell, C. E. Blunt and Michael Dolley: 'Sylloge of Coins of the British Isles, 19: Bristol and Gloucester Museums', 1973, published for the British Academy by Oxford University Press.

CHAPTER 5

WINCHCOMBE AT THE
DOMESDAY SURVEY

During Edward the Confessor's reign (1042-1066) Winchcombe prospered as a borough, administered by a 'port-reeve' or 'borough-reeve'. The titles derived from Old English terms, in which 'port' meant any trading centre and 'reeve' ('gerefa' in its earlier form) applied to an official with a wide range of administrative functions.[1] These could include the collection of tolls for markets, ensuring the coinage's purity and preventing its counterfeiting, and acting as a witness to important legal transactions. The port-reeve might also function as presiding magistrate. The administrative area for which this official was responsible appears to have been smaller than the former county of Winchcombeshire. It consisted of a number of sub-divisions of the unified Gloucestershire, each known as the 'hundred', already mentioned in Chapter 4. By this time the hundred had become a territorial and administrative unit within the shire, with responsibility for taxing, judicial and military functions; and where the freemen of the hundred attended the hundred court.

In the district around Winchcombe, the port-reeve probably administered the hundred of the town and the hundreds of Holford and Greston, including land comprised in Sudeley and Postlip manors, with a total area of some 44,000 acres.[2] These areas are shown on the map at Plan 2.[3]

The practical effect of the Norman conquest on Winchcombe is difficult to assess. The general picture is of William the Conqueror expropriating Saxon England for the benefit of his Norman followers. While this seems largely accurate, the local reality may have been more varied.

The thirty-five autonomous communities of black monks in England, of which Winchcombe abbey was one, were an obvious target of expropriation. In 1054 king Edward had appointed one of his chaplains, Godric, as abbot. Perhaps because he continued to show Saxon sympathies in defiance of the Normans, Godric (along with five other abbots) was removed by king William and temporarily imprisoned at Gloucester in about 1072. He was subsequently transferred to English custody, in the hands of the pro-Norman abbot Aethelwig of Evesham, who was also entrusted with Winchcombe abbey's administration for the three-year period after Godric's removal.[4] Thereafter, the next two abbots of Winchcombe, Galand and Ralph, appointed in 1075 and 1077 respectively, were of Norman origin. Nevertheless, despite these presumed signs of Norman disfavour to the abbey, there is no evidence that it was deprived of property, amounting in 1086 to some 25,300 acres.[5]

The Domesday Survey (commissioned by William the Conqueror at his council meeting in Gloucester soon after Christmas 1085 and completed by his clerks at Winchester before the end of 1086) might be expected to provide a complete account of the condition of Winchcombe at this time. But William's main purpose in the Survey was probably to assemble as much information as his officials could quickly and reliably obtain for taxation purposes. He was therefore interested in knowing the extent of land and property held in the time of his predecessor, king Edward, so that it could be compared with what was held, and by whom, in 1086. So it is perhaps unsurprising that the information recorded about Winchcombe (which may be less than was collected) tells us very little about the town's condition at that time.

The first thing to notice about the town's Domesday entry is its description as the Borough of Winchcombe: with this status, it ranks second in the county to Gloucester which is described as a city.[6] There is also a reference in the entry for land held in Gloucestershire by Evesham abbey to the 'ferding' (or quarter) of Winchcombe. This reference seemingly looks back to the former Winchcombeshire, before its absorption into the unified county, when its territory was about one-quarter of the area of Gloucestershire.

The Survey's information about the town's wealth is that, in king Edward's time (before 1066), it produced £6 from the Borough. At some unspecified later date, it produced £20, together with the whole hundred of the town. By 1086, taking into account also the three adjoining hundreds, the total revenue was £28, consisting of the £20 already mentioned, together with 100 shillings (£5) added by Durand the sheriff and 60 shillings (£3) by Roger of Ivry. Deduction from this entry is speculative, although it seems unlikely that the increase from £6 to £28, between the time of king Edward and 1086, can be regarded as a measure of the town's increased wealth during this period. A more likely explanation is that, during William I's reign, separate hundreds were grouped together for taxation purposes. The figure of £28 may therefore comprise the value of the borough of Winchcombe itself, together with three associated hundreds, which may have been Greston, Holford and Tibblestone (also shown on the map at Plan 2). The Tibble stone is traditionally believed to have been placed at the crossroads of the Tewkesbury to Stow-on-the-Wold and Cheltenham to Evesham roads, where it provided the meeting place for the men of that hundred.

The Survey's meagre information on Winchcombe can be supplemented with details recorded in what are known as 'satellite' texts. The most important such text for Gloucester and Winchcombe was compiled in about 1100 and preserved in Evesham abbey's archive, from which its title 'Evesham K' is derived. This text shows that, in Winchcombe borough, there were 60 burgesses, or burgage tenants, in king Edward's lordship (paying tax of 41 shillings), of whom 52 were living in inherited property and 8 had other residences in the town. The abbot of Winchcombe had 40 burgesses; and various other manorial lords had a total of 41 burgesses between them (including 10 owing service to Harold of Sudeley), making a total of 141 burgage tenancies.

Expert opinion differs on how this information can be reliably translated into population estimates for a late-eleventh-century borough. One estimate puts the number of burgesses in Winchcombe at Domesday as representing a total population, including wives, children, and monks and other inhabitants of the abbey, of perhaps 900 people.[7] A more recent estimate (emphasising that the Survey was not intended as a census and exact population estimates at this time are impossible) puts the Borough's secular population at 300 in 1066 and 410 in 1100, to which must be added some 50 to 75 abbey inhabitants.[8] Such widely differing estimates must clearly be treated with caution.

Another way of trying to understand how the borough functioned as the market centre for a quite extensive area is to examine the manors which had one or more burgesses in Winchcombe in 1086 and 1100. The underlying assumption is that these burgesses would act as agents for the sale of manorial produce in the borough's market and as buyers for their manorial lord's requirements. Using this approach, it has been shown that settlements as far away as Deerhurst (10 miles west), Broadwell (11 miles east) and Lechlade (24 miles south-east) looked to Winchcombe as a trading centre. This is illustrated in the map at Plan 3, showing the communication network between the town and places where one or more burgesses can be traced.[9]

The Survey's information can also be used to picture the appearance and way of life of the town's immediate surroundings.

The substantial manor of Sudeley, in Greston hundred, was immediately to the south-east. It was held before and after the Conquest by Harold, Earl Ralph's son, who possessed 10 hides on which tax was paid to the king and 4 ploughteams. There were also 18 villagers and 8 smallholders with 13 ploughteams, 14 slaves (male and female), 6 mills valued at 52 shillings, and woodland described as 3 leagues long and 2 leagues wide. This entry suggests that the area of arable land on the manor was substantial in order to justify 17 ploughteams. But perhaps the most distinctive feature of this holding was the extensive area of woodland, measuring about 4½ miles by 3 miles. If these measurements are correct, the woodland must have extended from somewhere in the area of Greet Grove (to the north) to Humblebee How or Bespidge Wood (to the south) and from Langley or Corndean in the west to the Saltway in the east. The greater part of the combe to the east and south of the town must have appeared heavily wooded.

Turning south towards Postlip (probably derived from the Old English words 'Pottes-lepe', meaning Pott's chasm or deep hollow[10]), there were 3 hides assessed to tax and the manorial lord in 1086, Godric, had 3 ploughteams. There were 3 villagers and 5 smallholders with 2 ploughteams, as well as 11 slaves, 2 mills valued at 15 shillings, and woodland measuring 1 league in length and width. The considerable area of woodland is again a distinctive feature of this manor.

Another prominent landscape feature resulted from the need to transport salt in commercial quantities. During Lent the inland population who could afford it would eat much salt fish; and for about half the year the great majority of people who could obtain meat would eat it salted. The supply of salt was brought from the salt pans at

Droitwich in Worcestershire to the highest point of navigation on the river Thames at Lechlade. This involved extending and adapting the former Roman route north-wards from Corinium which probably took its name, the White Way, from the transport of salt by pack horse. The result of this trade was that, by the end of the eleventh century, Winchcombe stood close to a recognised trade route, the Salt Way, running northwards beyond Hailes, through Toddington and Hinton-on-the-Green, and further into Worcestershire. Travelling southwards, the route followed the White Way until it diverged a little north of Compton Abdale to go by way of Coln St Dennis and Coln St Aldwyns to the salt quay at Lechlade. From there, river communication with London was possible.

Another clue to the landscape's appearance around the town is the number of mills. Mills recorded in the Survey include at least one owned by the abbey (probably a water-powered mill situated at the foot of what is now Mill Lane), one at Greet, two at Postlip, and as many as six on the manor of Sudeley. If these were all corn mills (rather than, for example, a fulling mill), substantial areas of land must have been under arable cultivation in the valleys to justify such investment in mill buildings and the employment of millers.

The picture emerging towards the end of the eleventh century is of an urban settle-ment at the centre of a comparatively extensive trading area. The borough's importance as a centre of Mercian kingship would already have become a fading memory and king Kenulph's former palace may well have been adapted to some other purpose or fallen into decay. Although the abbey church would have been the town's most impressive building, its vulnerability was shown on 15 October 1091 when, during a fierce storm, lightning severely damaged the tower and set light to a beam so that the building was filled with suffocating smoke.[11]

1   H. P. R. Finberg: 'The Genesis of the Gloucestershire Towns' in his 'Gloucestershire Studies', page 62

2   Rev. C. S. Taylor: 'An Analysis of the Domesday Survey of Gloucestershire', 1889, pages 31-32

3   This map is reproduced, with permission, from John S. Moore's paper entitled 'The Sudeley and Toddington Area in Domesday Book', published in 'The Sudeleys – Lords of Toddington' by the Manorial Society of Great Britain, 1985, pages 49-72

4   G. Haigh: 'The History of Winchcombe Abbey', page 27

5   Rev. C. S. Taylor, op cit, page 99

6   'Domesday Book, Volume 15 Gloucestershire', edited and translated by John S. Moore, Phillimore, 1982

7   H. P. R. Finberg, op cit, page 61

8   J. S. Moore, op cit, page 58

9   J. S. Moore, op cit, pages 69-70

10   A. H. Smith: 'The Place-Names of Gloucestershire – North and West Cotswolds', page 35

11   William of Malmesbury: 'Gesta Regum Anglorum', reproduced in G. Haigh, op cit, page 30

CHAPTER 6

THE TWELFTH CENTURY: UNQUIET TIMES

Winchcombe probably experienced comparative stability during the reign of the first two Norman kings and of William the Conqueror's son, Henry I (1100-1135). Henry I left no legitimate son; and, on his death, was succeeded in 1135 by his nephew Stephen. The result for southern England was a period of increasing, and ultimately terrifying, lawlessness as locally powerful barons took advantage of attempts by Henry's daughter, Matilda, to gain the English crown.

The years from 1135 to 1154 (the year of Stephen's death and the accession of the Plantagenet Henry II) were described by chroniclers of the time as the Anarchy. A modern historian has summarised the conditions experienced during this period by many towns in southern England as follows:

'While the disorders were, in the end, instructive to the English nobles in that they showed them that orderly government was in the long run to their own best interests, the nobles, who after all were only a minute fraction of the population of England, learned their lesson at a dreadful cost to the common people. Every chronicler, without exception, paints an appalling picture of the misery that prevailed during Stephen's reign, and the graphic account in the English Chronicle is only the most vivid of a whole series. The type of warfare that was practised during this period, whilst it was economical of the lives of knights, inflicted untold suffering upon the common people of the area in which it took place.'[1]

The plundering of towns and wasting of the country around them were at their most intense in Wiltshire and Gloucestershire because Earl Robert of Gloucester, the empress Matilda's half-brother and leader of her supporters, had strongholds at Gloucester and Bristol while Stephen's base in this area was at Oxford. The king sought to prevent Earl Robert from extending his control further eastwards and to inflict a heavy defeat on him.[2]

Winchcombe during the Anarchy

As a royal borough with a fortified castle, Winchcombe represented a significant prize to the king's opponents, quite apart from its strategically commanding situation in the north Cotswold foothills. The importance of controlling the town may have been increased by the fact that the first of the four abbots of Winchcombe named

Robert (abbot from 1138 to 1151) was related to king Stephen and would presumably have supported his cause.

A key figure in the struggle between king and empress was Miles of Gloucester, formerly Henry I's constable, who had initially recognised Stephen as king but later transferred his allegiance to Matilda and became one of her staunchest supporters. Miles was well placed to control the surrounding area from his base at Gloucester. On 7 November 1139, he attacked and captured Worcester, burning part of the town, and went on to capture Hereford later in the year. On 31 January 1140, Miles's forces fiercely attacked Winchcombe. It is impossible to say how well fortified the town and its castle (probably situated on the southern side of the abbey, perhaps on the slightly raised site now occupied by Jacobean House) were then. In any event, they could not withstand the fierce assault which resulted in burning the greater part of the town and driving out its inhabitants or taking them prisoner.[3]

When Miles of Gloucester transferred his allegiance from Stephen to Matilda he was followed by John de Sudeley, who (as lord of the manor) had fortified a castle at Sudeley. However, this change of allegiance soon proved a serious error of judgement because, in reprisal for Miles's partial destruction of Worcester, the Earl of Worcester (who supported Stephen) attacked Sudeley and captured its castle towards the end of December 1139. Consequently, when Miles's forces turned their attention from Winchcombe to Sudeley, at the beginning of 1140, they met with stiffer resistance than in the town and were forced to retreat. By the end of February 1140, the fighting in Winchcombe had left much of the town, except the abbey, in ruins and under the control of forces installed by Miles of Gloucester; whereas Sudeley was occupied by forces loyal to the king, while its lord (John de Sudeley) was in the service of Miles elsewhere in the county.

Winchcombe's remaining inhabitants might have hoped that the death of Miles of Gloucester, on Christmas Eve 1143, when one of his knights accidentally misdirected an arrow which fatally struck him in the chest while hunting deer, would bring relief from his marauding forces. However, Miles's place as one of Matilda's chief supporters was taken by his son Roger, whom she created Earl of Hereford. In 1144 the rival forces of king and empress were preparing for a decisive battle at Tetbury when the sudden appearance of Roger and Robert, Earl of Gloucester, at the head of 'a cruel and savage army of foot-soldiers' from Bristol persuaded the king and his supporters to avoid the engagement for the time being. Instead, realising that the area of north Gloucestershire formerly controlled by Miles and now by his son was temporarily vulnerable, Stephen changed tactics and marched northwards from Tetbury, aiming to lay siege to Winchcombe.

The exact date of these events in 1144 is unknown, but the chronicler of Stephen's reign has left a graphic account of them.[4] Roger had greatly strengthened the castle in Winchcombe since his father had captured it four years ago, so that it was now 'on a shelving precipice, with a very high wall, surrounded on all sides with defences of exceeding strength'. But Stephen had the advantage that many of the garrison had been withdrawn and ordered to Tetbury: this probably proved decisive to the outcome. Stephen assembled his best soldiers for the attack on Winchcombe and is said to have given them the following orders:

'Some were to keep up a thick and continued shower of arrows, others were to scale the mound on their hands and knees; whilst all the rest were to keep up a constant and untiring circuit round the walls. Every missile that came to hand was to be discharged into its interior. The besieged (but a scanty garrison, for many at the news of Stephen's sudden approach had taken fright), unable to endure the impetuous attack, surrendered the Castle, under mutual pledges.'

Thus the king regained the borough and used it as a garrison from which to restore his control over a large area of Gloucestershire.

Postlip during the Anarchy

Postlip's description in Domesday Book has been mentioned in Chapter 5. By Stephen's reign William de Solers was lord of the manor, where he probably occupied

a substantial house at the centre of a small agricultural estate. As no place of worship then existed at Postlip, its inhabitants had to travel to the nearest church in Winchcombe. While this arrangement was presumably satisfactory in peaceful times, conditions prevailing during the Anarchy made the journey too perilous. So William de Solers, 'moved by the tears and prayers of his tenants, built the chapel of St James at Postlip for a refuge from robbers, malignants and the fearful ravages in Stephen's days'.[5]

Before carrying out this building work William had to obtain the consent of abbot Robert of Winchcombe abbey. The legal agreement between them provided for William to meet the costs of providing a priest from the abbey to attend at St James's chapel by endowing it with tithes transferred from the house of St Peter in Gloucester. William also provided a house and a half yardland (possibly as much as twenty acres) at Postlip for the priests's residence. William's tenants themselves also gave a half yard-land. In return, the priest was to hold a daily service at the chapel when the lord of the manor was present and three services per week in his absence. These arrangements were subsequently renewed by William's son, Roger de Solers, in another legal agreement. Tradition maintains that the weathered stone figure of a man standing at the western gable-end of the splendid tithe barn at Postlip represents William de Solers.[6]

Hailes during the Anarchy

One consequence of the widespread lawlessness during the Anarchy was that local barons established their own fortified buildings in which they and their tenants could defend themselves against marauders. At the small hamlet of Hailes (where the abbey was not founded until the mid-thirteenth century), Ralph of Worcester decided to fortify a castle. He then took the controversial step of building a church, presumably for his tenants to worship in, and having it dedicated by Simon, bishop of Worcester from 1125 to 1151. As Winchcombe and Hailes were both in the diocese of Worcester until 1539, the bishop must have realised that, because Hailes belonged parochially to Winchcombe abbey, the abbot would resist Ralph's demand that this church at Hailes should have the right to bury the dead. However, abbot Robert probably did not antic-ipate the drastic measures Ralph would take against the abbey to enforce his claim.

Ralph responded to the abbot's objections by blockading the abbey and effectively preventing the community from living a normal life until they agreed to concede the right of burial to the church at Hailes. Faced with this show of force, abbot Robert had no alternative to giving up the abbey's claim: this concession is recorded in a legal document which provides for an annual payment of seven shillings to the abbey.[7] Ralph of Worcester had succeeded in humiliating the monastery at a time when it could not rely on the king for protection against a determined adversary.

The fire of 1151

A far more disastrous experience for the abbey occurred on 29 August 1151. At that time, the monastic buildings were apparently not enclosed by any boundary wall; and, as some form of fortification, numerous cottages had been built closely around the abbey on all sides. Fire was an ever-present danger in flimsy domestic buildings, probably consisting of wood, wattle and daub, and thatched roofs. When fire broke out in some of these cottages, apparently due to the occupants' carelessness, the abbey buildings, including the church, were engulfed and substantially destroyed.[8] The borough's inhabitants seemingly failed to heed the lesson as another fire, at some time in the 1160s or 1170s, also seriously damaged buildings in the town.[9]

The borough in the late twelfth century

The evidence of the itinerant justices appointed to assess the tax-paying capacity of Gloucestershire is that Winchcombe was steadily declining in the late twelfth century. In 1188, the justices assessed Gloucester at 100 marks (the mark was equiv-alent to thirteen shillings and fourpence, or two-thirds of one pound sterling), Cirencester at 20 marks, Cheltenham at £5, and Winchcombe at 4 marks. By 1196, the tax-paying capacity of the burgesses of Winchcombe had fallen to 3 marks.[10]

Despite this decline, what appears to have been an extremely important transac-tion took place between the borough's citizens and the abbey. It is recorded in the abbey's cartulary and, in English translation from the Latin, reads as follows:

'In the reign of Henry II, the men of Winchcombe, by common assent, on the advice of Nicholas de Brueria, then bailiff of the Hundred, exchanged with our Almonry the Booth Hall, situated below the Castle, and the Guildhall, which is in North Street, held communally by the townspeople themselves, for a plot of land close to the Almonry, in order to build an aisle and altar dedicated to Saint Nicholas on the north side of the Church of St Peter.'[11]

This document ends rather confusingly by stating that the Booth Hall (or market hall) is in North Street and the Guildhall in Here Street.

There are a number of possible interpretations of this transaction. Perhaps the most plausible is that the townspeople wished to provide a place of worship for themselves and the abbey agreed they should be enabled to do so by constructing an additional, external north aisle to St Peter's church which had remained the abbey's church until this time. If that interpretation is correct, it may also help to explain the persistent tradition of a Saxon church of St Nicholas. Although that church is supposed to have been at the junction of Bull Lane and Chandos Street, it may have been no more than a chantry chapel; and the 'aisle and altar dedicated to St Nicholas', which the towns-people presumably financed themselves, may subsequently have been customarily referred to as a separately dedicated church of St Nicholas, although no parish of that name can now reliably be traced in the available documentary records.

This transaction between the abbey and the townspeople also gives us the earliest intriguing glimpse of a secular figure responsible for the borough's government, namely Nicholas de Brueria. As bailiff of the hundred of Winchcombe borough, Nicholas would have been responsible for the king's affairs in the town. His name appears as a witness to numerous legal documents in the abbey's cartulary in the latter part of the twelfth century. As well as advising the townspeople collectively, he would have undertaken many property transactions. In one example, he sold a plot of land in the town which had been void since the fire of the 1160s or 1170s to Henry de Stanton for eighteen shillings, so that a house could be built on it.[12]

At some time before 1181 Nicholas made an agreement with abbot Henry to benefit from fraternity with the abbey. The basis was that, in return for paying ten marks in silver, Nicholas would receive accommodation and food in the abbey at the same standard as a monk, including bread, beer, thick pottage from the kitchen and whatever commons were provided for the monks in the evening. Towards the end of his life, Nicholas was also to be granted 'the habit of St Benedict' which was intended to ensure that, by clothing himself in monastic garb, he would deserve salvation as much as any other member of the monastic order.[13]

Towards the end of the twelfth century it seems that, although Winchcombe was a borough in decline from the effects of two disastrous fires, the abbey provided a stable core in the town. Moreover, the inhabitants apparently benefited from compe-tent civil government in the trusted hands of the king's bailiff.

1   J. T. Appleby: 'The Troubled Reign of King Stephen', Bell, 1969, page 206
2   A. L. Poole: 'Domesday Book to Magna Carta, 1087-1216', The Oxford History of England, 1955, page 151
3   G. Haigh: 'The History of Winchcombe Abbey', page 36
4   'Gesta Stephani', cited in Landboc, Volume I, page xvi
5   Landboc, Volume I, page 81
6   E. Adlard: 'Winchcombe Cavalcade', page 71
7   Landboc, Volume I, page 65
8   Landboc, Volume I, page 83, footnote 1
9   Landboc, Volume I, page xvii
10   Landboc, Volume I, page xviii
11   Landboc, Volume I, pages 231-232
12   Landboc, Volume I, page 147
13   Landboc, Volume I, pages 213-214

CHAPTER 7

REBUILDING IN THE
THIRTEENTH CENTURY

As late as 1181 Winchcombe abbey was in such poor physical condition that the monks lacked even the basic essential of a cloister for meditation, exercise and education within the community. During his lengthy rule from 1194 to 1221, the third abbot named Robert, previously a monk in the abbey, was responsible for providing the funds and overseeing the building work which would eventually result in provision of a new abbey church, monastic offices and a cloister. This laborious task was probably carried out by local masons in the solid Norman style, using stone from local quarries owned by, or leased to, the abbey. One such quarry was situated at 'Londeley', almost certainly the quarry later known as Monk Holes on Langley Hill.

The abbey's water supply

The rebuilding work was also an opportunity for the abbey to improve the monks' quality of life. One such improvement was the installation, between 1190 and 1200, of a piped supply of fresh water, brought from a spring known as Honeywell, now believed to be the site of St Kenelm's well on the Sudeley estate. For this purpose, Robert Russell and his son William granted the abbey permission to construct and maintain an underground water pipe across their land. A similar grant was obtained from Robert, then the parson of a chapel at Sudeley, for the length of pipe passing under his land.[1]

But any legal difficulties involved in obtaining these wayleaves must have seemed minor in comparison with the civil engineering problems involved in providing the water supply. The abbey records show that a lead pipe had to be laid underground throughout its course, including a short section beneath the bed of the river Isbourne. Nonetheless, the twelfth-century water engineers' skill was such that, when the town's mains water supply was being laid in 1887, some of the original one-inch bore lead pipe was found intact. There is no extant record of who constructed this pipeline; how long the operation took; or exactly how the abbey financed a civil engineering project on this scale when there were other major building works to be carried out as part of the restoration. But the town's inhabitants, laboriously drawing water from wells in houses and yards, must have envied this essential amenity the monks had provided for themselves. The townspeople had to wait almost another seven hundred years to obtain a piped water supply.

The abbey's property acquisitions

Abbot Robert also seems to have been concerned to strengthen the abbey's financial base. In 1201, he initiated the monastery's largest single property venture until then by acquiring from William de Béthune, an advocate from Arras, the Cotswold manors of Hawling, Haselton and Yanworth costing £208, together with £12 for livestock and payments of £5 and £3 respectively to William's wife and children.[2]

The abbey's land acquisitions were not concerned only with substantial Cotswold sheep-rearing manors. Abbot Robert and the abbey's prior Thomas appear to have been sharp commercial operators, with a quick eye for property acquisition in the borough. In about 1220, prior Thomas seized an opportunity to acquire a parcel of land in Winchcombe's North Street, with the object of building a house with a stone-slated roof at a cost of seven marks. This was regarded as unusually expensive because of the roof's superior quality. However, as the foundation of the house was being laid, a woman known only as Goda, and her husband Johannis le Franceis, tried to stop the building work by alleging that the site had been illegally acquired. The outcome of this dispute appears to have been that, through the wise counsel of the king's bailiff, who was then Thomas Smelred, Goda gave up any claim she might have had to the land; and the house was presumably completed.[3] Perhaps this is an early example of the serious tensions which subsequently developed between the abbey and the town.

Abbot Robert's death in 1221 preceded two events which greatly enhanced the abbey's prestige. First, in 1223, Henry III granted to the abbot of Winchcombe (by then, abbot Thomas) the hundred of the borough, together with the hundreds of Kiftsgate, Holford and Greston, at an annual rent of £50, payable at Michaelmas.[4] For practical purposes, this grant considerably increased its control over the town and a large surrounding area in administering justice and collecting tithes.

Rebuilding the abbey church

Secondly, the elaborate rebuilding of the abbey church was completed in 1239. As part of that operation, Henry III had given orders for timber from the royal forests in Gloucestershire to be used: in August 1233 twenty oaks were sent from the Forest of Dean; and in 1235 the constable of St Briavels was ordered to supply forty oaks.[5] This may mean that, despite the extensive woodland on the Sudeley estate, sufficient timber of suitable quality for such uses as roof beams could no longer be obtained locally. On 18 October 1239 Walter de Cantilupe, bishop of Worcester, was present in Winchcombe to dedicate the newly built abbey church in the names of the Blessed Virgin and St Kenelm. There is no information about how many monks then belonged to the monastery, but the community presumably hoped for increasing prosperity by attracting substantial numbers of pilgrims to St Kenelm's re-dedicated shrine.

The life of the borough

The thirteenth century's early years were probably also a time for rebuilding in the town as the voids resulting from the fires in the previous century were gradually filled. Numerous documents in the abbey's cartulary enable the names of the town's main

Plate 1

streets to be identified, although some have since ceased to exist. The town's main crossroads was probably at the junction of High Street (also called Magnus Vicus or Magna Platea) and North Street, with Hailes Street leading eastwards from High Street eventually to the ford through the river Isbourne at what later became known as Footbridge. The streets would have been narrow and largely unpaved: many are referred to as Lanes and were probably no wider than, for example, present-day Mill Lane and Bick's Lane. Cottages, barns and outhouses would have stood close together on either side, so that no space within a curtilage was wasted. Typical examples of such cottages were the pair known as 'King John's houses' which stood in the lower part of Hailes Street, almost opposite 'The Follies', until they were condemned as unfit for human habitation in the early-twentieth century. The site of these cottages is now occupied by the dwellings known as 1 and 2 Easter Cottages. The two older cottages can be seen in the photograph of Hailes Street at Plate 1 on the right hand side of the street.

The following streets and lanes are identifiable in legal documents: Beater street (seemingly on the course of the present Gloucester Street), Bodeford street (possibly leading towards Sudeley by way of a ford across the river Isbourne, roughly on the course of the present Castle Street), Cangerslane, Capuneslane, Colestrete (probably on the course of the present Cowl Lane, alongside the abbey's eastern boundary), Cuffeslane, Herestret, Mullelane (probably on the course of the present Mill Lane, leading to a corn mill owned by the abbey), Peticrueslane and Pillokeslane.

Outside the abbey complex, the most important public building would have been the town hall, almost certainly situated on or near the site of the present town hall at The Cross. There was also a market place, with an uncertain location. One possibility is that markets were held on land in front of the main gateway to the abbey, approximately on the site of the present Queen Square. The town's principal trading occasion was the feast of St Kenelm, originally held on 17 July but moved to 28 July when the calendar was reformed.[6] A merchant's attendance at St Kenelm's Fair might involve serious personal risk. In 1221, a Cirencester merchant, Simon de Sègre, was robbed and murdered on his way to the fair; but, although William de Camera was charged with the murder, in conspiracy with Simon's wife, he maintained that the merchant was alive and well.[7]

Winchcombe was also nationally recognised for its horse fairs. During the latter part of the nineteenth century, horse fairs were held in North Street, on either side of the junction with Chandos Street, where iron tethering rings can still be seen on the walls of some houses. The photograph at Plate 2 shows a horse fair in progress. A document from the abbey's cartulary during abbot Ralph's rule (1184-1194) enables the approximate location of the medieval horse market to be established.

This document records that the abbot granted to the abbey's sacristy a parcel of land situated under the monastery's wall, 'on the north side near Gastebroc', for the purpose of building 'a grange' (probably meaning a farmhouse). A traditional site of one of the abbey's barns, corresponding broadly to this description, is the building situated towards the eastern end of Back Lane, now known as Tythe Barn Cottages and previously occupied by Mr. Sam Bayliss as a blacksmith's forge. This barn may well have been associated with the sacristy's grange. 'Gastebroc' was probably the stream known much later as Tarrant Brook, which flowed across Back Lane at about that point and then crossed the northern end of North Street before it was culverted in the 1850s. The same document then refers to a parcel of land owned by Robert Cnotte which is described as 'in the northern part of the town, next to King street, near Horsmarket, and against the sacristy's grange, which was mentioned above'.[8] From these descriptions, it seems likely that there was an open area towards the northern

Plate 2

end of what is now Cowl Lane (where the Lane possibly intersected with a subsequently lost, west-to-east road, known as King street) which served as the borough's horse market in medieval times.

The horse fair undoubtedly attracted buyers from far afield. In 1256, during Henry III's reign, there is the following reference to horses being bought for the queen in Winchcombe:

'Allocate to William de Lasseberg, sheriff of Gloucester, in the issues of the king's fair at Winchcombe 18l. 16s. 8d. spent in purchase of a palfrey and two pack-horses for the queen in the said fair by view and testimony of Master Walter, the queen's farrier (marescalli) and Master John, the king's farrier.'[9]

Another example is provided by Roger de Marlowe, rector of Harwell in Berkshire, writing to a friend who was a monk at Hailes abbey to ask for help in buying a horse at Winchcombe fair, to replace lost horses, as follows:

'Also, since having lost some of my horses I am hardly able to go about, and there is at present a fair at Winchcombe near you, where as I have often heard, many horses are to be found, I earnestly beg you to look about and get some of your people to give their advice and help to the bearer [of the letter] and Sir Thomas de Sandford, canon, and also to assist them yourself, so that I may be provided with some suitable horse there, costing not more than four or five marks ...'[10]

Tension between abbey and borough

An early sign of tension between the abbey and its neighbours in the town occurred in about 1230, involving the vicar of Winchcombe who was Henry de Campden at that time. The parish church was then what the monks described as a chapel dedicated to St Peter in which the vicar officiated separately from the abbey church, although the land this St Peter's church occupied may well have been within the abbey's curtilage. Although the conflict's initial cause is unclear, Henry de Campden showed his displeasure by causing his church's bells to be rung so noisily that the monks were seriously disturbed during their observance of the canonical hours. As this dispute could not be resolved mutually, Pope Gregory IX delegated authority, on 7 March 1231, to the priors of Llanthony and St Oswald's and the dean of Gloucester to determine the charge against the vicar of disturbance by bell-ringing and other harmful actions. No record of this dispute's outcome appears to exist: perhaps the Pope's three wise men found a formula for concluding it satisfactorily to the parties. However, another Pope would have to return to the same matter in 1399.

About sixteen years later, Henry de Campden was involved in another dispute with the abbey over a proposal to enlarge by some 12 feet the chancel of the parish church of St Peter, and to add a south aisle, measuring 30 feet by 12 feet, which would have encroached on the abbey's access through its main gate and partially obstructed the road. As this dispute involved the highway in a royal borough, the matter was referred to Henry III whose reply to the vicar's request was as follows:

'If the chancel be lengthened by 12 feet, it will be to the damage of the Abbot and Abbey, because the said Abbot will not be able to have free ingress and egress for his carts and horses and to carry his timber; and if Henry enlarges the aisle as is aforesaid, and the wall of the church be made towards the highway, two carts will not be able to pass there at the same time, and this would be of the greatest harm on the market days of the said vill.'[11]

However, on 18 September 1246, the king's permission was given for carrying out the proposed work, provided the abbey's entrance was not reduced to less than 30 feet wide and the public highway to less than 18 feet.[12] This may be the earliest example of planning control in Winchcombe.

This permission is interesting for its topographical detail when no maps or plans of the borough are available. Assuming that the abbey's main gate was at the western end of what is now Abbey Terrace, the location of the church Henry de Campden wished to enlarge was probably about the same as the present parish church of St Peter, although a somewhat smaller building. Lengthening by 12 feet the chancel at the eastern end of that earlier building (which may well have had a lower level foundation than the present church) would therefore have encroached on the western flank of the abbey's main entrance. Similarly, if the highway on the southern side of the earlier church ran closer to the building than the present course of Gloucester Street at that point, a new south aisle 12 feet wide might well have resulted in some unacceptable reduction in the road's width. In any event, the king's permission presumably satisfied all parties sufficiently to enable Henry de Campden to have his proposed improvement carried out, subject to the king's modification.

The foundation of Hailes abbey

Not long after this dispute was settled the monastic community at Winchcombe may have been surprised, and perhaps concerned, to find that another house of a different religious order, the Cistercians, was to be established less than two miles east of the town, at Hailes.

The decision to found Hailes abbey resulted from a religious vow made by Richard, Earl of Cornwall, king John's son and Henry III's brother, when he was in danger of drowning at sea during a return voyage to England from Gascony in October 1242.[13] In 1245 Henry III granted his brother the manor of Hailes to provide land where he could fulfil his vow appropriately. The building work must have proceeded rapidly because the abbey church at Hailes was completed and ready for dedication by the bishop of Worcester, Walter de Cantilupe, on 5 November 1251. The chronicler Matthew Paris described the ceremony as follows:

'There was present the Earl Richard, the King and Queen with the Lord Edward, their noble first born. There were thirteen bishops at the church and many others, both abbots and priors of various orders, and over and above that, the great men of England, earls, barons and other nobles who came to the said monastery on the same day.'[14]

No doubt abbot John Yanworth of Winchcombe was among this throng, perhaps feeling some misgivings about his own abbey's future, alongside this new and well-supported foundation, when, earlier in the year, the grant of the hundreds of

Winchcombe borough, Holford and Kiftsgate had been withdrawn from the abbey and placed in the sheriff's keeping.

Although Earl Richard was said to have spent 10,000 marks on building the abbey and to have given 1,000 marks to acquire land or buildings, his new foundation of twenty Cistercian monks and ten lay-brothers did not flourish immediately. It was only after 1270, when the abbey received the gift from Edmund, Earl Richard's second son, of a phial of the Holy Blood (guaranteed as authentic by the Patriarch of Jerusalem, later Pope Urban IV), that Hailes abbey's future as a place of pilgrimage was secure. On the day before the relic was to be placed in a shrine at Hailes, Edmund brought it personally to Winchcombe abbey where he spent the night while the phial was guarded by two Cistercian monks. The next day's events (Holy Rood day in September 1270) have been reconstructed as follows:

'On the following morning a procession was formed, Edmund and the Abbot of Winchcombe heading it, which made for Hailes. The monks of the two Convents met in the field still called "Rowley", where a tent and an altar having been raised for the occasion the entire populace of the neighbourhood adored the Relic. The Abbot of Hailes preached an explanatory sermon, and after it, the procession re-formed and with hymn and jubilation carried the sacred treasure to the monastery.'[15]

Winchcombe abbey's building work continues

Whatever Winchcombe abbey's monks thought of the arrival of another monastic house at Hailes, new building work was commissioned at Winchcombe until the end of the thirteenth century and beyond. Two documents in the abbey's cartulary refer to a Lady Chapel then being built in the abbey's cemetery.[16] And another document mentions that this Mary Chapel had been completed and was situated in the cemetery beside the abbey church.[17] These documents were to enable donors to fund the provision of a light to burn continuously in the chapel, suggesting that the cult of the Blessed Virgin was as important as the Kenelm legend by the end of the thirteenth century.

Very little is known about the architects, then called master-masons, who were responsible for building and maintaining the abbey's fabric. But there is a brief glimpse, towards the end of the century, of one of these highly skilled craftsmen, Walter Herford. Master Walter probably came from the medieval village of Harford, between Naunton and Upper Slaughter.[18] After supervising the new building work at Winchcombe abbey, he undertook the building of Vale Royal abbey in Cheshire and was the architect for Caernarvon castle.[19]

Master Walter agreed to a contract, on 22 January 1278, with the abbey which provided in great detail for his terms of employment. He promised to serve the abbey faithfully and to carry out the new work competently; and, except for the king's building works, he was not to undertake any other work without the abbey's permission. In return, the abbey was to maintain Master Walter at the same standard as one of the abbot's chief servants. If he became ill, he was to receive daily two monks' loaves, two noggins of ale and two dishes from the abbot's kitchen. His two grooms were to receive the same fare as the abbot's grooms; and his two horses were to have a nightly bushel of oats when they were at work during the day. In any long-term sickness, or his old age, there would be the same provision of loaves, ale and meat, but he would only be entitled to one groom and one horse. As to clothing, he qualified annually for a robe of the same kind as the abbey's steward; and his grooms would have the same dress as the abbot's grooms. For his accommodation Walter was permitted to build a chamber near the abbey's granary, but he would have to meet the cost of the building work himself, except for the stone and timber which the abbot would provide. To light and heat this accommodation, he was to have two wax lights nightly from the abbot's chamber and four tallow candles, between Michaelmas and Easter, together with a weekly quantity of firewood.[20] Such were the rewards a skilled and experienced architect-craftsman could command.

1   Landboc, Volume I, pages 237-238 and 242
2   Landboc, Volume II, pages 310-311
3   Landboc, Volume I, pages 99-100
4   Landboc, Volume I, page xix
5   G. Haigh: 'The History of Winchcombe Abbey', page 64
6   Landboc, Volume I, page xl
7   Landboc, Volume I, page xli
8   Landboc, Volume I, pages 93-94
9   Calendar of Liberate Rolls, Volume IV (1251-1260), page 313
10   cited by Rosalind Hill in Berkshire Archaeological Journal, Volume 41 (1937), pages 18-19
11   cited by L. F. Salzman: 'Building in England down to 1540', page 383
12   Close Rolls, 1242-1247, page 462
13   Doreen Winkless: 'Hailes: The Story of a Gloucestershire Abbey', The Spredden Press, 1990, page 1
14   cited in D. Winkless, op cit, page 16
15   W. St. Clair Baddeley: 'A Cotteswold Shrine', John Bellows, 1908, page 58
16   Landboc, Volume I, pages 245-247
17   Landboc, Volume I, page 245
18   David Verey: 'Cotswold Churches', Batsford, 1976, page 29
19   John H. Harvey: 'Henry Yevele', Batsford, 1944, pages 4-5
20   Landboc, Volume I, pages 136-138

CHAPTER 8

PROSPERITY OVERCOME BY PESTILENCE AND UNREST

A t the beginning of the fourteenth century the borough of Winchcombe and its abbey displayed a veneer of prosperity. In 1273, one of the juries Edward I appointed to provide information about every hundred in the land found that the manor of Winchcombe was 'independent, extra-corporate of the County; in the hands of the King and of ancient demesne.'[1] This presumably meant that the sheriff of Gloucestershire had to account to the Exchequer for revenue from taxes payable to the king as lord of the borough. By the 1270s, the sheriff had become accustomed to granting the town to the bailiffs for the sum of five marks (representing the sheriff's profit margin) more than the annual rent owing to the king.[2] This arrangement made the borough effectively self-governing and contrasted with the situation of Cirencester, which lacked borough status and was dominated by its abbey until the dissolution of the monasteries in the 1530s.[3]

An indication that the physical condition of the borough was being gradually improved is Edward III's writ, issued on 18 December 1327 to the bailiffs of Winchcombe, authorising them to levy a local customs duty, for a three-year period, in order to help finance the paving of the town.[4] This document mentions the wares which were presumably expected to be brought for sale in the town's markets. Some of the items listed are a commonplace of trade in a market town at this time: a levy of 2d. on each sack of wool; $^1/_2$d. on each horse, mare, ox or cow; $^1/_4$d. on each horse-load of corn; 1d. on each weigh of salt; and 8d. on every 52 gallons of wine. But some items appear to show a more sophisticated taste on the part of the buyers in Winchcombe's markets: examples are 1d. on each bundle of squirrel skins; 1d. on 20 salmon; $^1/_2$d. on each hamper of figs and raisins; and $^1/_4$d. on each lamprey from the Severn, between Christmas and Easter. Although it is arguable that these are simply items on a standard list used by Exchequer clerks in granting a right to levy customs duties, the references to bundles of teazles (which were used in the cloth-fulling process) and lampreys from the Severn suggest that the list may well have been compiled by someone who was familiar with the range of products actually brought for sale in the borough's markets.

It seems likely that the town had already developed a diversified economy which required the services of craftsmen and tradesmen possessing a range of skills. An

Exchequer Roll of 1313, listing the names of Winchcombe's inhabitants owing lay subsidies to Edward II is revealing.[5] By this time the custom of naming men by their town or village of origin was gradually lapsing and references to their trade or craft, such as John the cutler, Gerard the slater and Henry the hooper, were being introduced. In this 1313 tax return, the following trades are represented by some of the names: four millers, three slaters, two weavers, a cutler, a cook, a maltster, a hooper, a tailor, a skinner and a tanner (indicating the probable existence of a tannery), a bowmaker, a saddler, a turner (presumably of wood), a carter, a 'horsenail' (presumably a blacksmith), and a horse dealer. A particularly interesting name is Nicholas le catour, which is an abbreviation for 'achatour' or buyer. His presence may indicate that buying and selling of commodities in the borough's markets were on a sufficient scale to support a small group of merchants; or he may have been a buyer of provisions for the abbey or for a manorial lord who held a burgage tenancy in the borough.

Winchcombe and the surrounding district relied on the two staple activities of arable farming and wool production. Although there may have been a very small group of prosperous individuals who did not need to produce their own crops, the great majority of inhabitants, including the skilled craftsmen, would also have tilled some land. As the abbey was a major landowner, some of them may have owed agricultural services on the abbot's land, while others may have been able to commute their services for a lump-sum payment freeing them to work on their own plots. Some would have had to rely on cultivating a small strip of the 'in-field', from which Enfield Farm is named. Even with the help of a ploughteam, this type of cultivation would have involved unremitting toil throughout the year, overshadowed by the fear that crop failure or a poor yield would result in food scarcity or famine. And, when such an essential crop as corn was successfully harvested, the additional burden of compulsion to have it ground at the abbey's, or a manorial lord's, mill had to be borne.

The importance of wool production

The production and marketing of wool in the district around Winchcombe were almost certainly monopolised by the abbey throughout the medieval period, although the arrival at Hailes of the Cistercian Order (who specialised in sheep rearing and wool production, particularly at their three great Yorkshire abbeys) would have provided an alternative source of material from the mid-thirteenth century. The Cistercians' greater competence in wool production probably explains why F.B. Pegolotti, one of the wool-buying agents in England for the Florentine Bardi company at this time, recorded that he could buy annually from Hailes abbey twenty sacks of wool, comprising first, second and third quality sorted wool at 19, 10 or 7 marks per sack (depending on the quality), whereas Benedictine Winchcombe abbey produced forty sacks of wool annually which was cleaned but not sorted by quality and could therefore not command more than 13 marks per sack.[6]

Fulling mills

The raw material from Winchcombe abbey's wool clip was not sold as such entirely to foreign buyers. Some of it appears to have been used to produce raw cloth, which was then put through the fulling process. This involved scouring, cleansing and thickening the cloth by beating it in water, which was carried out in a fulling mill. As early as king John's reign (1199-1216), a document in the abbey's cartulary mentions an overflow of water 'from our fulling mill, situated next to John Blundell's court-yard'.[7] It seems that some unexplained overflow of water from the abbey's fulling mill, which was presumably powered by water channelled from the river Isbourne, had damaged John Blundell's property, for which the abbey agreed to pay compensation of 8d. annually. Subsequently, John Blundell agreed to grant the abbey the right to use this water course so that the fulling mill would operate more efficiently.[8]

In about 1317 William Aderwyne of Cotes-juxta-Winchcombe granted to Master William de Bosco, who is described as 'clerk' (that is, a cleric) a fulling mill he owned in the village of Cotes, at a place called 'Le Dom'.[9] This arrangement was short-lived because the next document shows that William Aderwyne then granted the same fulling mill to the abbey, with William de Bosco's agreement.[10] Cotes was then a sepa-rate hamlet from Winchcombe and this fulling mill was probably on or near the site of what later became Coates mill, at the foot of present-day Corndean Lane, where water power from the river Isbourne was available. Although it is not known who operated this fulling mill, it was most likely leased to local cloth fullers. It has also been suggested that St. Kenelm's fair was the occasion for a great sale of cloth and that weavers, dyers and fullers worked in a Winchcombe cloth industry at the beginning of the fourteenth century.[11]

Further evidence of a flourishing cloth industry in the area is provided by John Waupol of Wenlond's grant to the abbey, at some time between 1282 and 1314 (during abbot Walter's rule), of his property in the village of Throp-juxta-Winchcombe, valued in total at £100, indicating that he was a landowner of considerable wealth. The list of John Waupol's property includes a fulling mill oper-ated by four (at least) of his tenants.[12] The exact location of Throp (or Thropp as it was also spelt) is uncertain, although another document from abbot Walter's time, in which Lord John of Sudeley grants extensive property rights to the abbey, including some in Throp-juxta-Winchcombe, suggests that it was in the manor of Sudeley.[13] If that is correct, this other fulling mill may have been outside the town's southern boundary where it could have relied on water power from the Beesmoor Brook.

Fulling mills replaced the earlier process of beating, kneading or treading the woven woollen fabric in a water-filled trough to close the threads together. Instead of this manual process, or walking repeatedly on the pieces of cloth, the fullers used large water-powered wooden hammers to beat the cloth in a trough. As a fulling mill involved considerable capital investment, only justified by processing substantial quantities of cloth, the existence of at least two fulling mills in these hamlets near Winchcombe appears to confirm that there was a well-established cloth-making industry in the area at the beginning of the fourteenth century.

Consolidating the abbey's property in the borough

The abbey evidently continued to take every affordable opportunity to extend and consolidate its estate in the borough. A good example of this incremental process occurred in September 1294 when abbot Walter wished to enlarge the area of the abbey's garden in the northern part of its curtilage. This involved obtaining from the king, Edward I, authority to stop up a road (known as Peticrueslane) on a west-to-east course through the abbey's grounds and compensating users of the road for that obstruction by providing another route to the west of the abbey's gardens on its own land.[14]

Dr. Steven Bassett has suggested that Peticrueslane followed the course of the former west-to-east road into the centre of the town and, before its stopping-up in 1294, continued eastwards to cross Cowl Lane and North Street, where it may have extended further east into what is now Chandos Street. Dr. Bassett traces the probable course of this road in his plan of the medieval borough which is reproduced, with his permission, in Plan 4.[15] It may be significant in this context that the house (52 North Street) on the western side of North Street, opposite the western end of Chandos Street, is a narrow infilled property, perhaps suggesting that it was built on the former course of Peticrueslane. However, the title of the king's grant of permission for stopping-up Peticrueslane seems to suggest that, despite its previous importance as part of a west-to-east highway through the town, it had been superseded by 1294, perhaps by Gloucester Street which, in its probable guise as Beater Street, can already be identified in a document of 1216.[16]

The abbey's domestic economy

In the early fourteenth century Winchcombe abbey probably consisted of about twenty monks. However, the abbey functioned as a substantial, largely self-contained estate within the borough, where the abbot and prior would have been regarded as wealthy and influential figures. The scale of the abbey's domestic economy can be measured from a list of the abbey's staff in about 1330, divided between servants of the monastery and the abbot's personal servants.

The abbey's servants included the following: the Provider for the Cellarer (the cellarer was the monastery's chief steward), the Porter, the Underporter, the Master Sergeant of the Church, the Subsergeant of the Sacristy, the Refectory Sergeant, the Master Sergeant of the Infirmary, the Undersergeant, the Convent Cook, the Buyer for the Kitchen, the General Sergeant, the Supervisor of crockery and tableware for the Convent and (a different servant) for the abbot's crockery and tableware, the Guest Hall Sergeant, the Undersergeant, the Stabler, the Master Brewer and two Undersergeants (indicating brewing on a large scale), the Master Baker and two Undersergeants, the Winnower, woodcarriers, carters, the kitchen door Porter, the Swineherd, the Tannery Sergeants, the Master Tanner and an Undersergeant, the Carpenter and the Sergeant of the Parlour. This list in the abbey's cartulary specifies the wages payable to each servant.

The abbot's personal staff are listed as: the Butler, the Sumpter, the abbot's Squire, the Messenger, the Padgroom, the Chaplain's Groom, the Cook, the Cellarer's Squire, the Cellarer's Groom, the Under-Butler, the Farrier, the Abbey's Smith, the Smith's boy, the Miller and the Carpenter. Their wages are also specified.[17]

The abbey's inhabitants were not confined to the monks and their servants. Additionally, there was a group of lay people benefiting from accommodation and food, and occasionally an income, provided by the abbey in return for their faithful service, or gifts of property, or cash payments. This arrangement, always detailed in a legal agreement, was known as a 'corrody': perhaps the nearest present-day equivalent is the purchase of an annuity. There was also a recognised custom that, where a monastery was a royal foundation, the king had the privilege of nominating such people as clerics who were temporarily without a benefice, or retired servants or ladies-in-waiting, to a corrody. These royal requests eventually became so numerous that abbeys were obliged to refuse them; and, by virtue of the Statute of Westminster in 1327, Edward III undertook that 'he will hereafter no more such things desire, but where he ought'.[18] At Winchcombe abbey it has been estimated that these people probably represented between one-quarter and one-half of the monastic community, excluding the servants, in the early fourteenth century.[19] So great a proportion of secular inhabitants (which most of these people were) probably distracted the monks from their true purpose and invariably strained their material resources.

The details recorded in these corrodies provide vital information about the standard of living expected by people who benefited from them and, in some cases, topographical information about the accommodation they were granted. From the many available examples in the abbey's cartulary, three will suffice.

One of the most generous corrodies was granted on 3 February 1320 to Matilda of Sydenham, who may have been a retired lady-in-waiting from Edward II's court. She was to have daily a monk's loaf of ancient weight and a small white loaf, a gallon of convent beer and another from the abbot's cellar, two full dishes from the abbot's kitchen and two dishes of convent pottage. She was also entitled to an annual allowance of three marks, payable in quarterly instalments, of which two were to provide a robe and the remaining mark was for necessaries. Matilda's accommodation is especially interesting: she was to have the house and garden in 'Le Winzardstret' which had previously been occupied by Thomas Walssch, 'the painter'. It is therefore clear that present-day Vineyard Street existed by 1320 and the abbey owned property in it. To light and heat this accommodation, Matilda was to have 12lbs. of Paris candles annually, or two shillings to buy candles, and two bundles of firewood carried to her house weekly by the abbey's servants. Finally, if she needed it, she was to have litter for her bed twice a year.[20]

The corrody granted to Master William de Bosco (described as 'our cleric' and presumably the same William de Bosco, mentioned earlier in this chapter, who had obtained a fulling mill at Cotes in 1317) for his services to the abbey is very interesting in its description of his accommodation. He was to occupy the chamber to the west of the abbey gate, with a chapel and a cellar below the chapel, a stable, a wardrobe and a plot of land situated between St Peter's church and his chamber.[21] This description appears to confirm that, by this time, the church of St Peter was entirely separate from the abbey's property and was situated to the west of the abbey's main gate, with a plot of garden land between the church and the chamber William was to occupy. If that interpretation is correct and the abbey's main gate opened on to what is now Queen Square, it seems very probable that the present parish church occupies approximately the same site as the fourteenth century St Peter's church. Dr. Steven Bassett makes a most persuasive case for his own conclusion, from this and other topographical evidence, that the chapel William de Bosco was to occupy was the chapel of St Pancras which the antiquary John Leland mentioned in his mid-sixteenth century account of a visit to Winchcombe; and that the cellar beneath the chapel was originally built as a crypt in which the body of Cynhelm (St Kenelm) was first interred in what had been a Mercian royal mausoleum.[22]

There is an intriguing reference in the corrody granted to Robert Bernard of Dumbleton on Thursday after Epiphany in 1322. His accommodation is described as the chamber situated 'below the Royal Chamber'.[23] This description appears to imply that the abbot kept a particularly sumptuous apartment for the king or other royal persons to occupy when visiting the abbey.

The agrarian crisis

The years from 1315 to 1322 were a period of profound agrarian crisis throughout much of England.[24] The crisis was initially due to appalling weather in 1315 and 1316, resulting in disastrous harvests and widespread famine; but it was not confined to arable farming. Livestock farmers experienced a serious sheep murrain, resulting in heavy losses of animals between 1313 and 1317. Abbot Richard of Idbury has been strongly criticised for mismanagement of the abbey's property and finances during the period of his rule from 1316 to 1340; but even the most competent abbot would probably have experienced great difficulty in coping with the effects of the economic forces threatening the monastery's financial stability.[25]

Other local landowners were probably suffering equally serious financial problems. For example, at Easter 1325, John de Sudeley decided to mortgage 40 acres of meadowland between Toddington and Wormington to the abbey for £136 at an interest rate of six marks per year (about 3%). But he was apparently unable to pay even this comparatively low interest and the meadowland was sold to the abbey in 1332.[26]

By 1329 the abbey's affairs were so disordered, perhaps through combined mismanagement and the medium-term consequences of the agrarian crisis, that a formal 'visitation' (or inspection) by the bishop of Worcester, Adam de Orleton, resulted in a series of 'ordinances' (or directives) aimed at achieving a more disciplined monastic life and improved financial management. The monks were required to attend services regularly; to be silent in the abbey church and cloister, instead of gossiping, especially with women; to spend their time in meditation, study, reading, writing and repeating the appointed prayers and offices; and not to wander about the town and countryside unless they were sent on the abbey's business. As to the abbey's finances, the bishop ordered abbot Richard to ensure that proper accounts were kept and not to use some of the abbey's property as if it were his own. As part of this firmer discipline, the abbey's seal was to be held securely and only used when the community's members, on a majority vote, had approved a particular course of action.[27] The bishop also forbade the private sale of any more corrodies.

Despite his apparent shortcomings as abbot, Richard of Idbury was granted what appears to be most generous pension provision when he retired in 1339. His accommodation was to be a chamber in the infirmary, together with adjacent buildings. For food, he was to receive three monks' loaves of the usual weight and two trencher loaves daily, four jugs of the better ale, meat and fish from the abbot's kitchen when he chose, and a half-weigh of cheese annually. For his chamber, he was entitled annually to 5lbs. of wax, 12lbs. of Paris candles and whatever fuel he needed. For his personal staff, he could choose a chaplain, a squire, a servant and a groom who were to receive the same benefits as their counterparts in the abbot's household.[28] Perhaps this generous settlement is a medieval example of paying over the odds to secure an under-achiever's early retirement?

However, Richard's life in retirement may not have been entirely peaceful. In 1346, during local disorder in the district, an armed band of more than twenty men, including Hugh de Beycyn, Thomas Symcykyns, John de Tredington and John Telemon, described as 'chaplains', broke into the abbey, assaulted the monks and servants, and took away a quantity of valuables. The marauders followed up this attack by blockading the monastery and preventing its inhabitants from obtaining provisions and carrying out their normal religious observance. On 20 July 1346, a warrant was issued for the arrest of Hugh de Beycyn and his accomplices who were to be taken to the Tower of London; but there is apparently no record whether they were caught or imprisoned.[29]

The Black Death

A new and deadly form of plague, pneumonic in some areas and bubonic in others, but generally referred to as the Black Death, reached England in August 1348 and spread across the country during the rest of the year and 1349. A second and less severe epidemic, known as the children's mortality, occurred in 1361 to 1362, and a third in 1369.[30] An overall estimate of its national effect is that the population was approximately halved by 1400. Although no specific record of the plague's effect on Winchcombe's population exists, there are apparent hints that the abbey experienced serious financial difficulties in the years following the Black Death. On 24 July 1353, after an appeal for help to the king as the abbey's patron, Edward III appointed four commissioners to administer the monastery and all its possessions. The document appointing the commissioners declares that 'By defect in past administration, it is burdened with great debt, and its state from various causes is so miserably impoverished that it is necessary to place the temporalities in the hands of a commission appointed by the crown'.[31] The commissioners remained in control of the abbey's finances until the appointment, in 1360, of Walter of Wynforton as abbot. Walter had been the chief steward of the cathedral church at Worcester and was the personal choice of bishop Reynold Brian of Worcester, with the aim of putting the abbey's finances on a sound footing.[32]

Although abbot Walter seems to have been remarkably successful during his thirty-five years' rule, continuing difficulties resulted in the bishop of Worcester's grant, in 1379, of permission for the abbey to appropriate the income from the benefice of Twyning. The permission refers to the abbey's 'compulsory ceaseless hospitality; vexatious, wrongful and costly lawsuits; barren lands; services and rents less by nearly half, from death of tenants and past pestilence; the ruinous decay of the monastery's buildings and manors through age and frightful gales; and many corrodies, pensions and burdensome debt'.[33]

The Black Death's main economic consequence was to reduce the number of agricultural labourers and thus increase the payment for services the remaining work-force expected. Together with natural distress at the death of a substantial proportion of the population, the demands for increased payments produced great social tension in various parts of the country, culminating in the Peasants' Revolt of 1381. The events of June 1360 in Winchcombe are perhaps some evidence of that tension. The abbot sought a judicial remedy for an attack on the abbey by John, vicar of Winchcombe, John Panter his curate, and twenty-nine other townsmen. These marauders broke down the abbey's gates, made off with the monks' goods and assaulted their servants; and followed up the raid by besieging the inhabitants so that they dared not go out of the abbey to obtain food and other essentials.[34]

Quarrels between the abbey and townspeople

Indications that the abbey and townspeople were increasingly at odds with each other become more numerous in the later fourteenth century.

Perhaps surprisingly, Thomas Power, vicar of Winchcombe from about 1388 to 1415, was the catalyst for some of this ill feeling. Shortly after his induction, the vicar embarked on a lengthy and costly legal dispute with the abbot about which of them was responsible for repairs to the parish church's chancel, including its window glass. An earlier judgement on this issue had gone against a former vicar, John Brighampton, in about 1360. Despite this precedent, Thomas Power insisted on pursuing the case; and, when the initial judgement was given against him (including an award of costs of 45 gold florins in the abbot's favour), he refused to accept the result and was consequently excommunicated by bishop Henry Wakefield of Worcester. After a failed appeal to the archbishop of Canterbury, Thomas Power appealed to the Pope who ordered the abbot of Gloucester and the archdeacons of Worcester and Gloucester to inquire discreetly into the matter. The eventual outcome was another judgement against the vicar, with a further award of costs against him. Pope Urban VI confirmed this judgement in February 1389 and it was finally executed on the abbot's behalf in October 1400.[35] The vicar thus lost the case completely and expensively, as he should perhaps have anticipated at the outset.

There is also some evidence that the abbot and prior were involved in certain legal sharp practices, sometimes amounting to attempted fraud, in their dealings with other owners and occupiers of property in the town. One such incident is recorded in the report of an inquisition (an inquiry into the facts) held in Winchcombe on 12 April 1368 by the king's escheator, John Benet, to ascertain what property in the borough was held from the king. Part of the report is as follows:

'The vill of Wynchecombe is held of the King in chief, and the King has a number of tenements there, which are held of him in chief, and not of any other person ... Henry Keys held a toft of the King in chief in the said vill, in the street called Northstret, by the service of 5½d. a year. The now abbot of Wynchecombe craftily brought a writ of cessavit against Thomas, son of the said Henry Keys, as though the said toft was held of him in chief, whereas it was never held of the said abbot nor of his predecessors, but only of the King in chief; and the said abbot, by means of an inquisition taken at Gloucester at Eastertide, 40 Edward III (1366), by the oath of strangers and his own tenants, before Henry Grene and his colleagues, then the King's justices, coming to take assizes in the county of Gloucester aforesaid, fraudulently recovered the said tenement in the absence of the said Thomas, without any warning given to him. The said toft is worth 6d. a year.'[36]

Such unworthy business practices must have caused the townspeople greatly to resent the abbey's control over property in the borough and devalued whatever credit the monastery earned for its charitable and educational work.

Quarrelling reached a climax in the fourteenth century's last decade, when a series of grants from the king and the pope considerably increased the abbey's standing. First, on 11 June 1391, Richard II granted the hundreds of Kiftsgate, Holford and Greston to the abbey on the death of Sir John atte Wood, to whom Edward III had granted them for life. This grant included the profit obtainable from farming out the town's fairs and markets and the abbey steward's right to hold courts in the borough, to which the burgesses were obliged to bring their grievances. These privileges were obtained for an annual rent of £50. Henry IV confirmed the grant on 25 July 1400.[37]

However, the townspeople were given an even more unwelcome sign of royal favour to the abbey in 1398. During a visit to the abbey in March of that year, Richard II was apparently persuaded to grant the abbot a licence to appropriate the vicarage and tithes of the parish church of St Peter at an annual cost of £10, on condition that a suitable sum was distributed annually to the town's poor parishioners. Although the vicarage was only valued at 50 marks at this time, the abbot was probably also keen to obtain the right to institute a vicar of his own choice in future and to remove a priest whose conduct was intolerable.[38]

Unsurprisingly, Thomas Power and the townspeople again showed their resentment of the abbey by vigorously ringing the parish church's bells at times when they knew the monks would be at prayer. The abbot's response to this disturbance was a direct appeal to the pope; and, by the issue of a bull in 1399, Boniface IX directed how the bells of the parish church were to be rung in future. The main limitations were that the bells should not be rung after the evening curfew (probably about 7.30pm in winter and 8.30pm in summer) or before the abbey's morning worship known as 'prime' (probably about 7am); and all bell-ringing should be performed moderately.[39] Although these requirements were to be enforced, if necessary, by the penalty of excommunication, Thomas Power and his parishioners were undeterred. On 22 March 1401, the archdeacon of Gloucester (Richard of Winchcombe, suggesting that he originated from the town) held an inquiry from which he concluded that the papal ordinance had been disobeyed. The archdeacon therefore placed the vicar, clerics and parishioners under excommunication.[40]

Another sign of papal favour to the abbot at this time was Boniface IX's grant of the privilege of wearing a mitre and ring and carrying a pastoral staff and other pontifical insignia, which was received on 1 July 1398.[41] By this grant, the abbey's spiritual authority over its resentful neighbours was further enhanced.

1   Hundred Rolls of 2 Ed I, cited in Landboc, Volume I, page xxiii
2   Hundred Rolls of 2 Ed I, cited in Landboc, Volume I, page xxiv
3   H. P. R. Finberg: 'The Genesis of the Gloucestershire Towns' in his 'Gloucestershire Studies', page 79
4   Patent Roll of 1 Ed III, cited in Landboc, Volume I, pages xxx-xxxii
5   Landboc, Volume I, pages xxvi-xxx
6   R. H. Hilton: 'A Medieval Society', Weidenfeld & Nicolson, 1966, pages 82-83
7   Landboc, Volume I, page 63
8   Landboc, Volume I, page 64
9   Landboc, Volume II, pages 454-455
10   Landboc, Volume II, page 455
11   R. Perry: 'The Gloucestershire Woollen Industry, 1100-1690', Trans BGAS, 1945, Volume 66, page 53
12   Landboc, Volume II, pages 155-156
13   Landboc, Volume I, pages 324-328
14   Landboc, Volume II, pages 105-106
15   reproduced from S. R. Bassett: 'A Probable Mercian Royal Mausoleum at Winchcombe, Gloucestershire', page 83
16   Landboc, Volume I, pages 106 and 113
17   Landboc, Volume I, pages 363-366
18   Landboc, Volume I, pages 344-345
19   G. Haigh: 'The History of Winchcombe Abbey', page 117
20   Landboc, Volume I, pages 337-338
21   Landboc, Volume I, page 339
22   S. R. Bassett, op cit, pages 89-90
23   Landboc, Volume I, pages 343-344
24   Ian Kershaw: 'The Great Famine and Agrarian Crisis in England, 1315-1322' in 'Peasants, Knights and Heretics – Studies in Medieval English Social History' edited by R. H. Hilton, Cambridge University Press, 1976, pages 88-108
25   G. Haigh, op cit, page 117
26   Landboc, Volume II, pages 284-288
27   G. Haigh, op cit, pages 106-108
28   'A Calendar of the Register of Wolstan de Bransford, Bishop of Worcester, 1339-49',

compiled by R. M. Haines, Historical Manuscripts Commission, 1966, pages 65-66

29   G. Haigh, op cit, pages 120-121

30   May McKisack: 'The Fourteenth Century, 1307-1399', The Oxford History of England, 1959, page 331

31   F. A. Gasquet: 'The Great Pestilence', Simpkin, Marshall, Hamilton, Kent & Co, 1893, page 189

32   G. Haigh, op cit, page 130

33   Landboc, Volume II, pages 97-98

34   G. Haigh, op cit, page 129

35   Landboc, Volume II, pages 45-76

36   'Abstracts of Inquisitiones Post Mortem for Gloucestershire', Part VI, 1359-1413, by Ethel Stokes for British Record Society, 1914, pages 51-52

37   Landboc, Volume II, pages 28-31

38   G. Haigh, op cit, pages 143-144

39   Landboc, Volume II, pages 31-34

40   G. Haigh, op cit, pages 144-145

41   G. Haigh, op cit, page 145

CHAPTER 9

WINCHCOMBE IN THE HIGH MIDDLE AGES

A tax return for the borough of Winchcombe for 1381 puts the taxed population at 201.[1] It is difficult to know how reliable this information is for calculating the town's actual population since there would undoubtedly have been some tax avoidance. However, using an accepted multiplier of 3.5, a reasonable estimate may be that, not counting the abbey's inhabitants, the population was between 700 and 800 people. It seems likely that, as the district's market centre for agricultural produce, the population was either stable or slowly increasing as the numbers lost in the Black Death were gradually replaced.

The town's governance appears to have been divided uneasily between the abbey, which held the grant of the hundred of the borough and was thus responsible for holding the hundred court, and the town's corporation consisting of the two bailiffs (known as the high bailiff and low bailiff) and ten burgesses, all of whom were elected by their fellow burgesses. The corporation was responsible for such matters as maintaining public highways in the town, collecting tolls at markets and fairs, and regulating the activities of craftsmen and traders. In 1445 the two bailiffs, also known as port-reeves, were Nicholas Hawkeslowe and Nicholas Boteller.[2]

The hundred court dealt with such routine matters as alleged debts, assaults, affray and the commission of nuisances. The court was held fourteen times a year, on specified Tuesdays and on the Monday in Christmas week. At some time during Henry VI's reign Robert Carpenter acknowledged that he owed Walter Bacare a pewter pot worth xviii d. and the court ordered him to return it to Walter, with a fine of ii d. The various bakers in the town appear to have been fined regularly for selling loaves which were below the standard weight. Those convicted of this offence included the baker of Pershore (who presumably brought loaves for sale in the town's market), John Bacare, and William Bacare senior and junior (presumably, father and son). The offenders were not always men. Agnes Hert, Juliana Wodledare, Margery Carter and Alice ffylle were each fined iiijd. for drawing the blood of Joan Evesham; but this fine was perhaps less than usual because the jury said, on oath, that Joan was a common scold, a grievous nuisance and against the king's peace. Robert Bacare was fined vjd. for leaving dung 'opposite the High Cross'; and if it was not removed by St Bartholomew's day, William Kempe was to be fined xijd. for committing the same offence 'under the Walls'.[3] The site of this last offence implies that, as late as the mid-fifteenth century, the town's previously fortified external walls still remained in some places.

The abbey's economy

There appears to have been a recovery in arable farming on the abbey's estates, although much of the arable demesne was leased to tenants by this time. On the abbey's Sherborne manor more than 400 acres were devoted to arable, probably on the usual two-course crop rotation. The bulk of grain production was kept for the abbey's own use rather than sold for cash. Most of the wheat, pulses and oats were consumed by the abbey or used to supplement the wages of labourers who had to be hired for such activities as haymaking and harvesting. Much of the coarser grain (154 of 270 quarters in total in 1426) was transported to the abbey for use in the brewery, where large quantities of ale were produced.[4]

Sheep-farming was the main source of the abbey's cash income. Cotswold wool's reputation was still high with Italian dealers who came regularly to the area, where Northleach was the wool trading centre, to buy a portion of the annual wool clip for export. In the six-month period between Michaelmas 1443 and Easter 1444 Laurence Marconovo of Venice bought forty sacks of wool for £400 from the abbots of Gloucester, Osney and Winchcombe and the prior of Gloucester.[5]

Wool production on the abbey's estate was concentrated on the manor of Sherborne, some twelve miles south-east of the town, where the Sherborne brook provided suitable conditions for washing large flocks of sheep. The annual sheep shearing was a major event, taking place after Easter and requiring the removal of the abbot and his chief servants from Winchcombe to the manor house to supervise it. The abbey's Master Shepherd and other shepherds responsible to him would drive the flocks from the abbey's grazings on the high wolds to Sherborne, where they were washed and sheared; and the fleeces were folded and packed for sale to the Italian and other dealers. In 1468 and 1483, 1,900 sheep were washed and sheared; and, in 1485, the number had risen to 2,900. In the latter year the entire operation took four days and the wool was placed in fourteen sacks each containing about 200 fleeces.[6] The abbot would be concerned to dispose of the wool clip quickly at the best price. He might also negotiate with the buyers as a middleman on behalf of some of the smaller wool producers on the abbey's estates. In 1436 there is evidence that Bernard Lumbard, one of the travelling Italian wool merchants, was present at Sherborne. He and his fellow merchants were doubtless used to hard bargaining with the abbot of Winchcombe and other Cotswold wool producers.

Between 1398 and 1402 the valuations of the abbey's income increased from 800 marks to 1,000 marks (one mark was still valued at 13s.4d., or two-thirds of one pound sterling): again allowing for the usual tax avoidance in declared income, the actual income may have been appreciably higher. But increased income appears not to have resulted in any rise in the number of monks. When John Cheltenham was elected abbot in 1423 he ruled a community of only twenty members, including himself and the prior John Bryan.

The abbey must have flourished under John Cheltenham's rule because, at a visitation on 16 October 1428, bishop Thomas Polton of Worcester found that the monastery was 'out of debt, prosperous, peaceful, an example to other monasteries, and a comfort and relief to himself'.[7] The bishop's report also urged the monks to abide by St Benedict's rule and to turn away from novelties. The last remark may be a veiled reference to the Lollard preachers who were active in various parts of the country during the fifteenth century's first two decades. The Lollard priest Thomas Bagley accused people who went on pilgrimages and trusted in and prayed to images of idolatry. Such heresy struck at the heart of popular religious beliefs and practices.[8] Locally, Winchcombe's abbot ordered the arrest in 1425 of John Walcote, curate of Haselton, on the ground of heresy; but, after being sent for trial by the bishop of Worcester, the curate admitted his errors and was reconciled with the church.[9]

Pilgrims to Winchcombe and Hailes abbeys

Provision for pilgrims to St Kenelm's shrine in the abbey church was a ceaseless demand on the abbey's resources. While the abbot's guests would have been lodged in his own house, within the abbey's grounds, pilgrims would have been accommodated at the 'hospitium', or hostel. Although this building's whereabouts cannot now be established, the reference in the list of the abbey's servants to the Guest Hall Sergeant ('Serviens de Sala Hospitum') suggests that this normal arrangement in a Benedictine abbey existed at Winchcombe. It was probably not until the early-sixteenth century that the George inn (at the High Cross) was extended to provide a pilgrims' hostel outside the abbey's curtilage. The abbey would have obtained some income from the numerous pilgrims, for example from the sale of indulgences, or candles to light at St Kenelm's and other shrines in the abbey church, or some small memento of having made the pilgrimage. Whether such income ever sufficed to cover the cost of meeting the obligation of hospitality is impossible to assess.

There is no surviving record written by a pilgrim to Winchcombe abbey. But it seems probable that the proximity of Hailes abbey would have encouraged pilgrims to St Kenelm's shrine also to visit the shrine of the Holy Blood at Hailes. This would have involved making their way down Hailes Street, through the ford in the river Isbourne, and then by Puck Pit Lane and the Pilgrims' Way to arrive at Hailes abbey. A short account by one pilgrim suggests that a medieval pilgrimage might turn into an unexpectedly boisterous occasion. Early in the fifteenth century Margery Kempe, from Norwich, was returning by way of Bristol from a pilgrimage to the shrine of St James of Compostella, at Santiago in Spain, when she decided to visit the Hailes abbey relic. She described her visit as follows:

'She abode not long there [at Bristol], but went forth to the Blood of Hayles, and there she was shriven and had loud cries and boisterous weepings. Then the religious men had her in amongst them, and made her good cheer, save they swore many great oaths and horrible. And she rebuked them therefor, after the Gospel, and thereof had they great wonder.'[10]

Partnership in a major project

Thomas Power's difficulties, as vicar, in raising enough money for essential repairs to the parish church have been described in Chapter 8. After he ceased to be vicar in 1415 the church's dilapidation worsened to the point where the parishioners were allowed to worship in the abbey church's nave, which was probably equally unsatisfactory for the townspeople and the monks. This was a time of increasing prosperity in the north Cotswold towns, largely due to wool production and cloth making. Winchcombe probably shared in this growing wealth. The borough has no domestic building of this period to compare with the splendid house in Chipping Campden, reputedly built in about 1380 for the wool dealer William Grevel. Although such conspicuous wealth was apparently absent from Winchcombe, there may have been a small group of local merchants who exploited its situation as a market for the district by trading as middlemen in wool produced by the tenant sheep farmers who preferred to sell their wool clip independently of the abbey. Together with others who obtained a living from wool production, the processing trades, and cloth weaving, and a probably increasing number of craftsmen and artisans, these people made up the burgesses from whom the town's corporation was drawn.

The lord of the manor of Sudeley was also more involved in the borough's affairs at this period. The male line of the de Sudeley family had ended in 1367 when John de Sudeley died while serving the Black Prince in Spain. His wife, Joan de Sudeley, had then married William, Lord Boteler of Wem, and the Sudeley estate passed into the Boteler family. The family's most distinguished member was Ralph Boteler, who was created Baron of Sudeley by Henry VI in 1442 for his services to the king in the French Wars. Ralph Boteler was also for a time an admiral of the fleet: he was reputed to have used a captured French admiral's ransom to pay for rebuilding Sudeley castle in such magnificent style that, in the later words of the mid-sixteenth century anti-quarian John Leland, 'it had the prize of all buildings of those dayes'. Ralph held the post of Governor of Calais from 1450 to 1456, but he helped the townspeople of Winchcombe to realise one of their ambitions before his eventual fall from royal favour in 1469.

From 1454 to 1474 the abbot of Winchcombe was William of Winchcombe: little is known about him, except that he was one of the monks who had elected his prede-cessor in 1423.[11] It may not be too fanciful to imagine that, because he was evidently a native of the town, he was well aware of the quarrels between some previous abbots and townspeople and wished to help reconcile the abbey and its neighbours.

Rebuilding the parish church of St Peter

The only surviving account of how the present parish church was built is John Leland's record of his inquiries about the borough's past during a visit to Winchcombe in 1540 or 1541, some seventy years after the building's probable date of completion. Although Leland's account is mainly hearsay, it is worth giving in full, as follows:

'... There was of ancient tyme a Church of St. Nicholas in the East part of the Towne, decayed many Yeares since.

In K. Hen. 5 tyme, the Paroch Chyrch of the Towne was kept in the Body of the Church of the Monastery. But in K.H.6. tyme one William Winchecombe, Abbot of Winchelescombe, beganne with the Consent of the Towne a Paroch Church at the West Ende of the Abbey, where of ould tyme had beene and then was a little Chappell of St. Pancrace.

Abbot William made the East Ende of the Church. The Parishoners had gathered a 200 l. and began the Body of the Church; but that Summe being not able to performe soe costly a Worke Rafe Boteler Lord Sudeley helped them and finished the Worke...'[12]

Despite its possible shortcomings as historical evidence, this account must be interpreted in an attempt to date the building of the parish church.

The major portion of Henry VI's reign was from 1422 (when, as an infant, he succeeded Henry V) until 1461, thus overlapping the initial seven years of William of Winchcombe's rule as abbot from 1454. Since the abbot played such an important part in initiating the church's rebuilding a reasonable conclusion may be that the work on the chancel (Leland's 'East Ende') would have started no later than 1460, or possibly a year or two earlier. The early 1460s probably saw the major part of the project (namely the nave and 90 feet high tower) carried out before the sum of £200 the parishioners had collected was spent.

The financial rescue made possible by Lord Ralph Boteler's generosity presumably followed immediately, in order to ensure continuity in construction and in employment of the workforce. Ralph Boteler was disgraced by the Yorkist Edward IV for his continued support of the Lancastrian Henry VI and was forced to surrender Sudeley castle in 1469, never to return to his estate or the borough. It therefore seems reasonable to conclude that the church would have been completed before 1469, so that Ralph Boteler would have financed the remaining work before his disgrace. Assuming that this major building operation probably required some ten years from start to completion, and depending on the number of masons employed on the site and the time lost through bad weather, the probable period of construction would have been from about 1458 to 1468, at the latest.

The rebuilt parish church is one of the splendid wool churches adorning the north Cotswold market towns. The dilapidated former church may well have been demolished and the site levelled, so that the new church could be constructed as a single building operation, in one architectural style (Perpendicular). It thus has a constructional unity unusual in Gloucestershire parish churches. The master mason who designed the church and was responsible for building it is unknown; but, in view of the abbot's close involvement with the project, he may well have been the master mason then in the abbey's service. The main building material, oolitic limestone, was probably quarried under his watchful supervision from one of the abbey's quarries on Langley hill or at Postlip. It was then transported to the site by horse-drawn cart or packhorse, to be worked on by a small army of masons, craftsmen and labourers. Some of these workpeople would have been locally recruited; but others may have been itinerant workers, living in the town for the duration of their employment, possibly in temporary huts providing accommodation on the site while the project lasted.

The parish church's rebuilding was no doubt partly intended to reflect the aspirations of the burgesses and townspeople at a time of comparative prosperity. The building's nave was perhaps deliberately made larger than that of its comparable neighbours at Chipping Campden and Northleach. But the absence of elaborate detailing and finely carved stonework suggests that the townspeople had to give up any idea of expensive ornamentation. When this superb building was finally completed bishop John Carpenter probably journeyed to Winchcombe from his palace in Worcester to dedicate it again in the name of St Peter. Although no documentary record survives, there was probably a day of elaborate ceremony, bringing together abbot William, Lord Ralph Boteler of Sudeley and the vicar, bailiffs, burgesses and townspeople, in thanksgiving for the project's completion and admiration for the skills and craftsmanship devoted to its accomplishment.

For the next seventy-five years these two dominant ecclesiastical buildings, the abbey church and the rebuilt parish church, stood together on the highest land in the heart of the borough, each a symphony in stone exemplifying their patrons' piety and testifying to their builders' skill in eye and hand. To pilgrims trudging wearily down Sudeley hill, or from Postlip, towards Winchcombe, the two churches must have been a spectacular sight at their journey's end. But, ironically, enthusiasm for rebuilding the parish church eventually contributed in part to the abbey church's disastrous loss. At the dissolution of Winchcombe abbey and other monasteries in 1540, the parishioners of the town, unlike Tewkesbury, already had their own parish church. Consequently, the borough did not need the abbey church, which was completely demolished, along with many of the other monastic buildings; whereas Tewkesbury's abbey church survived to become the town's parish church.

Soon after the parish church's rebuilding Tewkesbury was the scene of the fierce battle, on 4 May 1471, resulting in the decisive Yorkist victory over the house of Lancaster and finally enabling Edward IV to supplant Henry VI as king. The massacre of some 2,000 Lancastrian supporters at Bloody Meadow was a gruesome occasion; but the battle did not spill over into the surrounding district and there is no evidence that Winchcombe suffered directly from it.

1   R. H. Hilton: 'Winchcombe Abbey and the Manor of Sherborne', in H. P. R. Finberg: 'Gloucestershire Studies', page 90
2   Landboc, Volume I, page 1xxxviii
3   Landboc, Volume I, pages xlvi-xlvii
4   R. H. Hilton, op cit, page 108
5   E. E. Power and M. M. Postan: 'Studies in English Trade in the Fifteenth Century', 1933, page 52
6   R. H. Hilton, op cit, page 111
7   Landboc, Volume II, pages 499-500
8   E. F. Jacob: 'The Fifteenth Century, 1399-1485', The Oxford History of England, 1961, pages 282-283
9   G. Haigh: 'The History of Winchcombe Abbey', pages 152-153
10   W. Butler-Bowden: 'The Book of Margery Kempe', 1936, page 163
11   G. Haigh, op cit, page 151
12   'Itinerary of John Leland', edited by Thomas Hearne, Oxford, 1769, 3rd edition, pages 74-75

CHAPTER 10

THE ABBEY'S ZENITH

In the early years of Tudor England Winchcombe abbey was probably more prosperous, influential and secure than ever before. This achievement was principally due to one man, Richard Kidderminster, who became the penultimate abbot in 1488.

Kidderminster was born in about 1462, in the Worcestershire town whose name he bore, and was admitted to the monastery as a novice at the age of fifteen. In about 1484 abbot John Twyning arranged for him to enter Gloucester Hall (subsequently incorporated in Worcester College), in the University of Oxford, where there was a foundation for members of the Benedictine Order and the abbey owned an apartment called Winchcombe Lodgings. At Oxford he studied the humanities until abbot John summoned him back to Winchcombe and appointed him a 'scholar or pastor' of the monastery. On the abbot's death in 1488 Richard Kidderminster was chosen by his fellow monks as successor, at the comparatively early age of about twenty-six.[1]

From the outset the new abbot was concerned for his community's spiritual welfare. He established a thoroughly disciplined rule, based on prayer, monastic study and teaching. It was perhaps his reputation as a teacher and preacher which enabled him to increase the number of monks from fewer than twenty in 1488 to twenty-eight by the end of the fifteenth century.[2] Kidderminster left his own slightly self-satisfied description of life in the abbey under his rule, of which part is as follows:

'It was a fine sight to see how the brethren devoted themselves to sacred learning, how they made use of Latin even in their familiar conversations, and how the cloister at Winchcombe at that time had all the appearance of a young university, though on a minute scale. Added to this, regular observance was so ardently observed among us, and brotherly charity was so honoured, that you would have said that there could not possibly be another such family, so united, so harmonious and yet so small, in the whole of England. The good God alone knows what a joy it was then for me to be immersed in sacred studies with my brethren in the cloister. There day and night I passed the time at my books in a little study I had constructed; would that I had allowed it to stand till the present day!'[3]

Although Winchcombe abbey's comparatively small establishment prevented it from being a foremost community of the Benedictine Order, its scholastic reputation at this time must have been recognised well beyond Gloucestershire. This enhanced reputation may also have increased its popularity as a place of pilgrimage.

Between 1500 and 1520 Kidderminster made his national reputation and must have become a familiar figure in the corridors of monastic and royal power. By 1500 he was a doctor of divinity and, in that year, he travelled to Rome where he studied for more than twelve months. On his return he became a frequent preacher and, eventually, an influential adviser at Henry VIII's court. The king was sufficiently impressed to describe him as 'a man of remarkable learning and experience'; and, in February 1512, Henry sent the abbot, together with bishop John Fisher of Rochester and the Prior of St John's Hospitallers, as ambassadors to the Lateran council convened by Pope Julius II.

These were also years of increasing tension between the ecclesiastical authorities and those lay people who had come to resent many of the privileges and exemptions enjoyed by monks and priests. In February 1512 Parliament enacted a law which denied the benefit of clergy to men in minor religious orders who committed murder. This law was to remain in force until the next Parliament when it was theoretically possible that it would not be re-enacted because the lords in Parliament then comprised 49 spiritual lords (including Richard Kidderminster), 42 lay peers and the prior of the Order of St John.[4] The act alarmed the clergy as an encroachment on their privileges and Kidderminster was appointed to deliver a sermon against it at St Paul's Cross on 4 February 1514. The abbot declared that this law 'by which murderers, robbers of churches and housebreakers were deprived of the benefit of clergy unless they were in Holy Orders was against the law of God and the liberties of the Church; that all the lords who were parties to that Act had incurred the censures of the Church; and that all clerks who had received any manner of orders were exempt from temporal punishment'. Those who opposed clerical privileges greatly resented the abbot's views and he was severely censured in the next session of Parliament.[5] But these robust opinions probably increased his standing in the religious establishment since he was apparently present at the ceremony held to celebrate Thomas Wolsey's elevation as a cardinal in November 1515.

In these years preceding the Reformation Richard Kidderminster naturally took a close interest in doctrinal matters, although his personal opinions may have appeared ambivalent since his friends included both those who supported the new learning and ecclesiastical conservatives. In 1521 he published a work entitled 'Tractatus contra doctrinam M. Lutheri', clearly indicating that, whatever sympathy he felt for humanist doctrine, he was strongly opposed to the heresy, as he presumably regarded it, being spread from Germany by Martin Luther.[6]

Despite the onerous responsibilities frequently compelling his absence from the abbey for long periods, Kidderminster never seems to have lost his firm attachment to the monastery and borough of Winchcombe. He took a keen interest in the abbey's origins and history which prompted him to compile a register including as much detail as he could find about the abbey's past, a collection of its surviving charters and other documents, and brief lives of the abbots. This vital source material passed into the hands of a High Court judge, after the Reformation, and was unfortunately destroyed in the judge's lodgings in Serjeants' Inn during the fire of London in 1666.[7] The abbot's own scrupulous regard for historical fact is shown by his refusal to make any unsupported statement. Referring to the hearsay on which some of the abbey's history was based, he wrote: 'What truth there may be in these things I know not, for as I have never read them among our antiquities, I should not dare to write them.'[8]

The abbot was also keen to see that the monastery's assets and fabric were well managed. On 30 March 1509 these assets were substantially increased by Henry VII's grant of the manor of Sudeley to the abbey at an annual rent of £60. The extent of this property at that time is shown in the deed of grant, part of which is as follows:

'... the manor and lordship of Sudeley with the advowson of the church or chapel of Sudeley and 20 messuages, 400 acres of land, 80 acres of meadow, 200 acres of pasture, 100 acres of wood and £20 in rents in Sudeley, Toddington, Stanley, Greet, Gretton (Catesthorpe), Throp and Naunton, sometime of Ralph Boteler and Alice his wife. Also all the lands of the king with the said manors and towns, the castle excepted, to hold for ever at fee farm by the yearly rent of £60 with courts and all other privileges and exoneration from repairs and support of the castle.'[9]

Henry VIII confirmed the grant, with some modifications, in the following year.

The recital of this land grant shows that it was a substantial addition to the abbey's property, enabling it to control an area around the town where it had not previously possessed authority. Abbot Kidderminster was probably well pleased with what he may have regarded as a logical rounding-off of the abbey's estate. For example, whatever grange or farmstead and other farm buildings were then on the site of the present Almsbury Farm, on the south-eastern bank of the river Isbourne, may well have been included in this acquisition. Within the Sudeley estate, the castle did not come into the abbey's ownership because, following Ralph Boteler's disgrace in 1469, the king had taken possession of it and appointed a constable (who was Sir John Huddleston from 1478 to 1486 and from 1505 to 1510) as the royal agent.

On his visit to Gloucestershire in 1540 or 1541 John Leland recorded what he was told about Richard Kidderminster's improvement to the abbey's fabric as follows:

'Rich de Kiddermister, the last Abbot savinge one, did great cost of the Church, and enclosed the Abbey towardes the Towne with a maine stone-wall "ex quadrato Saxo".'[10]

As it seems most unlikely that the abbey's southern boundary with the town was not defined by a boundary wall before the early sixteenth century, this account may mean that abbot Kidderminster was responsible for having an earlier wall re-built in ashlar (squared and finished blocks of limestone) by the abbey's mason.

The abbot may also have decided it was time to provide lodging for pilgrims to the shrine of St Kenelm elsewhere than on the abbey's premises. Although the earliest documentary reference to the George inn at the High Cross is not until 1550, it has been suggested that Kidderminster acquired the property on the abbey's behalf in the early sixteenth century and arranged for extensive building works to be carried out to provide suitable accommodation for pilgrims.[11] Possible evidence of his involvement in this project is that, throughout the inn's successive refurbishment and conversion, the carved initials of the abbot's name have remained on the spandrels on either side of the building's main entrance off High Street, where they can still be seen. The property at Nos 5 and 7 High Street, now known as Abbot's House, with a carved angel supporting the abbey's coat of arms on the right-hand frontage, might also have been associated, in its earlier form, with the pilgrims' hostel, perhaps as a house for the abbey's servants who managed the hostel.

Plate 3

There are other signs that Richard Kidderminster may have countenanced a minor personality cult in the town as his carved initials appear elsewhere. A drawing by Edmund Thomas Browne

illustrates the front of an old house in High Street, before its demolition in 1830, where the barge boards displayed the abbot's initials. This house is traditionally believed to have stood at the corner of High Street and North Street, opposite the present town hall site.[12] The drawing is reproduced at Plate 3: a fragment of the barge board can

be seen in Winchcombe Museum in the town hall. There is also a well-preserved oak door, now kept in the parish church, on which the initials 'R' and 'K' have been elaborately carved by the abbey's carpenter.

In 1520 the abbot was still communicating with the most senior and influential figures in the Church. On 8 March 1520 he addressed an over-effusive letter of gratitude to Wolsey, referring to the cardinal's 'resplendent divine virtues' and offering him what was presumably intended as a suitable present in these terms:

'I send moreover to your sacred lordship, most gracious father, by the present bearer, in token of my love and faithful service to you, eight lampreys distributed in four pasties, with certain other things cooked in an oven after the manner of the country. I should have sent a larger number, both now and frequently heretofore, if either by prayers, money, or any other way I had been able to do so; but those persons who are near to the fish ponds where this kind of fish is taken are in the habit of taking what they want themselves before they will permit those who live at a distance from the Severn to take anything out of them ...'[13]

By this time, it seems that Kidderminster's involvement in affairs of state had lessened appreciably, although he was third president of the chapter of black monks with whom Wolsey discussed proposed reforms to the Benedictine Order at an assembly at Westminster on 26 February 1520.[14] Perhaps he had realised that the strength of the forces for reform of the Order, and indeed of the entire Church in England, was so great that his own further resistance would be ineffectual.

Late in 1525 Richard Kidderminster resigned as abbot of Winchcombe, at the probable age of sixty-three, having ruled the abbey for thirty-seven years. He continued to live in the monastery until his death, late in 1531, when he was buried in the abbey he had loved and served so diligently. Despite the increasing momentum of the reforming tide within the Church, it must still have seemed inconceivable that, within ten years of his death, Winchcombe abbey would have ceased to exist as a monastic institution and its buildings would have been largely demolished.

1   Dictionary of National Biography, Volume XXX, 1892, edited by Sidney Lee (cited below as DNB); and David Knowles: 'The Religious Orders in England', Volume III, 'The Tudor Age', Cambridge, 1971, pages 91-93

2   G. Haigh: 'The History of Winchcombe Abbey', page 167

3   D. Knowles, op cit, page 92

4   J. D. Mackie: 'The Earlier Tudors, 1485-1558', The Oxford History of England, 1952, page 291

5   G. Haigh, op cit, page 163

6   DNB, op cit

7   Emma Dent: 'Annals of Winchcombe and Sudeley', page 146

8   Victoria County History of Gloucestershire, Volume II, 1907, page 71

9   G. Haigh, op cit, page 162

10   J. Leland: 'Itinerary', page 74

11   City of Hereford Archaeology Unit: 'George Hotel, Winchcombe', An interim report by Richard K. Morris and Ron Shoesmith, Hereford Archaeology Series No 46, March 1989

12   E. Adlard: 'Winchcombe Cavalcade', pages 13-14

13   E. Dent, op cit, pages 139-140

14   G. Haigh, op cit, page 165

CHAPTER 11

WINCHCOMBE IN 1500

This chapter attempts to describe the condition of the town and its people about five hundred years ago. No town map or street plan is known to have survived from then: it is therefore necessary to piece together references to streets or buildings in documents primarily intended as property conveyances, tax returns and wills. Such a descriptive process inevitably involves a certain amount of guesswork. Accuracy in every detail is not achievable, not least because some of the evidence appears conflicting. The street map at Plan 5 attempts to draw some conclusions from the discussion of Winchcombe's topography that follows in this chapter.

The street pattern

The main crossroads was at the centre of the town, as it is today, where High Street and the southern end of North Street meet. The highway may then have continued southwards on a course which would have taken it through what was soon to be the main entrance of the pilgrims' hostel at The George, to intersect with what is now Silk Mill Lane, and then to cross the river Isbourne at a ford in about the position of the present bridge at the foot of Castle Street. The length of the highway south of The Cross, as far as this ford, may thus possibly have been the 'Bodefordstret' which is mentioned twice in the abbey's cartulary. To the east of The Cross, High Street continued for a short distance before it became Hailes Street, which probably followed its present course to reach another ford through the river for travellers entering the town from the east.

North Street took its present course to the town's boundary, where separate highways led, respectively, northwards to Gretton and north-eastwards to Greet. At this junction there were probably gated tolls where travellers and merchants entering the town had to pay the stipulated charge, depending on what commodities they were transporting. North Street had been so named before 1190 and there is no reason to suppose that its name subsequently changed, although Eleanor Adlard maintains that it was later named Horse Fair Street.[1] It may well have been referred to colloquially by this name when the horse fairs were held towards the street's northern end in the nineteenth century. There is no documentary evidence to support her other statement that North Street had previously been known as Betre Street.[2] Documents in the abbey's cartulary refer to 'Beatestret' three times between about 1190 and 1217. On the first occasion it is described as being 'in the western part of the town', which informs the supposition that it may have been on the course of the present Gloucester Street. The second reference is to a parcel of land in Beatestret situated 'near the abbey's orchard', which was probably in an area to the north-west of the parish church. Thirdly, the *same* document refers *separately* to a parcel of land in 'Norhstret', owned by a man called Everard, and another parcel which Thomas Smelred owned in Beatestret.[3]

Narrow lanes probably led eastwards off North Street on the course of the present Bull Lane and Chandos Street. There is a persistent tradition that Chandos Street was previously known as Nicholas Street or St Nicholas Street.[4] Evidence to support this tradition is unpersuasive: it appears to consist of the references in a Court Roll of 3 October 1534 to a close 'in the parish of St Nicholas' belonging to James ap Thomas and a similar reference in subsequent Letters Patent.[5]

High Street continued westwards of The Cross as far as the junction with what is now Cowl Lane, which ran northwards on its present course along the eastern boundary of the abbey's curtilage in the town. This boundary was probably defined by a stone wall, rebuilt on abbot Richard Kidderminster's initiative at about this time. Cowl Lane has had a variety of names in the past, including Colestret, Cow Lane, Cold Lane, and Chapel Lane. It may not be too fanciful to suppose that the name Cowl Lane was given because black-cowled monks of the Benedictine Order were frequently to be seen there during the abbey's heyday.

What road, if any, ran southwards from High Street to the west of The Cross is difficult to establish. There is a reference in a late-thirteenth-century document in the abbey's cartulary to a property situated 'on the western side of the street which descends from Winchcombe High Street towards Sudeley' ('qui est ex parte occidentali in Vico, qui descendit a Magna Platea Winchecumbe versus Sudleiam').[6] This may possibly mean that, some two hundred years later, there was a street leading towards Sudeley on the course of the present Castle Street (which was previously known as Sudeley Street). However, there is also a very puzzling reference in an indenture dated 6 August 1529 in which Henry Hodgkins holds a property 'in Birportestrete, alias Sudeley strete'.[7] This appears to conflict with much later documentary evidence about the location of Bearport Street in the nineteenth century. A Court Roll of 3 October 1534 also refers to a street called Berryportestret.[8]

In the central stretch of Cowl Lane there may possibly have been a west-to-east highway, known as King Street, on the course of the present accessway to the former abbey property now known as The Abbey Old House, although there is no documentary evidence that this street (if it existed) continued eastwards to intersect with North Street. Towards the northern end of Cowl Lane, where it forks eastwards, the stream previously known as 'Gastebroc' flowed across it.[9]

High Street, by name, did not extend further westwards than the junction with Cowl Lane. The 1815 enclosure map (entitled Greet and Sudeley Tenements Map) shows that there was then a double right-angled bend in the highway as late as that date, which must have been extremely inconvenient for heavily loaded carts and waggons to negotiate. It seems probable that this road layout had existed for centuries and was not altered until Abbey Terrace was created in 1835. The highway to the west of this double bend was comparatively narrow for a main street through a market town. The plan drawn in 1835 to show how the new Abbey Terrace would be laid out indicates that, at its narrowest point (about 100 feet east of the junction with what is now Vineyard Street), the former carriageway was only 10 feet 3 inches wide and the footpath 7 feet 6 inches wide. This is shown in the measured drawing reproduced at Plan 6 (of which the master copy is in the Gloucestershire County Record Office).

The name of this road in 1500 is a puzzle. A collection of leases and conveyances in the County Record Office dating from 1811 to 1863, relating mainly to The Bell inn before its landlord moved from Abbey Terrace to Gretton Road in 1863, refers to Abbey Terrace 'heretofore called Bearpot Street' (in one document) or 'Bearport Street' (in the others).[10] This evidence appears to show that the highway between Cowl Lane and what is now Queen Square was known, at least in the early nineteenth century, as Bearport Street. Documents relating to grants of land in July and August 1543 refer to a tenement and a barn in Birporte Strete which had belonged to Winchcombe monastery.[11] Thus, although these references are some three hundred years apart, this length of the highway may have been known as Birporte Street throughout that time. A further clue to this puzzle's solution may be given by the suffix 'porte'. This seems unlikely to derive from the Latin 'porta', a gate, as the town's gates would not have been in this central area. It more probably derives from the Old English legal term 'port', meaning an unfortified market centre.[12] If that is correct, and it is also valid to conclude that the open area (of which the present Queen Square is now part) in front of the abbey's main gate was the borough's open-air market place in medieval times, Birporte Street may have been so called because it led from High Street to the market place. It may also have continued further westwards out of the market place along the course of the present Almshouse Lane to an intersection with Mill Lane.

Vineyard Street undoubtedly existed on its present course in 1500. The earliest reference (as already mentioned in Chapter 8) to this street is in the corrody granted to Matilda of Sydenham on 3 February 1320. The name itself is a reminder that a vineyard belonging to the abbey was probably situated on this south-facing slope at some time between 950 and 1300, a period known to meteorologists as 'the Little Optimum', when the climate of western Europe was appreciably warmer. But, in 1500, the slope of the highway down to the river Isbourne was considerably steeper than it is now and the river was crossed by a ford.

The now lost Herestret, which appears in two documents in the abbey's cartulary dated about 1221, presents another puzzle.[13] It is impossible to tell from these documents exactly where this street was. The name may derive from the Old English word for a military road or highway, indicating that it had at one time been a main road into the town.[14]

Any speculative conclusion about Here Street's possible location in about 1500 has to be examined in the context of the information about Winchcombe's main streets in 1550 contained in an augmentation (for tax purposes) compiled in that year, which does not mention this street's name. This return lists the borough's main streets as: Hailes Strete, North Strete, Le Spitle Ende, Sudeley Strete, Hye Strete, Under the Cawseway, Wyneyarde Street, Before Le Abbey Yate and Gloucester Strete (in that order).[15] It is also puzzling that Birporte Street is not included in this list; and, where it should logically appear (namely between High Street and Vineyard Street), a street named Under the Causeway is listed. A possible explanation is that none of the occupiers of properties in Birporte Street in 1550 was a freeholder or copyholder, so that they were not assessable to tax. A less likely explanation is that whatever cottages or tenements had previously fronted the southern side of Birporte Street (the northern side of the street was defined by the abbey's boundary wall) were so dilapidated by 1550 that they had been demolished to make way for rebuilding, or had burned down and had not yet been rebuilt. In either event, it might help to explain how the street called (in 1550) Under the Causeway got its name. The land to the south of the presumed Birporte Street slopes quite steeply down to the river Isbourne, so that a road running parallel to Birporte Street – perhaps on the course of the earlier medieval Here Street – may have been temporarily called Under the Causeway because the occupiers used it as a description of their location at a level below that of the carriageway in Birporte Street.

Continuing further westwards beyond Vineyard Street, the street named Before the Abbey Gate was probably a row of tenements in the area on the southern side of the present Queen Square, assuming that (as previously suggested) the abbey's main gate faced on to that area, which was then used as the borough's open-air market place.

The highway layout to the west of the presumed market place in 1500 is uncertain. There is a reference in the abbey's cartulary, in about 1280, to a cottage situated at the corner of the street leading towards the abbey's mill and the southern side of 'the king's highway leading towards Gloucester'.[16] But this grant does not name the highway as Gloucester Street. Moreover, Dr. Steven Bassett has pointed out that Gloucester Street appears to be a 'non-conformist' street, running counter to the predominant, loosely rectilinear street pattern of medieval Winchcombe.[17]

It is clear from numerous references in the abbey's cartulary that an important street known as 'Betarestret' (with some variations in spelling) existed in medieval times in the western part of the town. As late as 1422, Alice Newman of Winchcombe granted to Robert Bushell and William Ashton 'her burgage with garden adjoining, in Betar Street, between a tenement of the Almonry, towards St Peter's Church, on one side; and a tenement of the Almonry on the other side: ...'[18] This description appears to confirm that Betar Street ran alongside the parish church in 1422. This grant is particularly interesting in referring to another parcel of land Alice Newman owned, described as a half-acre in Hide furlong 'between Gloucester Way and land formerly John le White's'. A possible inference from this description is that, in the early fifteenth century, the highway leading into Winchcombe from the west was already being called Gloucester Way; and the name Betar Street would eventually be superseded by Gloucester Street.

Two further pieces of evidence are relevant. On 22 November 1350, William Hooper granted to Margaret, daughter of John Thorsteyn, 'a cottage situated in the town of Winchcombe in the street which is called "Beterstret", between the tenement of the Vicar of Winchcombe on one hand, and the tenement formerly of Ralph the Palfreyman on the other hand: and another cottage situated in Mulestret, between the tenement of the aforesaid Ralph on the one hand and the tenement of the lord abbot of Winchcombe on the other'.[19] If Ralph the Palfreyman's tenement referred to in this grant is the same one in each place, it can be inferred that it stood at, or close to, the intersection of Mill Lane (Mulestret) and Beterstret, perhaps not far from where Mill Lane now runs south from Gloucester Street. There is a similar grant in 1400.[20]

In a document dated Easter 1324, Hugh (the son of Robert of Gretton) grants to John of Cheltenham, a cleric, and Margaret his wife, a parcel of land in the town of Winchcombe in 'Beteristret' where it abuts 'Kyngesmore', between tenements belonging respectively to the abbey's refectorer and almoner.[21] On 28 July 1858 Charles Lapworth (at that time master of the Chandos grammar school in Winchcombe) drew a plan of the land then within the abbey's grounds. Interestingly, the plan shows an area on the northern side of Gloucester Street, westwards of the parish church's cemetery (approximating now to the northern area in the back gardens of Nos. 15 to 37 Gloucester Street), which was called 'Kingsmoor' in 1858. If the Kings Moor in the 1324 land grant and the 1858 plan are virtually the same parcel of land, it would also suggest that Betar Street was re-named Gloucester Street.

Why Kings Moor was so named is puzzling. Perhaps it had been a small area of rough pasture which the occupiers of neighbouring cottages leased from the king and used for grazing domestic cattle.

In the south-west corner of the presumed market place there was almost certainly a road leading westwards, possibly on the course of present-day Almshouse Lane, eventually intersecting Mill Lane and perhaps continuing further westwards. The course of this road may possibly be defined by the southern (rear) boundary of the burgage plots fronting Betar Street. If, as Dr. Steven Bassett has suggested, Gloucester Street is a non-conformist street, this westward road from the market place may have been one of the main highways into the town from the west during the medieval period, although its use for that purpose had probably been superseded by Gloucester Street before 1500. Whether this road had been a westward continuation of Birporte Street in earlier times is impossible to establish from surviving documents.

Travelling further west along the present Gloucester Street, it is highly probable that Mill Lane existed on its present course in 1500 when it provided the main access from the town to one of the abbey's corn mills beside the river Isbourne. Although the first reference to Mill Lane as such is not until 1324,[22] there is a mention, in about 1202, of a street leading towards the mill which is opposite the street known as 'Cangereslone'.[23] It is thus possible that, in 1500, Cangeres Lane continued to exist as a northwards lane, leading away from Betar Street, and Mill Lane ran southwards from the same intersection to reach the mill.

Although Malthouse Lane is not mentioned as such in the medieval period, it seems possible that a lane on its present course ran alongside the western boundary of the abbey's curtilage in the town. Alternatively, the abbey's boundary wall on the eastern side of what is now Malthouse Lane may also have been the western limit of the borough so that, even as late as 1500, there was only a pathway around the exterior of the wall and no further settlement outside it. In that event, Malthouse Lane may be a later creation – perhaps when, in about 1550, the farmhouse which is now the Corner Cupboard inn was built.

The town's main buildings

Apart from the dominant ecclesiastical buildings (comprising the abbey church, its immediately adjoining monastic buildings and the parish church), the town's two main buildings in 1500 were probably the guild hall and booth hall (or market hall). These buildings were almost certainly situated at The Cross, approximately on the site of the present town hall and the building immediately to the west, now used as shop premises on the ground-floor and previously known as The Emporium. The Cross was not merely a term used to describe the intersection of High Street and North Street. There would have been a stone-built High Cross to remind all passers-by of man's higher purpose. As late as 1685, the town's bailiff Edward Harvey was authorised to spend money on maintaining The Cross, probably positioned within a wider opening into North Street.[24]

Although the town hall and booth hall were merged at the rebuilding in 1853, they were almost certainly separate buildings in 1500. The town hall would have provided a meeting place for the bailiffs and burgesses and accommodation for important civic ceremonies, while the booth hall would probably have been a covered market at a time when many traders would not have owned shop premises.

The recently refurbished and enlarged pilgrims' hostel also stood at The Cross, on the southern side of High Street. Although this building is referred to in a lease of 6 August 1531 as the inn called 'Le George', it may well have combined the functions of a pilgrims' hostel and an inn for any other travellers seeking accommodation in the town.[25] The lease of August 1531 also refers to a house in which four new shops have recently been built: this may possibly indicate a commercial venture by the abbey. Pilgrims travelling through the town would probably have seen mainly single-storey cottages, some no better than hovels, on either side of High Street and Hailes Street.

The same lease of August 1531 also refers to a 'close at Footebridge'. This suggests that, perhaps shortly after 1500, the river Isbourne was bridged by some rudimentary structure, enabling travellers on foot to cross it dry-shod, alongside the ford used by riders and livestock.

Although it was secluded within the abbey's curtilage, anyone venturing along Cowl Lane would have been greatly impressed by the sight of the abbot's house, about half way along on the western side and set well away from the highway. This was a beautiful, stone-built, richly ornamented manor house, comprising three storeys and attic rooms. Just before its demolition in 1815 Edmund Thomas Browne sketched the

two principal elevations of this impressive house which deliberately sought to emphasise the abbot of Winchcombe's status.

One of the most intriguing references in John Leland's description of his visit to Winchcombe, in 1540 or 1541, is as follows:

'... There was a Fortresse or Castle right against the South syde of St Peter's, the Parish Church of Winchecombe, called of latter dayes (as appeareth by Writinges in Winchecombe Abbey) Ivy-Castle, now a place where a few poore Houses bee and Gardeins. I think that the oulde Buildinges of it fallinge into ruine, and Ivy growinge in the Walles of it, caused it to be called by the Name of Ivy-Castle ...'[26]

The main reference to Ivy Castle in the abbey's cartulary is in a conveyance of 25 May 1393, between Thomas Webbeley of Winchcombe and the parson of Haselton, John Bradley, of a tenement 'which is commonly known as Ivycastel' in the street called 'Mullelone'.[27] This appears to suggest that, by the end of the fourteenth century, the building in Mill Lane to which Leland also refers was already ivy-covered, although its earlier use as part of a castle was still remembered.

The area of land to the south of the parish church, now occupied by Jacobean House and the Chandos almshouses (neither of which existed in 1500) slopes quite steeply down to the valley of the river Isbourne in this part of the town. It would there-fore have been a tactically astute location to build a castle and fortify the approach. Attacking forces from the direction of Sudeley, to the south, would have had to cross the river (which could have been artificially widened), where the town's defensive wall is likely to have been on the northern bank in Saxon times, and then to have scaled the upward slope beneath the castle's fortified wall. This area may also have been the site of the castle that king Stephen's forces attacked and captured in 1144.

At the southern end of Mill Lane the abbey's main corn mill in the town was undoubtedly situated on the northern bank of the river Isbourne. Two grants of land dating from about 1280 each refer to the curtilage of a cottage situated between Edith Colloch's tenement and the bridge called 'Knottepillesbrugge'.[28] It is impossible to tell from this description where the bridge was situated; but there may well have been a bridge over the river, in the vicinity of the mill, to enable corn to be brought in conve-niently from the abbey's arable land to the south. This supposition may be strengthened if Eleanor Adlard's statement that there was originally a road leading to the mill from the Brockhampton direction is correct.[29]

There were probably other corn mills in the town, using water power from the river Isbourne. One probable site is on the northern side of Castle Street on the town side of the river. The fulling mill at Coates-juxta-Winchcombe may also have remained in production in 1500.

John Leland gives the main descriptions of the interior of the abbey church and the parish church, enabling them to be visualised at least in part.

Although it had almost certainly been completely demolished by the time of his visit to Winchcombe, Leland refers to the tombs in the abbey church as follows:

'There laye buried in the East part of the Church of the Monastery of Winchecombe, Kenelphus and Kenelmus, the Father and Sonne, both Kinges of Merches. There lay in St. Nicholas Chappell at the East Ende of the High Aulter on[e] Henry Boteler, that covered the Body of the Church of the Monastery with Lead ... There laye other of the Botelers of Sudeley in the Church of the Monastery ...'[30]

This confirms that the Boteler family of Sudeley was even more strongly associated with the abbey than they had been with the town, to the extent of having given what must have been a substantial sum of money to meet the cost of re-leading the monastic church's roof. And the reference to a chapel dedicated to St Nicholas in the most sacred part of the church, to the east of the high altar, provides another possible source of the tradition of an ancient church of St Nicholas in the town.

Leland's eyewitness account of the parish church's interior is as follows:

'I marked in the South Isle of the Quire, first the Image of Tho[mas] Boteler Lord Sudeley. Then were three Images of these his Sonnes followinge, John, William, Thomas and Rafe, and an Image (as I take it) of Elizabeth Wife to Rafe Lord Sudeley. There was alsoe in the Glasse Windowes in the North Isle of the Quire Images of 4 Gentlewomen, whereof one was named Alicia, Da[ughter] to Thomas Boteler Lord Sudeley ...'[31]

As well as these images of Boteler family members in the parish church's choir, the will of David Jefferes, made on 12 February 1503, indicates that there were a number of altars and lights, apart from the high altar. This will leaves gifts to the altar of the Blessed Mary, separate altars dedicated to St Katharine, St John, St Christopher and St George, the light of the Holy Cross and the light in the middle of the Church.[32] Some of these altars may have been in richly decorated side chapels, complementing the wall paintings which would almost certainly have remained until the Reformation. The chancel was separated from the nave by the elaborately carved wooden screen (which was banished to the west end in 1984) and the screen would have been surmounted by the carved figure of the Holy Rood, depicting the Saviour's crucifixion in glowing colours. Stained glass in all the church's windows would have completed the atmosphere of mystery and reverence.

One building not to be found anywhere in the town in 1500 was a purpose-built school. As Chapter 13 will explain, no such institution existed until the 1520s. Although the abbey's master of the choristers probably instructed some half a dozen boys in song and may have been capable of teaching them grammar, this instruction would have been given within the abbey. No education was thought necessary for girls.

The town's surroundings

Much of the land around the town would have been devoted to arable production, especially wheat and barley. On Langley hill the signs of recent limestone quarrying for new building, the parish church in particular, would probably have been evident. But there was also valuable woodland. The main wooded areas were Depewood on Corage hill (370 acres), Humblebee How (50 acres), Farmcote wood and Westwood (70 acres). All these woods appear to have belonged to the abbey in 1500. They were a vital source of timber for housebuilding and repairs; and of fuel in a location to which coal from the Forest of Dean would have been difficult to transport.

The town's inhabitants

Apart from the monastic community, it is difficult to give a coherent account of the borough's people in 1500. The most important citizen was probably the high bailiff; but his identity appears to be unknown. The vicar was Thomas Butler, son of Sir John Butler of Badminton.

The nearest date for which information is available about the size of the town's population at this time is 1522. In that year commissioners carried out a fiscal and military survey on the king's behalf, in preparation for an anticipated Anglo-French war. As this was not a census and it is impossible to know how many of the male population might have avoided inclusion in it, the returns cannot be regarded as entirely accurate.

In the Winchcombe area, the male population is recorded separately for the town, Stanley Pontlarge, Postlip, Gretton, Greet, Sudeley and Coates. Allowing for repetition of two names, 117 non-clerical men are listed as the town's male inhabitants. This may possibly indicate a total population, excluding the abbey, of between 400 and 450, which seems surprisingly low. As very few surnames refer to an individual's trade or occupation, this survey cannot be used to analyse the range of trades and crafts practised by Winchcombe's male inhabitants in 1500. Twenty-five of the men listed were considered unfit or unable to undertake military service.[33]

1   E. Adlard: 'Winchcombe Cavalcade', page 14
2   E. Adlard, op cit, page 14
3   Landboc, Volume I, pages 31, 106 and 112-113
4   E. Adlard, op cit, page 14
5   Landboc, Volume I, pages xlix and liv
6   Landboc, Volume I, page 246
7   Landboc, Volume I, page lii
8   Landboc, Volume I, page xlix
9   identified by Dr. Steven Bassett in S. R. Bassett: 'The origins and early development of Winchcombe and its district', unpublished BA dissertation, University of Birmingham, 1977
10   GRO, D 7622/3/16 and 3/36
11   Letters and Papers, Foreign and Domestic of the Reign of Henry VIII, HMSO, 1901,

Volume XVIII, Part 1, Doc. No. 981, folio 20; and (1902) Volume XVIII, Part 2, Doc. No. 107, folio 56

12   H. P. R. Finberg: 'Gloucestershire Studies', page 80

13   Landboc, Volume I, pages 134 and 135

14   A. H. Smith: 'The Place-Names of Gloucestershire', Volume xxxviii, Part One, pages 17-18

15   Landboc, Volume I, pages lvii-lix

16   Landboc, Volume II, page 400

17   S. R. Bassett: 'A Probable Mercian Royal Mausoleum at Winchcombe, Gloucestershire', page 83

18   Landboc, Volume I, page xliv

19   Landboc, Volume II, pages 414-415

20   Landboc, Volume II, page 432

21   Landboc, Volume II, page 421

22   Landboc, Volume II, page 151

23   Landboc, Volume I, page 43

24   Landboc, Volume I, page xliii

25   Landboc, Volume I, page lx

26   J. Leland: 'Itinerary', page 74

27   Landboc, Volume II, page 430

28   Landboc, Volume II, pages 399-401

29   E. Adlard, op cit, page 74

30   J. Leland, op cit, page 74

31   J. Leland, op cit, page 75

32   Landboc, Volume I, page xcix

33   R. W. Hoyle (editor): 'The Military Survey of Gloucestershire', BGAS, 1993, pages 208-212

CHAPTER 12

THE ABBEY'S DISSOLUTION

When abbot Richard Mounslow succeeded Richard Kidderminster, in December 1525, he probably did not expect that the momentous upheaval within the Church constituting the English Reformation would limit his rule, as last abbot of Winchcombe, to fourteen years.

Although this is not the place to analyse this theologically and politically complex movement, three main forces can perhaps be distinguished. First, later medieval England had witnessed growing English nationalism, stimulating a view of the Papacy as an Italian secular state to which excessive financial tribute was being paid. An extension of this view regarded monasteries as an alien feature of English religious life. Secondly, although it was not true of Winchcombe abbey during Richard Kidderminster's rule, many members of the religious orders appeared no longer to live according to their profession of faith; and, in particular, some abbots behaved as rich and influential landowners, rather than leaders of a community dedicated to prayer, teaching and charitable purpose. This behaviour prompted envy and resentment of what was seen as their misappropriated wealth. Thirdly, the increasingly prosperous and influential merchants, or middle class, in the towns, who saw themselves as sturdily independent and thrifty, came to regard the monastic orders as lacking in vocation, or even irrelevant to their concerns. As there were some 563 religious houses in England in 1535, containing some 7,000 men in holy orders, 2,000 nuns and 35,000 laymen, any criticism could readily focus on some local institution.[1]

Such feelings were almost certainly expressed in Winchcombe where, despite its borough status and the measure of self-government exercised by the bailiffs, the abbey stood uncompromisingly at the heart of the town and its dominance was unmistakable. These factors help to explain why, in Winchcombe as in many other towns with a religious house in their midst, the assault on the monasteries launched by Henry VIII, and his vicar-general Thomas Cromwell, seems to have inspired little sympathy or support for monastic institutions from the local community.

On 15 January 1535, Henry VIII formally assumed the title of Supreme Head on earth of the Church in his realm. As vicar-general, Thomas Cromwell was enabled to exercise virtually complete control over Church government. In Winchcombe, abbot Mounslow appears to have been particularly unfortunate in experiencing Cromwell's close interest in the abbey's affairs. On 17 July 1535, the vicar-general arrived at Sudeley castle to prepare for a royal progress through the county to Berkeley castle, by Henry VIII and Anne Boleyn, lasting until September. The royal visitors arrived at Sudeley on 21 July and stayed for about five days: they may well have enjoyed the abbey's hospitality and used their visit as an opportunity to assess its condition and wealth.[2]

Almost immediately, Cromwell began the suppression of the smaller religious houses, defined as having an annual income of less than £200: their lands and property were transferred to the crown. Severe restrictions were then imposed on the larger monasteries' activities. This may have prompted abbot Mounslow, Winchcombe abbey's prior John Austen, and twenty-three monks to acknowledge the Royal Supremacy, on 25 August 1535, in the hope of prolonging the abbey's survival. But Cromwell was so unrelenting in his efforts to curtail the abbey's external influence on lay people that his injunctions even extended to limiting the monks to the use of one of the abbey's gates. Towards the end of 1535, when abbot Mounslow sought a relaxation in some of the restrictions, he reminded Cromwell that one of the two gates opened on to the town, where a porter was always on duty; while the other (presumably a gate in the northern boundary, providing access on to what is now Back Lane) opened into the fields. Thus, the restriction on the use of the back gate meant that the abbey's crops of hay and corn had to be carried on a half-mile detour.[3] However, since part of Cromwell's purpose may have been to make monastic life so uncomfortable that abbots would voluntarily surrender their houses, he was probably unmoved by abbot Mounslow's pleading.

Another of Cromwell's techniques in dealing with the larger monasteries was personally to select and appoint as local clerics men who would oppose traditional religious views and practices, and would try to persuade monks and local communities to follow enlightened opinion, based on reformist theology. For this purpose, Cromwell appointed in Winchcombe a lecturer named Anthony Saunders, towards the end of 1534 or early in 1535, who had graduated as M.A. from Merton College in the University of Oxford some two years previously.[4] Saunders 'held after the new world' in matters of religion and has been variously described as curate or roving preacher. His main function in the abbey was to lecture to the monks in an effort to persuade them to abandon traditional views. However, this proved to be an uphill task; and, as early as 3 February 1535, Saunders wrote to Cromwell seeking his patron's help in the following terms:

'As you have appointed me to be a pastor at Winchcombe to preach the Word of God and read it to the monks, I desire you to help me of the manifold lets and burdens which hinder me in the performance of my duty.'

Saunders goes on to complain of the size of his parish, amounting to a population of 2,000 (which must have included the parishes in the deanery of Winchcombe), and abbot Mounslow's unco-operative attitude to him.[5]

Despite the abbot's unhelpfulness, Saunders appears to have successfully stimulated some dissent among the monks, although it is impossible to say whether these views were based on genuine theological differences or were merely an expression of personal aversion to the sometimes irksome discipline of monastic life. At least two of the monks appear to have reported directly to Cromwell on alleged instances of the abbot's failure to observe the vicar-general's injunctions promptly. Perhaps in response to increasing signs of indiscipline, abbot Mounslow himself resorted to a complaint to Cromwell, in a letter of 7 December 1535, including the following passage:

'On Friday in the first week of Advent, two of my brethren, Dan Walter Aldelme and Dan Hugh Egwyne, ate flesh, contrary to custom. I called them before me and my brethren in the Chapter House and imposed penance, which they refused to obey, saying that they would eat flesh next Friday if they might have it. I told them that imprisonment was the punishment for disobedience, which they little regarded; and I have committed them in custody till I hear further from you.'[6]

This letter clearly conveys both the abbot's frustration at losing control over disobedient brethren and the vicar-general's pervasive influence over monastic life.

Unsurprisingly, abbot Mounslow and prior John Austen appear to have made some careful plans, from as early as 1533, to ensure that, in the event of the abbey's expropriation, they would not be left in poverty. On 14 December 1533, the abbey granted a ninety-nine year lease of the manor of Sherborne to Sir John Alleyn, described as knight, citizen and alderman of the city of London, in return for a substantial sum of money not specified in the lease.[7] The editor of the Dutton family's memoirs describes this transaction as follows:

'There is no doubt from the fact also that Henry VIII after trying other means in vain, offered as much as £1,400 for the surrender of the lease, that the amount paid by Sir John was at that time something considerable, and that each of the signatories to the deed received as "hush-money" a portion of the proceeds.'

The grant of the manor of Sherborne was not the only example of seeking to provide for anticipated leaner times. In June 1538, the abbey sought to convey one of its London properties, a house in St Bride's, to William Mounslow, a London mercer who was probably also one of the abbot's cousins or a closer relative, and Richard Rowndall, a lawyer of the Temple.[8] However, there was some difficulty in obtaining Cromwell's consent to this grant and whether it was completed is uncertain. This transaction may have amounted to a fictitious conveyance from the abbot to a close relative, with the object of eventually enabling the property to be regained after the dissolution.

Whatever expedients Winchcombe abbey or other monastic houses might use to safeguard their property, Thomas Cromwell was determined to follow up the Act of Dissolution of 1536, suppressing the smaller monasteries, with progressive seizure of the assets of the remaining houses. In 1538 he launched an attack on superstitious images and began the suppression of the pilgrimage saints, of whom the most venerated was St Thomas a Becket at the shrine in Canterbury. An early casualty of this attack was the relic of the Holy Blood at Hailes abbey. It was thoroughly investigated by Cromwell's commissioners, who sent him a certificate, in October 1538, confirming that the supposed relic had been 'tried according to our powers, wits and discretions by all means and by force of view and other trials.'[9]

The shrine in which sacred relics were usually encased was particularly valued by the commissioners because it often contained gold and silver ornamentation or precious jewels. There appears to be no record of the destruction which presumably befell St Kenelm's shrine in Winchcombe abbey. However, its loss seems to have been less important than was the removal of the relic of the Holy Blood from Hailes because the commissioners noted that Winchcombe abbey's income from St Kenelm's shrine was not worth recording; whereas the Holy Blood yielded an annual income of £10.[10]

On 17 August 1539, abbot Richard Mounslow made what was to be his last appeal to Cromwell against the monastery's dissolution, 'trusting that he [the abbot] has not done anything against the law of God and the king to merit the suppression of the monastery'.[11] But he was too late. When Parliament had met in April of that year, one of its first Acts had been to facilitate Henry VIII and his successors in obtaining the income and property gained from surrender of the remaining monasteries. This paved the way for Cromwell to overcome any further resistance from reluctant abbots.

Between August and December 1539, the abbot and his remaining brethren must have decided that surrender of the abbey on the best available terms was their only prudent course. Although there appears to be no record of the exact date of this decision, the reality of their situation may have dawned on them gradually as news reached the abbey of the surrender of other monasteries, sometimes grimly enforced. In 1538, the abbot of Woburn and the prior of Lenton (now a suburb of Nottingham) had been executed for criticising the royal supremacy; and, in autumn 1539, the abbots of Glastonbury, Colchester and Reading were hanged, partly for allegedly supporting the conspiracy against the king known as 'the Pilgrimage of Grace'.[12] It had become clear that the probable alternative to surrender was martyrdom.

The terms of surrender were accepted by the abbot, the prior and sixteen monks. The compensation paid for loss of office varied greatly between the abbot and other members of the house. The abbot received an annual pension of £140 and forty loads of wood from Depewood annually; while prior John Austen's annual pension was £8. Nine monks received an annual pension of £6 13s. 4d. and the remaining seven each obtained an annual pension of £6. It is virtually impossible to convert these sums to present-day money values; but an indication that most recipients found them insufficient is that they sooner or later took advantage of the permission to seek appointment to a benefice. As well as receiving a seemingly generous pension, the former abbot was given the rectory of Notgrove in 1541. On 14 November 1546, he was presented to a prebendal stall in Gloucester, but had his pension reduced by £20 on this account. Subsequently, on 27 September 1554, he was presented to the rectory of Radwinter in Essex and remained there until his death in October 1558. Prior John Austen (also known as Hancock) appears to have remained in the Winchcombe district until he was appointed rector of Shipton Oliffe in 1554, where he stayed until he died in 1562.[13] Others obtained benefices in Gloucestershire or further afield. Some ninety lay servants of the abbey were granted an annuity of a year's wages.

The abbey's property at the dissolution was valued at £766 10s. 7¼d. Its main components in Gloucestershire were the manors of Winchcombe, Twyning, Sherborne, Stanton, Snowshill, Honeybourne, Dry Marston, Admington, Yanworth, Haselton, Rowell, Hawling, Charlton Abbots, Naunton, Frampton, Cotes-in-Winchcombe and Sudeley; the Hundreds of Kiftsgate, Holford and Greston; rents from property in Winchcombe and Gloucester; and the rectories of Winchcombe, Twyning, Stanton and Bledington. The abbey also owned the manors of Enstone in Oxfordshire and Alne in Warwickshire.[14]

Cromwell's chief aim was to maximise the value of the abbey's assets to the crown. The king's commissioners were his willing accomplices: they thoroughly surveyed the fabric and divided the buildings into two main categories, namely those 'to remain undefaced' and those 'deemed to be superfluous.' They placed in the first category the abbot's lodging, with his kitchen, buttery, pantry and other lodgings within the same curtilage; lodgings on the west side of the court, the bakery, the brewery, and the abbot's stable, barns, oxhouse and sheephouse. The superfluous category included the abbey church, with its choir, aisles, chapels, steeple, cloister, chapter house, dormitory, frater, infirmary, library and other adjoining chapels and lodgings. The commissioners estimated that these surplus buildings would yield 121 'foders' (about 130 tons) of roofing lead, which was extremely valuable, together with the bells in the steeple. The list of 'jewels reserved to the use of the king's majesty' amounted to a mitre garnished with silver gilt and some 'ragged pearls and counterset stones'.[15] Perhaps these jewels had been stripped from the ornamentation of St Kenelm's shrine in the abbey church.

At the surrender the abbey's buildings became the king's property and Sir John Bridges was appointed as the king's custodian until the longer term future of those buildings 'deemed to be superfluous' could be determined. It is sometimes suggested that the surplus buildings became a quarry for building stone for the townspeople. Two factors suggest that this is unlikely. First, reusable building stone was valuable and part of the king's custodian's responsibility would have been to safeguard the site until the stone and other materials could be disposed of profitably. In practice, when the abbey and manor of Winchcombe were granted to Sir Thomas Seymour in August 1547, much of the reusable stone was probably transported to the Sudeley estate where it was intended to fulfil Seymour's ambition to rebuild the castle. Secondly, with the exception of the former farmhouse which is now the Corner Cupboard inn, there is almost no evidence of domestic buildings in the town with external stone walls dating from the mid-sixteenth century. This does not necessarily exclude the possibility that there are fragments of decorative stone from the abbey's buildings to be found inside and outside some domestic buildings: the string course incorporating carved rabbits at the front of the dwelling house which is now 94 Gloucester Street (Rabbit Box House) may be one such example.

Abbot Richard Mounslow surrendered Winchcombe abbey to the king's commissioners on 23 December 1539, reportedly 'a cold chilly day'.[16] The commissioners proceeded to Hailes abbey the next day, where they accepted the surrender of abbot Sagar and twenty-two monks. On 4 January 1540, the commissioners were able to report to Cromwell that they 'had despatched Hailes and Winchcombe and are at Gloucester, where they have taken the surrender … ' There is no surviving record of what Winchcombe's abbot or the townspeople thought about this momentous event in the borough's life. Just inside the abbey's main gate there had been a modest, stone-built structure known as Small-bread Hall, presumably used by the monks to distribute doles of bread to the poorest in the town. At Christmas 1539, that charitable purpose had ceased.

1   J. D. Mackie: 'The Earlier Tudors, 1485-1558', The Oxford History of England, 1952, page 373
2   Landboc, Volume I, pages xlvii-xlviii
3   G. Haigh: 'The History of Winchcombe Abbey', page 178
4   Nicholas Orme: 'Education in the West of England, 1066-1548', University of Exeter, 1976, page 214
5   G. Haigh, op cit, pages 171-172
6   G. Haigh, op cit, page 177
7   'Memoirs of the Dutton family of Sherborne', edited by Blacker Morgan, 1899, page 49
8   G. Haigh, op cit, page 183
9   D. Winkless: 'Hailes Abbey, Gloucestershire', page 57
10   G. Haigh, op cit, page 191
11   G. Haigh, op cit, page 185
12   J. D. Mackie, op cit, page 398
13   G. Haigh, op cit, page 187
14   G. Haigh, op cit, page 190
15   Landboc, Volume II, page xli
16   Landboc, Volume II, page xl

CHAPTER 13

FIRST STEPS IN FORMAL EDUCATION

The first steps towards providing children in Winchcombe with formal public education were taken almost by chance. Lady Joan Huddleston, widow of the former constable of Sudeley castle, Sir John Huddleston, maintained contact with the abbot of Hailes after her husband's death and his burial in the abbey church at Hailes in January 1512.[1] Lady Joan was also acquainted with Richard Kidderminster during his rule at Winchcombe abbey; and she appointed the abbot of Hailes as supervisor of her will (made on 18 April 1518) and the abbot of Winchcombe as one of her executors.[2] Among numerous other charitable bequests, she provided for the aisles of Hailes abbey church to be finished, leaded and embattled, if this work had not been completed at her death; and, similarly, for the Lady chapel at Winchcombe abbey to be finished at her expense.[3]

Lady Joan also left one hundred marks (£66 13s. 4d.) for the purpose of building and maintaining an almshouse in Winchcombe to accommodate thirteen poor people.[4] Following her death in the summer of 1519, Lady Joan's executors found that she had not provided sufficiently to carry out the almshouse project, for which no building plot had been allocated and no property left to endow it. After paying for her funeral expenses and fulfilling the terms of her legacies, the executors found that some £400 remained which would only provide an annual income of about £20. They decided to use this sum to found a grammar school for boys in Winchcombe as Lady Joan Huddleston's memorial. Recalling his strong personal interest in providing education for the monks in Winchcombe abbey, this decision probably owed more to Richard Kidderminster's inspiration, as one of the executors, than any other factor.[5]

By an indenture dated 7 September 1521, the monastery undertook, with the agreement of the community at Hailes abbey, to acquire land and property capable of yielding an annual income of £21 6s. 8d. and to seek the king's licence to found a school and schoolhouse in the town and to maintain six choristers in the abbey. This agreement provided for a schoolmaster to be appointed by the abbot of Winchcombe, who had discretion to remove him. The master's responsibilities were to govern the school, in accordance with the statutes drawn up by the abbot, and to teach all who came to him without payment, except for any voluntary sums he might be given. He was to reside permanently at the school, apparently teaching throughout the year, apart from four weeks' annual holiday and any period when attendance was prevented through plague or sickness. The schoolmaster's annual reward was to be £6 13s. 4d. and a gown, or 20s. instead of the gown; and he was to have a chamber, either within the abbey or outside, together with four loads of firewood and food and drink in the abbey appropriate to his status. The abbot also undertook to ensure that the sum of £10 from the annual endowment should go towards providing the grammar school and the schoolmaster.[6]

These arrangements were described in the 'Valor Ecclesiasticus' (valuation of the property of the Church in England commissioned by Henry VIII) of 1535 as follows:

'In alms and payments by foundation and ordinance of Lady Jane Huddelston, relict of John Huddilston knight, yearly to the Master of the Grammar School of Winchcombe, to the Master of the boys singing in the monastery aforesaid, and for the maintenance of 6 boys in the said monastery being instructed and taught in the art of grammar and of song; and also for keeping the anniversaries of the Lady Jane and the said Sir John her late husband at the monasteries of Hayles and Winchcombe yearly with distributions in bread to the poor on the said anniversary days, £21 6s. 8d.'[7]

As this description makes clear, the grammar school and its master were to be financed separately from the six boy choristers in the abbey choir, although out of the same endowment. (Why Lady Joan has been wrongly named Lady Jane is not stated.)

In 1532 the schoolmaster was Christopher Glanfield, who also officiated, from 4 March 1532 to 26 September 1541, as chaplain to the chantry of the Blessed Mary in the parish church, which had originally been established by Richard Chamberleyn and Walter Ponchard in August 1402.[8] However, by 1536, Glanfield had fallen out with abbot Richard Mounslow because he had apparently helped Anthony Saunders (Thomas Cromwell's appointee) to spread the gospel according to the new learning among the parishioners of Winchcombe. In response, the abbot allegedly reduced the schoolmaster's pay from £10 annually to 40s. and tried to set the parishioners against him, even going to the length of threatening Glanfield with a one shilling fine each time he deputised for the parish priest in services at St Peter's church.[9]

This hostility may have prompted Glanfield to resign as schoolmaster because, following the abbey's dissolution in 1539, a master of the free grammar school in Winchcombe called George Broke emerges on 13 February 1542, when the crown granted him a pension as if he had been one of the abbey's servants dismissed from their posts. The terms of George Broke's pension also included the schoolhouse in Winchcombe, the master's chamber, a life-time annuity of £5, and permission to charge his pupils the fees customary in other schools.[10]

This decision effectively privatised the school into George Broke's hands and made no arrangements for its future survival. But the decision was subsequently counter-manded – or, at least, a further decision was taken to restore the regular payment of £10 to an active grammar schoolmaster in Winchcombe. At Michaelmas 1543 the king's appointed bailiff for the abbey's property at the dissolution recorded a payment of £20, to a 'master of the common school' at Winchcombe, known as Humphrey

Dick, for two years' teaching. Teaching therefore continued, though there is no indication where the schoolhouse was kept after the facilities previously provided by the abbey had ceased. Perhaps the schoolmaster taught whatever boys presented themselves in his own accommodation. Nevertheless, these arrangements continued, with Humphrey Dick as schoolmaster until Michaelmas 1560, and again from 1563 to 1566, and Robert Hide between 1561 and 1563. In 1566 Thomas Angel took over from Humphrey Dick on the same terms as had originally been established in 1521, which suggests that, despite the disruption caused by the abbey's dissolution, another body – possibly the town's bailiffs – had assumed effective responsibility as governors of the school. The same salary as Christopher Glanfield had received also continued, but as a direct payment from the crown.[11]

This sequence of appointments suggests that, because Lady Joan Huddleston's original endowment had been administered by the abbey, it was mistakenly regarded as part of the abbey's assets in 1539 and passed, along with the rest, into the king's hands. Thus, when payments for the schoolmaster's maintenance were resumed, they came from Exchequer funds, albeit on the same terms as Lady Joan had effectively provided through her executors' arrangements. Although the grammar school was known as the King's school from the reign of Edward VI, it might more accurately have been called Lady Joan Huddleston's foundation.

The same arrangements seem to have continued without interruption into Elizabeth I's reign. In 1570 the bishop of Gloucester received a special commission requiring him to report on the condition of the grammar schools at Cirencester and Winchcombe. The required information for Winchcombe was submitted to the bishop in February 1571 by the town's two bailiffs, John Tockor and Thomas Boler, and four churchwardens, as follows (with modern spelling substituted for the original):

'Whereas we are charged with certain articles touching our grammar school, this shall be, for our discharge, to let you understand, that we have of the Queen's Majesty by her receiver, Mr Fludd, ten pounds, yearly, to the maintaining of good learning, and to the virtuous bringing up of youth in our School of Winchelcombe. Our schoolmaster is one Phillip Brode, a Bachelor of Arts, and not only allowed and admitted by the Ordinary, but, also for his good behaviour, conversation and diligence in teaching, well liked of the town. But we have no decent and convenient house, wherein our school may be kept, for, the Abbey being suppressed, a schoolhouse was taken away, and, since that time, we have had none, but upon sufferance.'[12]

In reply to another commission, in the following year, two statements reveal a little more about the school's management, as follows:

'Item, the school house is in a decent and convenient place but is not of duty but of sufferance and friendship.

Item, the election and placing of the Schoolmaster is at the discretion of the bailiffs of the town and other of the honest and substantial men there and at the confirmation of the bishop.'[13]

The whereabouts of this decent and convenient place for the schoolhouse cannot now be ascertained. But, as Valentine Blake was vicar of Winchcombe and master of the school from 1598 until his death on 29 September 1614, he may have used his own accommodation for teaching the boys. It is known that some later vicars also served as the schoolmaster.

By the early seventeenth century, it must have become irksome to the bailiffs and other 'honest and substantial men' who managed the school not to have a permanent, purpose-built school building in the town. At this juncture, John Barksdale, who was high bailiff in 1615 and 1616 and possessed considerable wealth, took the lead in re-establishing the King's school in a fine, new building in the town's centre. The financial transaction by which John Barksdale received a payment of £10 10s. from the town's stock towards some of the expense he incurred on this project is recorded as follows:

> 'John Barksdall received, of the Towne Stock, of Richard Harvey,
> 23 August, 1618 £3 – 20 Dec. 1618, £2 10s. 0d. – March, 1618,
> of Roger Symondes, then baylie, £5.
> Wch. said some is layed forth owte of the Towne Stocke of Tenn
> poundes, tenne shillings, uppon the Newe Schole Howse buylded
> in Anno Dni. 1618, by John Barksdale of Winchcomb.
>
> Witnessethe
>
> John Barkesdale   Arthur Bleeke
> Christopher Merrett   Ralphe Kempe
> Edward Massonne X his m'ke.'[14]

The people involved in this arrangement were clearly substantial men in the borough. Richard Harvey was a bailiff in 1618 and 1621, as was Roger Symonds in 1619. Christopher Merrett had been a bailiff in 1614 and 1615 and would return to that office in 1623. And Arthur Bleek (or Blake) would become a bailiff in 1622, 1623 and 1630.

The building they provided for the school is the anonymous Cotswold mason's masterpiece which survives as Jacobean House, facing eastwards across Queen Square. Despite the vicissitudes of alteration and restoration in almost four hundred

years, the building's original purpose can still be seen in its structure. The school was held in the large room which occupied the entire ground-floor; the schoolmaster's accommodation was on the self-contained floor above, with its own separate entrance at first-floor level from what is now the property's back garden; and the schoolboys from the surrounding district whose homes were too distant for daily travel to school were accommodated in dormitories on the second floor.[15]

Only three years after Winchcombe was provided with its first purpose-built school, arrangements were made for a second grammar school foundation. By a deed dated 13 November 1621, Lady Frances Chandos, wife of Lord Giles Chandos of Sudeley, gave certain property and stock which would produce an income of £13 13s. 10d. annually to maintain a free grammar school for fourteen children of the town of Winchcombe. This school was to be built in what the deed refers to as Nicholas Street (now Chandos Street). The scholars were to be instructed 'as well in the science of grammar as in other learning fit for their years'.[16] Although Lady Frances apparently relied on advice from John Tutty, who had been a bailiff of the town in 1600 and again in 1616, and she appointed him one of the school's trustees, it is unclear what relationship the Chandos grammar school and the King's school were intended to have to each other. Perhaps it was simply a question of providing more school places to meet an increasing demand for education.

In any event, by the mid-1620s, Winchcombe had two grammar schools, each occupying its own separate accommodation in the town, and providing education to some twenty-four pupils, probably without any parental obligation to pay teaching fees.

1   C. Roy Hudleston: 'Sir John Hudleston, Constable of Sudeley', Trans BGAS, 1926, Volume 48, Pages 117-132
2   Nicholas Orme: 'Education in the West of England, 1066-1548', Exeter University Press, 1976, page 188
3   C. R. Hudleston, op cit, page 130
4   C. R. Hudleston, op cit, page 131
5   N. Orme, op cit, page 188
6   N. Orme, op cit, page 189
7   Victoria County History of Gloucestershire (VCH), Volume II, 1907, page 420
8   Landboc, Volume I, pages cxiv and cxix
9   N. Orme, op cit, page 189
10   N. Orme, op cit, page 189
11   N. Orme, op cit, page 190
12   Landboc, Volume I, pages cxii-cxiii
13   VCH, Volume II, page 422
14   Landboc, Volume I, page lxxxiii
15   Philip Styles' Collection, GRO, D 3530/5
16   VCH, Volume II, page 422

CHAPTER 14

SURVIVING WITHOUT THE ABBEY

The effect on Winchcombe of the abbey's dissolution can be summarised in the oversimplified equation: the borough minus the abbey equals hardship. Although Winchcombe remained a royal borough, that status could not compensate for losing the institution which, despite its often-difficult relationship with the townspeople, had probably been economically and socially beneficial overall. The abbey had maintained a substantial staff; and its buildings must have needed continual refurbishment, which meant work for craftsmen and labourers recruited locally. St Kenelm's shrine in the abbey church and the commemorative well on Sudeley hill had been a notable pilgrimage destination. When pilgrims ceased to arrive in the town, its most important annual fair, held on the feast of St Kenelm, on 17 July, no longer attracted the numerous traders who had previously been assured of large numbers of visitors to this thriving market centre. The town's poorest inhabitants almost certainly suffered most from the abbey's loss since, despite individual monks' failings, the monastery had been a source of charity for the most needy.

The abbey's removal also emphasised that, without the artificial stimulus of a monastery at its centre, the borough lacked the natural resources – other than agriculture – needed for a sound economic base. This disadvantage was accentuated by the inevitable difficulty experienced in communications with the town from the south and east across the Cotswold scarp. The wool trade and cloth production had helped to make the borough comparatively prosperous during the fifteenth century; but, without the abbey's major organisational role, these vital activities declined. Although there were still some fulling mills in the Winchcombe district, the water power available from the river Isbourne and its even smaller tributaries could only sustain a cottage-style industry. Elsewhere, some former abbey buildings were acquired by cloth manufacturers for use as the earliest factories: for example, William Stumpe bought Malmesbury abbey and rented Osney abbey, and Tucker of Burford sought to obtain Abingdon abbey, for cloth production.[1] No such development occurred at Winchcombe, where the abbey buildings passed into the hands of successive owners of the Sudeley estate who were not entrepreneurs. It may be significant that, although he belonged to an earlier generation, the town's most famous son in Tudor times, Jack of Newbury, left to make his fortune in the cloth trade in Berkshire, where he died in 1520.

It is difficult to establish the size of Winchcombe's population immediately after the abbey's dissolution. The first available estimate is for 1549 when the king's commissioners were appointed on 14 February to survey the Gloucestershire chantries. Their statement for Winchcombe includes the following information: in the Deanery of Winchcombe, the Parish of Winchcombe 'where are of houseling people the nombre of viij C' [that is, 800 people].[2] Interpreting this figure of 800 is problematical: it may mean that the total population in 1549 was about 1,300. When that estimate is compared with estimated populations of Winchcombe (as a grammar school town) of 1,155 in 1551 and 875 in 1562, it appears that the number of inhabitants was gradually falling during this period.[3]

The chantry commissioners' 1549 return for Winchcombe is particularly interesting in recording that a priest then continued to serve in the chantry of Our Lady in the parish church. The priest at that time was 55-year old Sir Arthur Butterworth, who had an income of £7 per year. The commissioners also recorded that an acre of land had been given to maintain two tapers to burn before the image of 'St Nichas' in the parish church. This again suggests that the tradition of a parish of St Nicholas derived from a chantry chapel or altar dedicated to the saint in the parish church, rather than to any other church with that dedication elsewhere in the town.

It is equally difficult to establish the condition of the town and its people in the mid-sixteenth century. A court roll of 23 January 1540 indicates that there were freeholders, copyholders and tenants at will assessed in total at £44 2s. 11d.[4] The augmentation of 1550, which is a more detailed statement, produces a total assessment of £42 2s. 4d., which suggests that there had been little change in the inhabitants' financial circumstances during those ten years.[5] The latter document contains a brief description of the town's appearance in 1550 stating that 'the Towne of Winchcombe is a market Towne, and standithe almost altogether by housinge, which have noe landes belonginge to theme, more then apperithe in the particulers;...'[6] This account seems to suggest that the core area of the town comprised a closely grouped collection of cottages, each within its own confined plot.

As Chapter 11 mentions, one of the most interesting features of the 1550 augmentation is the list of tenants at will according to the street name in which their property was situated. The nine streets named in what is still the core area of the town are: Hailes Street (10), North Street (16), Le Spitle Ende (3), Sudeley Street (2), High Street (6), Under the Cawseway (5), Wyneyarde Street (7), Before Le Abbey Yate (5) and Gloucester Street (29).[7] The number of tenants in each street, some of whom leased more than one property, is given in the bracketed figures. This return lists only one shop, which belonged to Thomas Palmer in the street known as Under the Cawseway. In Gloucester Street, Henry Orpeyn was tenant of 1½ acres of pasture adjoining his tenement and garden: this pasture may possibly have been the remnant of the grazing known as King's Moor, also mentioned in Chapter 11.

The 1550 augmentation does not identify the trades or crafts of the tenants. However, it may be reasonable to assume that at least half of them were engaged in some form of agriculture, while the rest probably combined a trade or craft with raising crops for their own consumption in the common field. The same document mentions two inns.[8] The 'Crowne Inne' was owned by Richard Palmer and leased for eighty years to John Richards and his wife: the inn's traditional site is in Gloucester Street, at the junction with Mill Lane. It is believed to have been the home of the Merrett family during the seventeenth century. The other inn was 'Le George', situated at The Cross and probably experiencing leaner times in the absence of pilgrims seeking accommodation during their stay in Winchcombe.

It should be theoretically possible to compare the names of men recorded as living in Winchcombe at the time of the military survey of Gloucestershire in 1522 with those reported in the 1550 augmentation, in order to assess residential continuity in the town during this period of twenty-eight years. In practice, the comparison is unreliable because the information of 1550 relates to property occupiers, some of whom may have sub-leased to tenants who are not included in the survey. And, if a father and son lived in the same household in 1550, only one name would be recorded for the purpose of the augmentation. Nevertheless, for what it is worth, only ten (8.5%) of 117 names recorded in the 1522 military survey are identifiable with reasonable certainty in the 1550 augmentation. This appears to suggest that a substantial proportion of the male population had died or left the town during this period.

One of the remaining inhabitants' chief concerns must have been how disposal of the abbey's estate would affect the town. Before dissolution, the abbey's extensive properties had usually been well managed and provided employment over a wide area. They were therefore all the more attractive to predators who could obtain the king's favour in granting a manor or other property. As early as July 1540, Sir John Bridges, then constable of Sudeley castle and later to become the first Lord Chandos of Sudeley, obtained a twenty-one year lease of the house and site of the monastery, together with its property in the town, including the house known as 'le Amery' (probably the site of what is now Almsbury Farm) and the mansion called Corndean, all at an annual rent of £45 7s. 4d.[9] This lease did not run its full term. On 19 August 1547 Edward VI granted the abbey lands and the manor of Winchcombe to Thomas Seymour, whom Henry VIII had created Baron Seymour of Sudeley and appointed as Lord Admiral in February of the same year.[10]

Seymour's acquisition of the abbey's property in the town and the Sudeley estate might have been mutually beneficial if his ownership had resulted in purposeful management. But Seymour was preoccupied with other matters. As Edward VI's uncle and the brother of 'Protector' Somerset, who was for a time the youthful king's guardian and virtual ruler, Seymour was heavily and, in the end, fatally involved in affairs of state. Following Henry VIII's death, he had hastily and secretly married the king's widow, Catherine Parr, who died tragically at Sudeley castle on 5 September 1548 when she contracted puerperal fever after giving birth to Seymour's daughter. Seymour himself only survived until 20 March 1549 when he was executed in the Tower of London, having refused to attend before the Privy Council to answer charges of dishonesty and recalcitrance in his office of Lord Admiral.[11]

There is no evidence that Seymour took any personal interest in Winchcombe other than arranging to obtain reusable stone from the site of the abbey, so that Sudeley castle could be substantially rebuilt in Catherine Parr's honour. After

Seymour's death, Edward VI granted the abbey site and demesnes to the marquis of Northampton on 12 June 1550, who was himself accused of treason in 1553. Mary I then granted the estate once more to Sir John Bridges, whom she created Lord Chandos of Sudeley in April 1554. When the first Lord Chandos died three years later, the property passed to his son Edmund Bridges.[12]

Although the Sudeley estate was now firmly held by successive Lords Chandos, this stability could not compensate for the decline Winchcombe experienced during the remainder of the sixteenth century. Indeed, the fact that Edmund Bridges left the sum of £13 6s. 8d. annually to the poor of Winchcombe, when he died at Sudeley on 11 September 1572, suggests he was well aware of the town's plight.[13] This bequest was complemented by the decision of his widow, Lady Dorothy Chandos, to provide for the building of almshouses in the town to accommodate twelve poor

people in twelve apartments.[14] These almshouses, originally built in 1573 and substantially reconstructed in 1841, have survived in Almshouse Lane, between Queen Square and Mill Lane, alongside Jacobean House.

Elizabeth I reportedly visited Sudeley castle three times (in 1574, 1575 and 1592) while Giles, third Lord Chandos, owned it. The first visit may have resulted in the royal grant, on 7 April 1575, of a charter to the borough of Winchcombe, authorising an additional fair to be held on the feast of St Mark the Evangelist (25 April) and the preceding and following days, and enabling the bailiffs and burgesses to hold a 'pie powder court' at which any disputes resulting from trading during the fair could be settled quickly. In return for this privilege the borough was required to pay an annual fee of 10s. The charter's preamble reveals something of the difficulties Winchcombe was then experiencing, as follows:

' ... whereas our village or borough of Winchcomb in our county of Gloucester is in such a ruinous and decayed state, that the inhabitants of the same being very poor are unable to support and repair the aforesaid village or borough as it appears by the relation of Lady Dorothy Chandos, widow, and by the humble petition of the inhabitants of the aforesaid village or borough whereupon they have humbly besought us, that we, as well for the repairing as the enriching and relieving of the aforesaid borough or village who now are and who at any time shall be, would be pleased to grant one fair every year and one market every week to be held perpetually within the aforesaid village or borough of Winchcomb by the said inhabitants and their heirs inhabitants.'[15]

More evidence of the borough's problems during the last quarter of the sixteenth century is provided in the steps taken by the bailiffs and burgesses to control the town's trading activities. On 19 March 1588 the following resolution was made:

'It is ordered that ... no person, not being a Burgesse, or not lycensed and allowed (upon composicon) by the Baylieffs, Burgesses, Steward or under Steward of the same Burgh, shall, from and after Easter next, erect, sett up or open any standing, stawle or shopp, within the precincts or jurisdiccon of this Burgh, or utter, sett furth to be uttered, any maner of wares or merchandize, or use any Art, mistery, science, trade or occupacon, within the said Burgh, upon payne to forfect for every day (other than the usual fayres and markett dayes, wch are excepted, and not meant to be restrayned or in anything impeached by this ordinaunce), iis. vjd. The one moytye thereof to be to the use of the Quene, and the other moytye thereof to the use of the Burgh.'[16]

There is no indication how effective this licensing proved to be in practice. But it seems likely that it failed to protect what the town's bakers regarded as their legitimate interest in the face of competition from outsiders. On 6 October 1589 the two bailiffs, John Mutlow and John Tutty, recorded the following resolution in the Winchcombe corporation book:

'It is ordered and established by the Steward, Bailiffs and the whole Jury, this day impanelled, that no person, inhabiting or dwellinge within the precinct of the Burgh, shall att any tyme carry, fetch, badge or bring any bredd, of what sortt soever, from or furth of any Towne, villadge, Citie, burgh or hamlett, to thentent to retayle the same within this Burgh, uppon any daye other than the ordinary marckett and ffayer dayes, upon payne to forfect for every loaffe soe fetched &c. ijd. Provided allwayes, that yt may be lawfull for any Inhabitaunt to fettch bredd, from any place, to be spentt only in his owne howse, upon his owne family and servaunts.'[17]

The corporation probably did as much as they could afford to maintain the borough's fabric in reasonable condition. For example, on 28 October 1600, John Tutty was allowed the sum of 26s. 2d. for the provision of stone and sand for pitching and amending the pavement under and about the market place.[18] Nevertheless, a number of wills made during this period testify to the efforts its more prosperous citizens made to relieve the town's oppressive poverty. On 7 August 1560, Robert Kempe's will left 'To the poor at my burial, xxs.'; on 24 June 1614, the Reverend Valentine Blake left 'To the poor people of Winchcombe, xiijs. iiijd.'; on 18 April 1615, William Cowell left 'To the poor of the Towne, xxs.'; and, on 31 December 1624, Christopher Merrett left 'Forty shillings to the poor of Winchcombe'.[19]

1   J. D. Mackie: 'The Earlier Tudors, 1485-1558', The Oxford History of England, 1952, page 462

2   Sir John Maclean: 'Chantry Certificates, Gloucestershire,' Trans BGAS, 1883-84, Volume VIII, pages 280-281

3   Alicia C. Percival: 'Gloucestershire Grammar Schools from the 16th to the 19th Centuries', Trans BGAS, 1970, Volume 89, page 117

4   Landboc, Volume I, pages xlviii-lii

5   Landboc, Volume I, pages lvii-lxi

6   Landboc, Volume I, page lxii
7   Landboc, Volume I, pages lviii-lix
8   Landboc, Volume I, page lx
9   G. Haigh: 'The History of Winchcombe Abbey', page 195
10 Landboc, Volume I, page lvi
11 J. D. Mackie, op cit, page 488
12 W. St. Clair Baddeley: 'A Cotteswold Shrine', page 140
13 Landboc, Volume I, page lxiii
14 Landboc, Volume I, page lxiii
15 GRO, photocopy No. 890
16 Landboc, Volume I, pages lxxvii-lxxviii
17 Landboc, Volume I, page lxxix
18 Landboc, Volume I, page lxxix
19 Landboc, Volume I, pages xcii-xcv

CHAPTER 15

WINCHCOMBE'S GOLDEN LEAF?

In August 1608 the lord lieutenant of Gloucestershire was required to submit a return to the king listing 'all the able and sufficient men in body fit for his Majesty's service in the wars' in the county.[1] As this return was intended only to provide information about the availability of able-bodied men, it is unsurprising that, of 153 men listed in the borough of Winchcombe, only four were aged between fifty and sixty. Nevertheless, the return is a valuable source of information about how most of the male population of working age then gained a living, since only six are recorded without their trade, or as not following any trade.

Almost one-third of the men apparently relied wholly or mainly on agriculture: they included thirty-six labourers, nine husbandmen and five shepherds. The next largest occupational group, about one-quarter, were engaged in the cloth-making or the clothing trades: they included fourteen tailors, nine glovers, six clothworkers, five weavers and one collarmaker. As the town's estimated population in 1603 was only 1,182, many products of this clothworking industry must have been sold outside the town or even further afield. The next largest occupational group was eleven butchers, followed by six shoemakers and five smiths. Perhaps surprisingly, the building trades are poorly represented, comprising only one mason, one freemason, two slaters, four carpenters and one joiner: this may imply that demand for new building or refurbishment was low. Among the unusual occupations were one musician and one drummer: they may possibly have helped to provide music in the parish church where no organ had yet been installed. There was one physician.

The four mercers (dealers in cloth) included Christopher Merrett, who is described as in his twenties and 'of middle stature fit to make a musketeer'. Christopher Merrett exemplified the prosperity still obtainable from the cloth trade in Winchcombe. He was the borough's high bailiff in the years 1614, 1615 and 1623; lived in the house known as 'Le In or signe of the Crowne', at the corner of Gloucester Street and Mill Lane, where he also kept a shop; and had four sons and three daughters. His third son, also Christopher, born in Winchcombe in 1614, was educated at Gloucester Hall and Oriel College, Oxford; became an accomplished physician; and published numerous scientific works, including a catalogue of British animals, vegetables and minerals.[2]

The elder Christopher Merrett's wealth is exemplified by his will dated 31 December 1624, which refers to 'all my houses, lands and etc. in Winchcombe, Sudeley, Coates, Greet, Gretton and Cheltenham, or elsewhere in Gloucestershire, and my dwelling house in Winchcombe'. In addition to property bequests to his wife and children, he also left £250 to his son Christopher, £160 to his eldest daughter Anne, £150 to his second daughter Mary, and £120 to his third daughter Elizabeth. Among smaller legacies, he left 'Forty shillings to the poor of Winchcombe'.[3] He left the shop, which was part of the premises in Gloucester Street, to his second son George for life, provided he followed 'the art or trade of a mercer'. A brass plate still to be seen on the parish church's south wall records that Christopher Merrett was 'interred ye 9th of January 1624 & Awdery his wife (remarried to Thomas Hawkins) buried ye 7th of September 1654'.

Christopher Merrett's wealth was probably exceptional in early-seventeenth century Winchcombe. In 1612 James I granted the lordship of the manor and borough of Winchcombe to Sir George and Thomas Whitmore, sons of a highly successful London haberdasher and merchant adventurer, William Whitmore. The lordship of the manor subsequently passed on to their elder brother, also William Whitmore. The Whitmores were a family of successful London merchants. Although they appointed agents to hold manorial courts and collect the dues owing to the lord of the manor, there is no indication of their personal concern for the town's well-being during the following twenty-five years.

The other possible source of enterprise on the town's behalf was the local gentry. The Chandos family at Sudeley proved disappointing. Although Grey, fifth lord Chandos, was appointed lord lieutenant of the county in 1614, he apparently preferred to devote his energies to attendance at James I's court, where his substantial retinue earned him the title 'king of Cotswold'.[4] On his death in 1621, his son George was only one year old and no initiative on the town's behalf could therefore be expected from the Sudeley estate.

Instead, the badly needed commercial initiative was taken by John Stratford, second son of George Stratford of Farmcote. After involving himself and his London-based business partners in some unsuccessful ventures, John Stratford decided to try growing tobacco in the Winchcombe area and on the slopes above the Hailes abbey site, where unploughed old pasture was considered favourable for a tobacco crop. A contemporary described how John Stratford set about this project as follows:

'John Stratford, citizen of London, took a long lease of a house within the scite of the Abbey of Winchcombe: He bought lands thereabouts to the value of £300, and was of a great estate in his time: About five years past he fell to plant tobacco, and having the first year gained well thereby, he was so greedie after more gain thereby that (he) engaged his whole estate for tobacco, of which he had so much, was valued to be worth 20,000 li. His sale failing thereof he was by use of monie worn out of his estate; hath sold all his land and hideth his head and hath undone manie of his friends.'[5]

There are conflicting accounts of how tobacco smoking was first introduced into England. Most probably, the practice was brought from America by Sir John Hawkins in 1566. In any event, pipe-smoking had become a widespread indulgence by the end of the sixteenth century.[6] It is also doubtful when tobacco growing first began in the Winchcombe district. Although tradition maintains that the first crop was planted by Sir Walter Raleigh during his association with Brockhampton, no documentary evidence supports this possibility.[7]

John Stratford's tobacco growing enterprise began in 1619, when he assembled about 100 acres of rented land in Winchcombe, Cleeve and Cheltenham; paid about £1,400 in labour costs; and may have employed as many as 200 men between the beginning of May and the end of November.[8] Where the tobacco fields were is now uncertain; but land near the present Winchcombe hospital was known as Tobacco Piece, and Tobacco Close (leading northwards from Cheltenham Road, shortly after entering the town from the west) is a reminder of one area where the crop may well have been grown. John Stratford leased some of the land he needed from Giles Broadway of Postlip; and the magnificent tithe barn, situated below Postlip Hall, is said to have been used for wetting and drying the tobacco crop for the whole area.[9] Subsequently, some buildings in North Street were apparently used as tobacco warehouses.

However, despite the increased prosperity resulting from tobacco-growing in Gloucestershire, and Winchcombe in particular, the government was more concerned to maintain the lucrative monopoly for the tobacco crop exported to London by the Virginia settlers. Thus a proclamation was issued in 1619 making tobacco-growing in England illegal.[10] Although John Stratford petitioned against this proclamation, he immediately stopped cultivating tobacco and turned instead to flax with which he was already familiar from previous dealings with the Eastland company handling the Baltic flax trade.[11]

In 1623 Stratford planted flax on forty acres of land in Winchcombe and Cockbury and claimed to employ some 200 people in growing and dressing the crop. By 1627 he maintained that flax production had enabled him to pay off £8,000 of the debts previously incurred from taking long leases on parcels of land on which tobacco cultivation was forbidden. Stratford regarded flax-growing not simply as a means of achieving quick personal wealth, but as a way of helping to provide people in the Winchcombe area with badly needed new forms of employment. The following extract from one of his letters makes his intention clear:

'If our idle poor had flax raised here, as they might have, and [were] compelled to work, if they will not willingly otherwise, whereas now they are an intolerable burden to the abler sort by begging and stealing, they would contrariwise become profitable to the commonwealth, paying for food and clothing and live according to God's ordinance by the sweat of their face in a more religious order.'[12]

Although John Stratford had observed the government's ban on tobacco growing from the outset in 1619, others who had quickly appreciated the success of his enterprise defied the prohibition. Consequently, tobacco was grown on a large scale in the Winchcombe district for about another seventy years and a considerable proportion of the town's inhabitants must have relied heavily on the annual crop as their main source of income.

Despite James I's and Charles I's strong personal dislike for the tobacco habit, it was not until 1627 that a further proclamation was issued, on the Privy Council's authority, forbidding tobacco growing in England and ordering all tobacco crops to be destroyed.[13] This order proved ineffective, as did further royal proclamations in 1631 and 1634. It was about this time that William King, who bore the official title of messenger to the Chamber of the Council of State and had similar powers to those of a customs officer and bailiff combined, was appointed by the government to search for, and seize, any home-grown tobacco he could find in the county. The Privy Council exhorted Gloucestershire's justices of the peace to support the government's efforts at suppression; but there was a strong suspicion that some justices colluded with the tobacco growers in their area. In any event, William King complained to his superiors that 'the said offenders and divers others have gathered their said tobacco and daily bring it to London by secret ways and do usually sell it for Virginia and Bermuda tobacco'.[14] There is now no evidence to show what were the secret ways for transporting the dried and cured tobacco crop from Winchcombe to London; but, at a time when nearly all highways were atrociously difficult and often dangerous, it was probably not hard to lead pack horse teams by night along little known Cotswold trackways into Oxfordshire and beyond.

A much later description of how tobacco was grown in the Winchcombe area suggests that it was principally a cottage-based activity. Ralph Bigland's account of the operation is as follows:

'Its seed is smaller than mustard seed, it is sown upon a hill bed three yards high in horse dung in March, then some fine earth sifted upon it, the seed is mixed with ashes. About the latter end of May, they make fresh beds and replant it. The third time when 'tis as dry as a cabbage, they plant it again in a garden. In July they gather it and string it, and hang it up in the house to dry and then roll it up.'[15]

It is difficult to assess what effect the illegal tobacco growing and John Stratford's flax production had on the borough's economy. The parliamentary survey of church livings in 1649-1650 recorded that Winchcombe was a market town with about 350 families living in it.[16] The estimated population of the town in 1650 was 1,530.[17] Such evidence as exists suggests that the majority of these people probably lived at or near subsistence level, in poor housing. When the Whitmore family, as manorial lords, attempted to increase rents and enforce other obligations on their tenants, they met hostility mixed with pleas of poverty. Thomas Whitmore wrote from Pucklechurch in April 1637 to Sir William Whitmore, giving the following account of their Winchcombe tenants' possessions and attitude to authority:

'From Slaughter we went to Winchcomb and there kept a Courte, and made a particular view and demaunde at every house; and for herriots we might have had naked children, and for distresses for rents, patched petticoates, the Common pasture of all the quicke Cattle, and when we spake of ffines and raysinge of rents, we had a Charme of Scoulds, raysinge their voyces to "God save the Kinge and the lawes; and they and theire ancestours had lived there And they would live there:" and without the danger of hotte spittes and scaldinge water and fiery tongues, there is no gaineinge of possession: and we find that there is a Confederacye amongst the people to stand off, And when some of the most enclynable natures were cominge to compound, the others would put them by, and not suffer them ... '[18]

This hostility prompted Sir William Whitmore to seek an injunction in the Court of Exchequer against his tenants, maintaining that John Harvey of Gloucester Street, Richard Kite and John Evans had solicited 'other tenants of the Manor to take their parts against him; when his bailiffs or servants distrain, defendants run at them with spits, cast scalding water upon them – they buy and sell the houses, by delivering the key of the doors, giving £20, £30, £40 for a house, without conveyance'.[19] The defendants' response to Sir William's statement of case emphasised the townspeople's extreme poverty in the following terms:

'The inhabitants bene and nowe are poore Tradesmen, and such as gett their livinge by handicrafte trade, and by retaylinge of small merchandizes and commodities, and have payed all dutyes (ancient rents, and services at Leet and Courts Baron), assessed, as freehoulders or absolute holders, they have, in all time, sold away tenements without deede or writing, and delivered seizin, by the delivery of a key – that, terrified with threatenings of suits, the tenants, being, for the most part, very poor and maintained by charity, not daring to repair them, their houses are groune into such decay, as the danger is groune very great for the Kinges subjects to pass by the same – that the nomber of the poore is exceedingly incresed, there is not one housekeeper for them that is of ability to give almes, and this is occasioned by the Complainantes meanes ... '[20]

Unhappily for the tenants, the Court of Exchequer's judges were apparently unmoved by the recital of Winchcombe's poverty and were prepared to grant the injunction Sir William sought unless the defendants could show a contrary reason. In the event, this legal action failed to benefit Sir William Whitmore as parliament confiscated his estates in May 1645, in reprisal for supporting the royalist cause during the Civil War; and he died in December 1649.[21]

The breakdown in law and order resulting from the Civil War was probably a significant factor in enabling tobacco cultivation to continue undisturbed during the 1640s. But in April 1652 the long parliament, prompted by those wishing to protect the colonial planters' interests and the Virginia company merchants who imported their crops, enacted legislation to prohibit tobacco-growing in England. In response, a petition was submitted to the Council of State in May 1652 by the 'many landowners and labourers at Cheltenham and Winchcomb in ye County of Gloucester' engaged in cultivating tobacco claiming that:

'your petioners have for many years past grown in ye common fields ye weed called tobacco, and pray that your Highnesse and Parliament will permitt them through your Council to practice the same, as their crops will be perilled and lost and it will be ye ruin of very many labourers: our crops thereof growing and grown also into decay, with many other inconveniences, ... '[22]

This petition and other submissions apparently persuaded the long parliament to permit the tobacco growers 'to enjoy the tobacco by them planted, made or cured for this year only', but an excise duty of 3d. per pound in weight was to be paid by the buyer of any crop.[23]

The growers' reaction to this lenience was to continue tobacco cultivation beyond the permitted additional year. Consequently, in 1655, Oliver Cromwell, as lord protector of the Commonwealth, decided that the 1652 Act should be enforced. But, despite Cromwell's resolve and a specific warning from the Council of State to the justices of the city and county of Gloucester, in March 1655, that tobacco growing would not be tolerated, the crop was still cultivated in the Winchcombe district. The strength of resistance had been shown in June 1654 when Winchcombe growers raised 300 men on horse and foot to protect that year's crop.[24]

When law enforcement by the sheriff and local justices demonstrably failed in the following years, a decision was taken in July 1658 that sufficient force should be used to end the tobacco growers' defiance. But a court newspaper entitled 'Mercurius Politicus' described in its issue for that month what happened when the troop of horse sent to suppress the crop arrived in the tobacco growing district as follows:

'Cornet Wakefield with a party of horse marching out of Gloucester upon the last of July to Winchcombe and Cheltnam to destroy the tobacco plants in these parts, the country did rise against them in a great body, to the number of 5 or 600, giving them very reviling and threatening speeches, even to kill them, horse and man, if that he and his soldiers did come on, insomuch that the tumult being so great he was constrained to draw off, and nothing more done.'[25]

Oliver Cromwell's death in 1658 may partly explain why the use of force against the tobacco growers was not vigorously pursued in the two following years. However, with the monarchy's restoration in 1660, a further Act was passed on 21 December prohibiting tobacco planting; and, when it took effect in February 1661, a proclamation announced that crops would be forfeited and a fine of forty shillings imposed for every rod or pole of land planted with tobacco.[26] To show the government's determination in dealing with the Cheltenham and Winchcombe growers, the sheriff of Gloucestershire, Sir Humphrey Hooke, was ordered to go from London to the county, on 10 May 1662, at the start of the tobacco-planting season, to ensure that the new law was fully enforced. Although the sheriff appears to have had some success in 1662, the area of planting increased in the following year, prompting in return an increased fine of £10 for every rod or pole of land planted, of which one-third went, respectively, to the Exchequer, to the parish poor and to any informer.[27]

In 1666 the sheriff's attempts to destroy the tobacco crop resulted in serious riots and he was reportedly in danger of his life at the hands of the Winchcombe planters. Consequently, in the following year, a government official, Mr. J. Fitzherbert, reported to Mr. Secretary Williamson on 19 August 1667 that '120 Horse of the King's and Duke's Guards are making to Winscombe [sic] in Glos. to cut down the tobacco there in contempt of the law'.[28] By this time, Winchcombe and Cheltenham had gained national notoriety for tobacco growing. In 1675 John Ogilby published his survey entitled 'Britannia, or an Illustration of the Kingdom of England and Dominion of Wales' including the following reference:

'Winchcombe is a large town, containing about 300 houses; a place well known, for at this place and Cheltenham, the people are much given to plant tobacco, though they are supprest by authority.'

The unpopular duty of suppressing tobacco growing perhaps bore most heavily on the local constables who were required to assist the sheriff in carrying out the government's orders. In 1676, when tobacco was still being planted in Winchcombe, one of the constables, Nicholas Robinson, was roughly handled by the townspeople, and he and his family were persecuted and threatened in an effort to drive them out of the town, because he had tried to prevent the growing of that year's crop.[29]

Although tobacco growing continued in the Winchcombe area well into the 1680s it was by then experiencing a decline that neither legislation nor armed force had been able to achieve. Two factors probably contributed most to this decline. First, the increasingly plentiful supply and the fall in price of tobacco imported from the American colonies meant that it was no longer profitable to produce a home-grown crop. Additionally, home-grown tobacco was the variety known as 'nicotiana rustica', a smaller and hardier plant which was suitable for the English climate; whereas the variety known as 'nicotiana tabacum', grown in Virginia, had proved more popular for smoking. Secondly, the intensive cultivation of the comparatively small area of land in the Winchcombe district which was suitable, and could be spared, for tobacco growing eventually resulted in soil exhaustion and reduced production.

Although John Stratford praised his own efforts to relieve poverty in and around Winchcombe by introducing diversified crops, it seems doubtful whether tobacco growing and flax production benefited the town in the longer term. Winchcombe's estimated population increased from 1,530 in 1650 to 2,457 in 1676.[30] Since this increase considerably exceeds any likely increase resulting from an excess of births over deaths, at a time when high rates of infant mortality were normal, it seems probable that a substantial proportion of the additional 900 inhabitants in 1676 were incomers to the town, attracted by the prospect of a tobacco boom. If John Ogilby's statement that the town contained about 300 houses in 1675 is reliable, the overcrowding involved in accommodating some 2,450 people must have been considerable, even by contemporary standards. It is possible that the population was swollen to this number by itinerant agricultural labourers moving into the town during the tobacco growing season, between May and October, and returning to surrounding villages for the winter months: even if that were so, the temporary overcrowding, poor hygiene and additional demands for water from the town's pumps and domestic wells must have resulted in unpleasant living conditions.

It also seems doubtful whether the increased income from tobacco growing and flax production resulted in any increase in real wealth per head of the population. Apart from the entrepreneurs who leased the additional land needed for the new crops, the majority of those involved in cultivation were probably agricultural labourers living on incomes, when spread over the whole year, at little above subsistence level. And those who grew small amounts of tobacco in the common fields, for sale to a middleman, would probably have done so by sacrificing land which would otherwise have been devoted to producing corn or vegetables for their own consumption or for sale at market.

Although these agricultural experiments may have seemed highly commendable to contemporaries and probably produced some increased prosperity in their early years, tobacco growing must have been an increasingly risky enterprise. Apart from the ever-present danger of having the entire crop uprooted or destroyed on government orders, there must have been booms and slumps in some years, caused by crop failures at home or in Virginia; and the gradual soil-exhaustion must have made it obvious that sustained prosperity could not result from exploiting a single crop. Moreover, there is no indication – such as new domestic buildings dating from the second half of the seventeenth century – that any increase in personal incomes was sufficient to enable Winchcombe's inhabitants to achieve improved living conditions. On the available evidence, the verdict must be that these well-intentioned experiments failed to realise the hoped-for results and probably attracted still more poor people to the borough.

1   'Men and Armour for Gloucestershire in 1608', compiled by John Smith, 1902 edition, pages 76-78
2   Landboc, Volume I, page xc
3   Landboc, Volume I, pages xciv-xcv
4   W. St C. Baddeley: 'A Cotteswold Shrine', page 142
5   W. St C. Baddeley, op cit, page 147: quotation from original Gurney manuscript, 1627
6   J. B. Black: 'The Reign of Elizabeth, 1558-1603', The Oxford History of England, 1959, page 274
7   Eleanor Adlard: 'Winchcombe Cavalcade', page 69
8   Joan Thirsk: ' Projects for Gentlemen, Jobs for the Poor, Mutual Aid in the Vale of Tewkesbury, 1600-1630', in 'Essays in Bristol and Gloucestershire History', edited by P. McGrath and J. Cannon, BGAS, 1976, pages 158-159
9   Vincent Keyte – article in Gloucestershire Countryside, June/July 1963, pages 14-15
10   Godfrey Davies: 'The Early Stuarts, 1603-1660', The Oxford History of England, 1959, page 346
11   'Agrarian History of England and Wales', Volume IV, 1500-1640, edited by Joan Thirsk, page 177
12   Joan Thirsk, op cit, page 161
13   C. M. MacInnes: 'The Early English Tobacco Trade', Kegan Paul, 1926, page 84
14   cited in Gwen Hart: 'A History of Cheltenham', page 111
15   Ralph Bigland: 'Historical, Monumental and Genealogical Collections relative to the County of Gloucester', Part 4, edited by Brian Frith, BGAS, 1995, page 1461
16   cited in Gloucestershire Notes & Queries 1884, Volume II, page 217
17   Alicia C. Percival: 'Gloucestershire Grammar Schools from the 16th to the 19th Centuries', Trans BGAS, Volume 89, 1970, page 117
18   GRO, D45 M1
19   Landboc, Volume I, page lxxii
20   Landboc, Volume I, pages lxxii-lxxiii
21   Landboc, Volume I, page lxxiv
22   Norman's History of Cheltenham by John Goding, 1863, page 227

23   C. M. MacInnes, op cit, page 98
24   C. M. MacInnes, op cit, page 99
25   cited in Gloucestershire Notes & Queries, Volume III, 1887, page 511
26   C. M. MacInnes, op cit, page 104
27   C. M. MacInnes, op cit, page 104
28   V. Keyte, op cit, pages 14-15
29   C. M. MacInnes, op cit, page 120
30   Alicia C. Percival, op cit, page 117

CHAPTER 16

CIVIL WARS AND RELIGIOUS DISPUTE

It may seem arbitrary to separate the events of the first (in 1642 to 1646) and the second (in 1648 and 1649) civil wars from Winchcombe's history in the seventeenth century. The justification is that the civil wars' effects on the town were due mainly to the Chandos family's support for the royalist cause, for which Sudeley castle at times provided a stronghold. But the fact that tobacco growing continued in the Winchcombe district throughout this period suggests that serious disruption was intermittent in what was still an isolated borough.

Gloucestershire was inevitably involved in the wars because Charles I's headquarters were at Oxford and he needed to communicate with supporters in south Wales and control the port of Bristol. Like many other large towns, the populations of Bristol and Gloucester supported parliament against the king. Because Charles regarded Gloucester as strategically important for controlling the river Severn, he laid siege to the city from 10 August to 5 September 1643; and his failure to capture it was an important early setback for the royalist cause.[1]

One of the king's disadvantages was his reliance on prominent royalists to raise a regiment of foot soldiers or a troop of horse from their attendants and neighbours to make up his army. In the autumn of 1642 George, sixth Lord Chandos of Sudeley, raised such forces at his own expense and reported with them to the king at Shrewsbury in January 1643.[2] Exactly how and where Chandos recruited this force is unclear. He may have relied mainly on his tenants; and, although there is no documentary evidence to support this suggestion, some volunteers may have been men living in Winchcombe who supported the king's cause or were attracted by the mercenary soldier's life.

In its lord's absence, Sudeley castle was garrisoned by forces commanded by captain Brydges who were almost immediately besieged by a superior force, comprising eighty cavalrymen, 300 infantry and two artillery pieces headed by colonel Edward Massey, commander of the parliamentary garrison in Gloucester.[3] An assault on the castle was prepared under cover of a smoke-screen, made by burning hay and straw in a field near its weakest defences. However, captain Brydges decided that Massey's force was too strong for his garrison of sixty men to resist and surrendered the castle on 29 January 1643. What then happened is described in the following extract from a contemporary broadsheet by 'Mercurius Rusticus':

'… the Castle of Sudeley, upon composition, was delivered up to the rebels; they plunder … not only the Castle, the seat and house of the Lord Chandois, and Winchcombe, a neighbouring village, to the utter undoing the poor inhabitants, but in defence of the Protestant religion, and vindication of the honour of God, they profane His house [Sudeley church].'[4]

The parliamentary forces' occupation of Sudeley castle was short-lived. In February 1643, the royalist forces' most effective commander, the king's nephew prince Rupert, took Cirencester by assault and the parliamentary garrison decided to abandon Sudeley rather than face a likely siege by superior royalist forces under prince Rupert. By April 1643 Chandos had equipped another garrison force at the castle, under Sir William Morton's command.[5]

In July 1643 prince Rupert's forces compelled the city of Bristol to surrender. At this point, as already mentioned, the king decided to secure the whole county by capturing the parliamentary garrison in Gloucester before proceeding towards London. In an effort to delay the king's progress to the capital and strengthen the garrison in Gloucester, the earl of Essex set out from London on 26 August with a parliamentary force of 8,000 men to march to Gloucester, taking a route through the Cotswolds by way of Sudeley hill, Winchcombe and Cleeve hill in the final stages of their approach to the city. These relieving forces, mainly recruited from London's train-bands, a militia, were apparently soaked and exhausted when their commanders sought billets for them in Winchcombe, Prestbury and Cheltenham.[6] The Sudeley garrison is said to have attempted to delay Essex's forces, with the result that hand to hand fighting occurred in Winchcombe where, according to tradition, some royalists were imprisoned overnight in the tower of the parish church before supposedly being shot at dawn.[7]

The approach of the parliamentary forces is said to have been signalled by artillery fired from high on Cleeve hill; and, when the king learned that such overwhelming numbers were near, he decided to abandon the siege of Gloucester. The royalist forces retreated from the city on 6 September 1643; and Charles, accompanied by his sons and those remaining loyal to him, encamped at Sudeley castle while informers kept watch on the movements of Essex's force in the county. While staying at Sudeley, the king issued a proclamation to the people of Cornwall, thanking them for their endeavours on his behalf.[8] The text is preserved on a notice board displayed at the castle. The king did not stay long at Sudeley. On 20 September he engaged with Essex's forces, attempting their return to London, in the first battle of Newbury which ended in the king's withdrawal but no decisive victory for either side. George Chandos fought most bravely in this battle, having three horses killed under him and riding a fourth to lead a decisive charge against the parliamentary mounted soldiers. As his reward, Charles offered to create Chandos earl of Newbury; but this honour was refused 'until it might please God to restore his Majesty to the peaceable enjoyment of his crown'.[9] In reality, George Chandos probably decided that the future course of the war was too uncertain to bind himself so publicly to the king's cause at this stage.

Nevertheless, Chandos was again in action on 21 November 1643 when he led a force of 120 cavalry and 100 infantry in preventing a sortie by a small force from the Gloucester garrison who had been commissioned to collect rents in Cheltenham owing to the lord of the manor and, instead, take the money to colonel Massey.[10] But Chandos was not at Sudeley in June 1644 when combined parliamentary forces, under Sir William Waller and colonel Massey, laid siege to the castle which was still under Sir William Morton's command. Although Morton's garrison was small, it seems to have been a stroke of misfortune which quickly persuaded him to surrender.[11] The attacking force set up their artillery on the slopes of Sudeley hill, to the east of the castle, and began a heavy assault on it. A cannon ball directly hit the officer commanding the garrison's own artillery, decapitating him. This demoralising blow and inadequate provisions to sustain a prolonged siege compelled Morton to submit immediately. The commander himself, nine captains and twenty-two other officers were taken prisoner by the parliamentary forces, who also captured stores of cloth valued at £4,000. Sudeley castle was then garrisoned by a parliamentary force commanded by Massey's brother, captain George Massey.

One other recorded incident involving Winchcombe during the first civil war occurred in February or March 1645, when Chipping Campden was garrisoned by royalist forces commanded by the notorious Sir Henry Bard. An edition of the parliamentary paper entitled 'Perfect Passages' for 5 April 1645 contained the following report:

'I fear the way is something dangerous from Warwick to Gloucester. Some of Cambden's garrison went lately to Winchcomb, where they plundered them so there that the plundered had not a Sunday shift of clothes left them. All the cattle drove away.'[12]

When the final skirmish of the first civil war was fought on 21 March 1646 George Chandos had already given up supporting the royalist cause and was 'compounding' with the parliamentary leaders to retrieve what he could from his Sudeley estate. Chandos had surrendered in person to the earl of Essex on 1 April 1644 and begun negotiations for the terms of an eventual pardon. There was considerable difficulty in valuing the Sudeley estate; but agreement was finally reached in the sum of £1,789 per year. The opponents of parliament who agreed to 'compound' for their estates before the end of October 1644 were fined one-tenth of the estate's value, assessed over a twenty-year period. Chandos's fine was eventually set at £4,976, but a further complication arose from Sudeley castle itself. The parliamentary leaders were determined not to let the castle remain as a potential focus for royalist resistance in the county and, on 3 April 1649, the Council of State ordered the building to be 'slighted', or rendered useless as a military stronghold. On 29 September 1649 the Council acknowledged a report that the required demolition of fortifications had been carried out. Thereafter, much of Sudeley castle remained a desolate ruin for almost two hundred years.

Chandos attempted to gain something from the castle's destruction by petitioning the Council of State to reduce his fine to compensate for the damage: on 30 May 1650, the Council agreed to a provisional reduction of £1,000. The last five years of George

Sudeley Castle, in ruins.

Chandos's life were extremely unhappy. After spending some time abroad he returned to England, where his wife died in April 1651; he was convicted of manslaughter following a successful duel with colonel Henry Compton in May 1652; he re-married Jane, daughter of Earl Rivers, in May 1653; and died of smallpox on 1 February 1655, while living in his London house, near Covent Garden. After her husband's death Jane Chandos married twice more. The result of the second marriage was that the Sudeley estate eventually passed to George Pitt of Stratfield Saye in Hampshire, whose great grandson was created Lord Rivers of Stratfield Saye in 1776 and Lord Rivers of Sudeley Castle in 1802. But the removal of the Chandos family and the subsequent decline of the Sudeley estate had profound consequences for Winchcombe's inhabitants. There was no longer a manorial lord living on the estate, to whom the borough might look as a possible source of investment and employment.

The mid-seventeenth century was also a time of profound religious dispute. Nowhere is this more apparent than in the ranks of Cromwell's 'new model army', where the levellers sought to spread a doctrinaire radicalism amongst all ranks. It may have been about this time that the proverb 'as sure as God's in Gloucestershire' was coined to describe the evangelical fervour of the county's independents, congregationalists, presbyterians and anabaptists who each represented their sect's belief as the only true faith.

In Winchcombe, between 1639 and 1660, the minister was Carnshew Helme, an independent who described himself as 'preacher of the Gospel in this place'.[13] It may have been due to this minister's zealous radicalism that the communion table was positioned at the east end of the parish church's chancel, where it was surrounded by wooden rails on all four sides and seating for communicants against the three walls. This arrangement lasted until the major restoration in 1872.

Carnshew Helme is mainly remembered for a doctrinal dispute held in Winchcombe parish church, on 9 November 1653, with the Reverend Clement Barksdale, who was then minister of the church at Sudeley. Barksdale was the son of John Barksdale and was born in Winchcombe on 23 November 1609. Although his father had contributed substantially to establishing the town's first purpose-built school building in 1618, Clement was sent away to school in Abingdon from where he progressed to Merton College and Gloucester Hall, Oxford. He subsequently became master of the Free School in Hereford and vicar of All Saints church there, until he was rescued from the siege of Hereford and brought to Sudeley.[14]

The subject of the dispute between Helme and Barksdale was a seemingly obscure doctrinal issue, namely 'Whether it be lawful to administer the Holy Sacrament in Congregation called mixed'. Helme's view was that proof of godliness was required before someone could be admitted to partake in the sacrament, whereas Barksdale would admit anyone of whom he knew no harm.[15] Its importance was reflected by the fact that the public debate was attended by one of the justices, colonel Richard Aileworth, who was closely associated with Carnshew Helme, and by the independent ministers of the churches at Oddington (William Tray), Tewkesbury (John Wells) and Naunton. The minister at Toddington, William Towers, attended to support Clement Barksdale.[16] The record of the debate extends to many pages in which Biblical authority is generously cited; but, as so often in such matters, no satisfactory resolution of the disputed issue appears to have been achieved. Carnshew Helme remained in Winchcombe for another seven years but was reportedly ejected from the living in about 1660, following the restoration of the monarchy.[17] Clement Barksdale kept a private school at Hawling during his time as minister in the village, before becoming rector of Naunton in 1660 and remaining there until his death in 1687.

Thomas Markley (or possibly Markby) succeeded Carnshew Helme as minister for eleven years and was followed by Henry Thorne, the longest serving vicar of Winchcombe, from 1671 to 1714. Henry Thorne also held the post of schoolmaster, although whether he taught boys himself or farmed out the teaching duties is unknown.[18] By this time, doctrinal controversy appears to have ceased. Henry Thorne was probably more concerned about the parish church's fabric than about religious dispute. The building was now more than two hundred years old and had perhaps not been maintained as carefully as it would have been had the parishioners been wealthier. In 1690 a collapse of masonry in the chancel's battlements substantially damaged the roof of the chancel and the east end of both aisles. Presumably because full repairs were beyond the parishioners' means, the damage was remedied by substituting a barn-styled and gabled roof over the chancel which remained in place until the major restoration of 1872.[19] At the same time, Henry Thorne had to arrange for essential repairs to the top of the tower and for timber supports to strengthen the roof at the west end of the nave. The appearance of the church resulting from these alterations is shown in Plates 4 to 6.

1   Godfrey Davies: 'The Early Stuarts, 1603-1660', The Oxford History of England, 1959, page 134
2   Emma Dent: 'Annals of Winchcombe and Sudeley', page 257
3   Emma Dent, op cit, page 258
4   cited in 'Gloucestershire Notes and Queries', Volume III, 1887, page 136
5   Emma Dent, op cit, page 261
6   Emma Dent, op cit, page 262
7   Rev. T. E. Meurig-Davies: 'A Handbook to Winchcombe Parish Church', 1939, page 15
8   Emma Dent, op cit, page 263

9   J. Okell: 'A brief historical account of the castle and manor of Sudeley', 1844, page 26

10 J. Goding: 'Norman's History of Cheltenham', 1863, page 219

11 J. Okell, op cit, page 28

12 C. Whitfield: 'A History of Chipping Campden', 1958, page 125

13 T. E. Meurig-Davies, op cit, page 31

14 Landboc, Volume I, page lxxxviii

15 A. R. Warmington: 'Civil War, Interregnum and Restoration in Gloucestershire, 1640 –1672', 1997, The Royal Historical Society, The Boydell Press, page 115

16 GRO, D 2052 (Nonconformist Notes)

17 GRO, D 2052

18 Landboc, Volume I, page cvi

19 Emma Dent, op cit, page 304

CHAPTER 17

CHARITABLE PURPOSES

The years from 1680 to 1720 saw some of Winchcombe's inhabitants benefit from the charitable purposes of private individuals who sought to relieve some of the chronic poverty and lack of educational opportunity in the town. These gifts seem not to have had any concerted purpose, but were all carefully formulated to fulfil the donor's intentions.

George Townsend's charity

The first such charity derived from the will of George Townsend, made on 14 December 1682. Townsend was a barrister of Lincoln's Inn and eldest of the ten sons of Charles Townsend of Ford. There is no evidence of a particularly close association with Winchcombe; and, since the will also provides comparable legacies for similar purposes in Northleach, Chipping Campden, Cheltenham and Guiting Power, it seems that George Townsend intended generally to help these north Cotswold market towns.

The relevant part of the will provides for Winchcombe's poor as follows:

' ... From the manor of Wormington, ... I further will and appoint three shillings weekly to be disposed of in the Church of Winchcomb aforesaid, every Lord's Day, by the minister, bailiffs, churchwardens and overseers of the poor there, to such of the poor there present as shall be usual frequenters of the church, and then present at all, or most part of divine service, and not to any other poor, sick or impotent persons of the same town ...'[1]

As well as educational provision and relief of the poor, Townsend was concerned about improving conditions for pedestrians and horse-riders in Winchcombe. He owned a close (probably a dwelling house and its curtilage) in the town and specified that the rent from it should be used 'for and towards the making and maintaining of causeways for horse and foot, but not for carts and carriages, in the Parish of Winchcomb aforesaid, the parishioners finding stones and other materials for the doing thereof, so that the said rents be only paid to masons and labourers for pitch thereof ...'[2] Thus, while George Townsend was concerned that pedestrians and horse-riders should not have to walk or ride in the deep winter mire which was normal on the roads, he also wished to ensure that this bequest was spent on providing worthwhile work, and income, for stoneworkers and labourers, rather than on buying materials from quarry owners.

Unlike some other charitable bequests, George Townsend's intentions were still being largely fulfilled in 1829 when commissioners investigated the administration of charities in Gloucestershire. They found that the sum of three shillings was still being given to the poor attending divine service weekly at the parish church, according to the directions in the will. The income from the close in Winchcombe was then being paid to the parish surveyor of highways, who applied it to repairing and maintaining the footpaths through and around the town. And the master of Townsend's school in Winchcombe was being paid £20 per year for teaching between twenty and thirty children to read in what the commissioners considered a well conducted school. In one respect the trustees had exceeded George Townsend's purpose. He had provided for £5 to be spent annually on an apprenticeship for a poor boy in each of the five north Cotswold towns, including Winchcombe; but by 1829 the trustees had succeeded in increasing this sum to £15 annually, which enabled better masters and apprenticeships to be provided for the boys.[3]

George Harvey's charity

By his will of 12 February 1685, George Harvey gave two acres of arable land 'lying in Winchcombe Field' to be used by the town's bailiffs and other chief officers to produce an income to 'be disposed of at their discretion amongst the poor of the said town yearly, and every year for ever'.[4] This land, known as Puckpits, was eventually transferred to the town's bailiffs, by virtue of the Greet and Sudeley Tenements Inclosure Award 1815, but was still producing a payment of one shilling each to twenty poor widows in 1890.

Lady Juliana Tracy's charity

Lady Juliana Tracy was the wife of Sir John Tracy of Stanway. When he died in 1677 the couple were childless and she inherited his Stanway estate for life, but seems to have left the village for good on re-marrying and going to live at South Luffenham, Rutland. Nevertheless, she appears not to have severed all ties with Winchcombe because she made a deed of gift, on 17 March 1693, by which sixteen rudges of arable land in various fields in Winchcombe and Greet were to be held in trust to provide an income 'for the use and benefit of the poor of the parish of Winchcombe'. The trustees, who initially included lady Juliana herself and Richard Freeman of Batsford, then decided that the income should be used to buy 'such and so many coats or gowns for such and so many of the poor of the parish of Winchcombe' as the trustees might determine. These coats and gowns were to be handed out, appropriately enough, to the chosen recipients on Christmas Day.[5]

The 1815 Inclosure Award also affected this bequest. Although it too passed into the hands of the town's bailiffs, the commissioners investigating charities in 1829 found that it still produced an income of £20 per year with which the trustees bought coats and gowns for poor men and women of Winchcombe.[6]

Thomas Compere's charity

Thomas Compere is described as citizen and apothecary of London. Although he was a cousin of George Townsend, it is unclear what connection he had with Winchcombe or Stow-on-the-Wold, the two towns he chose to benefit from bequests of £150 for the poor of each parish. In his will of 30 June 1715, Thomas Compere carefully specified that his trustees should obtain the approval of the ministers, church-wardens and overseers of the poor in using the income his bequest was intended to provide as follows:

' ... either in the purchase of lands, or at interest upon securities, and that the rents of the lands so to be purchased, or the interest of the money so to be placed out, be disposed of in placing poor children of the said respective parishes to be Apprentices; or in materials for setting poor people of the said parishes to work; or in Bread to be given ... , upon the Lord's Day to such poor persons of the respective parishes as shall be of the communion of the Church of England, established by law, and constantly attend at Divine Service; ... but in no wise to any purpose that may encourage laziness or idleness.'[7]

The sum of £300 left for the benefit of the poor of both towns was used to buy some eleven acres of land in Winchcombe, known as Poor's Hill. As late as 1890, this land was being let to produce a net income of £10 8s. 9d., half of which was spent on bread distributed by the churchwardens in Winchcombe parish church, every Sunday morning, to poor men and women.

Several other important charities were established in the later eighteenth, and during the nineteenth, century. While they now seem steeped in the concept of the deserving poor, the proceeds were no doubt gratefully received by the intended beneficiaries – even if it meant listening to the unrelenting Sunday morning sermon. And what cannot now be assessed is the benefit, particularly in George Townsend's charity, almost certainly resulting from apprenticeships for young men who would otherwise have endured a working life of intermittent manual labour.

1   GRO, P 368 CH 6/1
2   The Winchcombe and Sudeley Record, Volume 1, No 2, February 1890
3   Further Report of the Commissioners for Inquiring concerning Charities, County of Gloucester, 1829, No. xxi, pages 164-165
4   The Winchcombe and Sudeley Record, Volume 1, No 3, March 1890
5   The Winchcombe and Sudeley Record, Volume 1, No 4, April 1890
6   Commissioners' Further Report, 1829, page 165
7   The Winchcombe and Sudeley Record, Volume 1, No 4, April 1890

CHAPTER 18

THE VESTRY TAKES CHARGE

A true estimate of Winchcombe's population during the eighteenth century is problematic. One estimate is of a decline from 2,715 in 1712 to 1,960 in 1779 and, further, to 1,888 by 1801.[1] However, the Gloucestershire historian Samuel Rudder, writing in 1779, thought that a more accurate figure for 1712 was 1,960. A further complication is that bishop Benson's diocesan survey of 1735 gives the number of Winchcombe's inhabitants as 1,300, although this figure may well relate to the area of the borough without adjacent parishes.[2] Whatever the true figure, there appears little doubt that the population was declining, whereas the populations of Chipping Campden, Cirencester and Northleach remained almost stable. The probable reason for Winchcombe's decline is that large-scale tobacco growing had ceased in the 1690s so that the town's inhabitants had to rely mainly on agricultural work and trade in its markets to survive. As these activities were insufficient to sustain a population of 2,700, and the town's physical isolation remained a serious obstacle to increased trade, those seeking better prospects probably left.

The institutions to which the townspeople might normally have looked for help were also in decline. The manorial lordships of Winchcombe and Sudeley were held by absentees. The manor of Winchcombe had passed from the Whitmore family to William Poulden and then to the Rev. Dr. William Lloyd, rector of the Worcestershire village of Fladbury. After Dr. Lloyd's death his daughters inherited the manor and it was subsequently sold in 1737 to George Pitt of Stratfield Saye in Hampshire. Although (as explained in Chapter 16) the manor and Sudeley estate stayed in this family's hands and George Pitt's great grandson became Lord Rivers in 1776, Sudeley castle remained substantially ruined. The Sudeley estate was occupied by tenant farmers and, towards the end of the eighteenth century, part of the castle's remaining structure was used as a public house, known as the Castle inn. When George III reportedly visited the site, in July or August 1788, he was saved from a serious fall down a dilapidated turret staircase by the presence of mind of Mrs Cox, who lived in part of the building.[3]

Winchcombe corporation

In the manorial lord's effective absence, the town's corporation, headed by the still influential figures of the high bailiff and low bailiff, might have been expected to assume some of his responsibilities. But this did not happen in practice because the corporation's functions were limited to supervision of the grammar school and the charities for which it was a trustee, regulation of the markets and fairs, and management of the town hall and booth hall – both still situated at The Cross, but needing repair. Moreover, because trade in the markets was declining, the corporation's main source of income in tolls from the markets and fairs was depleted, so that even essential expenditure probably had to be deferred.

A typical transaction involving the corporation's property took place on 30 April 1650, when the bailiffs and burgesses leased to Nathaniell Hyett (who was himself a bailiff for eight of the years between 1633 and 1662) 'All that loft or upper room over the Town Hall ... and also all that little room below the said Town Hall lately made in one corner of the Market House, next adjoining unto the shop now in the occupation of Thomas Dobbins, [who was himself a bailiff in 1659] butcher ... ' for ninety-nine years at a yearly rent of one shilling.[4] And, on 18 October 1680, the bailiffs and burgesses leased to Ralph Hulls, described as victualler, 'all that lower room under the Town Hall ... commonly called the Buttery and also the entry adjoining the same room or Buttery' for a term of twenty-one years at twenty-six shillings annually.[5]

The description of these premises suggests that the town hall and market hall comprised one building, in which the town hall was on the first-floor and at least one room suitable for use as a shop existed in the market hall on the ground-floor. Evidently, there was also a loft or attic room above the town hall which Nathaniell Hyett found it worthwhile to rent for some unspecified purpose in 1650. The butcher's shop occupied by Thomas Dobbins at that time presumably faced on to High Street, immediately adjoining the corporation's premises.

Despite the town's declining trade, the corporation sought to maintain its regulatory function. As late as 1765, it was involved in a lawsuit concerning a merchant's failure to pay tax on corn sold in Winchcombe market. This tax was levied at the rate of one pint of wheat or corn for every three bushells sold in the market; and it is clear from the terms of the lawsuit that the corporation retained the proceeds of this sales tax.[6]

The vestry's emergence

As Winchcombe corporation lacked the power and resources to provide effective local government and the manorial lords were generally absentees, the gap was increasingly filled during the eighteenth century by the institution known as the vestry. The vestry's origins in English local government are unclear. The most authoritative explanation is that it developed, from the sixteenth century onwards, particularly during Elizabeth I's poor law reforms, as an alternative to the decaying jurisdiction of the hundred and manorial courts.[7] Its main advantage for local government purposes was the ability to impose a church rate: it was a short step from levying this rate for maintaining the church to levying rates for some other purposes eventually to be fulfilled by local government.

Another advantage was that the vestry gradually gained control over the parish officers through its ability to 'allow', that is to approve, expenditure they incurred. Thus when churchwardens, at first, and then constables, surveyors of highways, overseers of the poor and other parochial officers, submitted their accounts for scrutiny, they enabled the parishioners, as ratepayers, to gain some control over the expenditure on local services they were obliged to fund. How the vestry's responsibilities developed in practice depended very much on local circumstances, although its officers were always subordinate to the justices, meeting in quarter sessions or petty sessions, who were given jurisdiction to deal with rating appeals in 1743.

In Winchcombe, records of vestry meetings date from at least 1602; and it is quite possible that the vestry as an institution was even older. In 1605, four churchwardens were elected for Winchcombe and there were four 'supervisors for the highways'. In a town of Winchcombe's size, overlapping membership between the corporation and the vestry was inevitable. For example, in 1605, one of the churchwardens was William Cowell (described as Gentleman) who had been a bailiff in 1588 and 1598; and one of the highways supervisors was Richard Harvey, who was to become a bailiff in 1618 and 1621. In 1629, the two churchwardens were Arthur Bleeke (or Blake) and Nathaniell Hyett: the former appeared in Chapter 13 as one of the corporation's witnesses in establishing the building for the King's school and was a bailiff in 1622, 1623 and 1630, as was the latter (mentioned earlier in this chapter) on eight occasions.

How the vestry functioned

The vestry was a corporate body. Its chairman was always the minister of the parish: in his absence from a meeting, a chairman was elected for that occasion on a majority of those present. The substitute chairman would be a senior figure in the town, perhaps one of the bailiffs. The Winchcombe vestry was an open vestry, which meant that all the parishioners who were ratepayers (thus excluding the poorest inhabitants) could participate in its proceedings. Vestry meetings usually took place in the parish church, although occasionally they were held in the town hall, and were well attended – especially when there was important business to discuss. In practice, they were public meetings for the ratepayers.

With the vicar as chairman, the other parish officers attending vestry meetings were usually the churchwardens (elected annually by the parishioners), the surveyors of highways and the overseers of the poor. As these officers were all men of standing in the town, they naturally served without payment, knowing that their fellow citizens relied on them for good government, provided as economically as practicable. The fact that the rates burden fell most heavily on the most prosperous parishioners, with no subsidy available from the national exchequer, provided an in-built mechanism to discourage financial extravagance.

The vestry's proceedings were recorded by the parish clerk. Until quite recently, these records were maintained in the enormous parish chest, still kept in the south aisle of the parish church. They are now deposited in the Gloucestershire County Record Office. The parish clerk was careful to record exactly what had been decided and to emphasise the collective nature of the decision. For example, at a meeting on 8 January 1764, the vestry considered whether to provide an additional pew in the parish church to accommodate excise officers then living in the town. The decision is recorded as follows:

'It is ordered by this Vestry ... that a proper and commodious pew be erected by the Churchwardens for the use of the Excise Officers now resident in the Borough, and their successors, behind the Great Door in Winchcombe Church, at the expense of the inhabitants of the said Borough only, and that a rate shall be made on the said inhabitants in proportion to the poor's Rate of the said Borough to re-imburse the Churchwardens all such moneys which they shall lay out by means of erecting such pew.'

The numerous witnesses to this decision were headed by the Reverend John Taylor, then vicar of Winchcombe.

Overseers of the poor

A principal concern of Winchcombe's vestry was how to provide for the borough's poor. Chapter 17 explained how a small number of charities had been established in the late-seventeenth century as a substitute for the former abbey's almsgiving. The overseers of the poor were originally responsible for collection of alms within the parish, but they gradually took charge of all the vestry's efforts to provide for poor people. Apart from administering cash payments for poor relief, the overseers' most exacting task was supervising the workhouse.

In March 1745 Winchcombe's vestry decided to set up a workhouse in the town, where the poorest inhabitants could be accommodated and given some employment to defray the cost of public provision. On 19 April 1746 an agreement was reached with William Smart of Winchcombe to lease Abbey House, off Cowl Lane (the former manor house occupied by successive abbots of Winchcombe until the disso-lution in 1539), for use as the workhouse, although that purpose is not specified in the lease.[8] The first named master of the workhouse was William Pearson whom the vestry elected to this post on 7 August 1764 at an annual salary of £10. Between April 1774 and April 1778 William Thomson, described as a yarnmaker of Fairford, was contracted to 'farm' the workhouse at the cost of £500 per year. But, by 1782, the Vestry resumed full control and seemingly felt sufficiently confident of their ability to manage the workhouse to make an agreement, the following year, with the parishes of Bishop's Cleeve and Woodmancote to accommodate their poor in the Winchcombe workhouse on a fee-paying basis, at the rate of £30 per year for each parish and 3s. per week for each person accommodated. This arrangement was short-lived: in about 1801 the two other parishes decided to provide their own workhouse building, on a site in Bishop's Cleeve.

By 1787 the vestry decided that responsibility for housing and maintaining the poor who could not remain in their own homes should be given to a full-time, salaried indi-vidual. Accordingly, on Saturday, 30 June of that year, the vestry resolved as follows:

' ... we do hereby impower the present Churchwardens and overseers of the poor of the said parish to contract with Richard White, of the parish of Winchcombe afore-said, for training the poor thereof at the sum of Four hundred and eighty pounds a year ... ' [9]

Richard White was expected to 'dwell and lodge regularly' in the workhouse. It is unclear whether he was master of the workhouse in the sense of the institution to which poor people were to be referred as the only available form of relief. However, the reference in his contract to 'training the poor thereof' suggests that his main task was to provide schemes of work for the inmates which would reduce the parishioners' financial burden in maintaining them. This appears to be confirmed by an entry in the vestry records for 1836, ordering that 'the pin-knobbing machinery lent to this Parish some years since for employing the Poor in the Workhouse be returned to the owner ... there being no further use of it'.

Maintaining law and order

The parish constable was an ancient office, to which appointments were made by the justices; but the vestry could decide how many constables there should be and how much to pay them. In the entire Winchcombe parish there were normally nine consta-bles in the early nineteenth century, of whom two were appointed for the borough. Their total annual cost in 1807 and 1808 was £21.[10]

The Winchcombe vestry seems to have been responsible for the town's bridewell, or local gaol, which was situated in the greatly dilapidated town hall in the 1770s. When John Howard, prison reformer, visited Gloucestershire in 1776 he found that prisoners in Winchcombe had previously been detained in a cellar of the bridewell, but were then accommodated in two garrets, one for men and the other for women, measuring fourteen feet square and having sloping roofs so that they were no more than eight feet high at the highest point.[11] This may have been the same accommo-dation in a loft or upper room of the town hall which Nathaniell Hyett had leased in 1650, as mentioned earlier in this chapter. Howard found that the prisoners had no straw for bedding and their food allowance was 3d. worth of bread per day. The bridewell's keeper was over eighty years old and received an annual salary of £12 and fees of 13s. 4d., together with a licence to sell beer to the prisoners. Because the town hall's courtyard was insecure, the keeper could not let prisoners out for exercise.

John Howard's recommended prison reforms resulted in Winchcombe bridewell's closure on 17 October 1791 and sentenced prisoners were subsequently detained in the newly built 'house of correction' in Northleach, where forty prisoners could be accommodated. (In 1981 the former house of correction took on a new lease of life when it reopened as a museum housing the Cotswold Countryside Collection, now renamed the Cotswold Heritage Museum.)

Public health

As there was no eighteenth century public health authority, the vestry became involved in reporting the course of epidemics and with such preventive medicine as was available. For much of the century, smallpox was a regular scourge. After one outbreak, the vestry's officers submitted the following report on 26 September 1758:

'We, whose names are hereunto subscribed, do certify that the smallpox, which lately raged amongst the inhabitants of the borough of Winchcomb aforesaid, is now entirely ceased; and that not one person has had the said distemper within the said borough, for the space of two months last past'.[12]

The report's signatories were the vicar, two churchwardens and two overseers of the poor.

Although Lady Mary Wortley Montagu had been persuaded, during a visit to Constantinople in 1718, of the efficacy of smallpox inoculation and had arranged for her own children to be inoculated, her persuasive efforts to spread the practice seem not to have resulted in widespread adoption.[13] However, at a meeting on 25 March 1770, the Winchcombe vestry authorised the overseers of the poor to employ Dr. William Reynolds –

'to inoculate [presumably against smallpox] at five shillings per head all such poor families being of the said parish, to begin from the day of the date hereof, and so to continue for the space of one month that are not immediately or now in the parish books which the overseers of the poor of the said parish shall think fit to be inoculated.'

Pressed into his majesty's service

The parish constables took the lead in maintaining law and order and kept the town's armour. They were also responsible for ensuring that men chosen by lot to serve in the militia reported at the muster. But, from 1757, the vestry became liable for administering the system of choice by lot. A fundamental flaw in this system was that paid substitution for militia service was permitted, so that some citizens who could afford it substituted for themselves an able-bodied man who might otherwise have served in the regular troops overseas. Winchcombe's vestry records provide examples of these problems.

On 28 April 1807, the vestry ordered payment of two shillings and sixpence to each person in the parish who had been chosen by lot to serve in the militia for the expense of journeying to Stow-on-the-Wold to attend the muster and be enrolled. The substitution arrangements were more troublesome. In the following year the vestry authorised the payment of ten guineas to their clerk, John Chadborn, 'for the trouble he lately had in providing substitutes to serve in the Militia of this County ... ' Nevertheless, substitution continued to be allowed, perhaps because the vestry found it profitable. On 5 May 1811 the vestry authorised the overseers of the poor to receive from John Roberts, who had been chosen by lot for militia service, the sum of £25, in return for which the vestry undertook to provide a substitute.

By an Act of 1795 the vestry became responsible for providing recruits for the royal navy when required. On 7 April in that year the vestry met in the parish church to consider 'the most effectual means of raising two men to serve in His Majesty's Navy'. The outcome was that 'William Cox of Sudeley Lodge hath agreed to procure the said two men who shall be approved and enrolled on or before the 17th day of April ... '

The vestry minutes do not record how William Cox would procure two, probably very reluctant, sailors to serve in the navy during the Napoleonic Wars where pay was at the rate of half-a-crown weekly and discipline normally enforced by lashings.

Fire fighting

Although there is no record of serious damage by fire to property in Winchcombe during the eighteenth century, the risk of domestic fires spreading quickly in the many timber-framed houses, particularly those with thatched roofs, was considerable. A Phillips fire engine was therefore bought by voluntary subscription, in 1789, for use only in the town. As the subscribers had made no arrangement for its upkeep, a meeting of the vestry on 9 February 1790 decided that the churchwardens should be responsible for its maintenance and the expense should be borne by the rate-paying parishioners. Since there was apparently no more suitable place in the borough, the churchwardens kept the fire engine in the parish church until alternative arrangements were made in 1846.[14]

Pest control

Legislation providing for the control of predatory birds, such as rooks, crows and choughs, had been enacted as early as 1532 and was subsequently extended to provide a bounty payable by the churchwardens, out of a tithe-based fund, for the heads of such birds and of animals regarded as pests.[15] Situated in a mainly agricultural area, Winchcombe's vestry took pest control seriously. Between 1757 and 1770 a bounty of one shilling was paid for every fox's head brought to the churchwardens 'to be cut in sunder or otherwise destroyed', with the result that fourteen shillings had to be paid in 1764 and twenty-one shillings in 1770. Payments were made regularly between 1798 and 1854 for sparrows' heads at a farthing per head. 1801 was a bumper year for sparrow netting: the churchwardens paid 16s. 1¾d. for 775 sparrows' heads brought to them.

A vestry dispute

In 1770 a serious dispute occurred between the then vicar and the vestry members. For many years the normal fee for each burial in the parish churchyard had been six shillings and eight pence. These sums were used by the churchwardens for essential repairs to the church's fabric. When the Rev. John Taylor tried to appropriate the burial fee for himself the vestry decided to summon a meeting on 17 April 1770 to discuss the matter. However, the vicar attempted to frustrate the discussion by preventing the parish clerk, John Lacey, from reading out the advance notice of the meeting and by deleting the name of one of the churchwardens, John Merryman, from the notice. Not to be outflanked by the vicar, the vestry responded by electing Samuel Smith as churchwarden for the ensuing year and authorising him 'to call the vicar to account, either at law or in equity, for fraudulently taking and imposing on the paymasters' [that is, the churchwardens'] property'. How this dispute was resolved is not recorded in subsequent vestry minutes. Perhaps the vicar decided that his claim was not legally strong enough to withstand the immemorial custom to which the churchwardens would be able to appeal if litigation ensued. In any event, although the Rev. John Taylor continued as vestry chairman in 1772, he ceased to hold the post of vicar at his death on 11 May 1774.

In Winchcombe, as in many other English towns, local government evolved during the eighteenth century to suit local circumstances. Elections to the various parish officers' posts seem to have been mainly uncontested. Decision-making was kept firmly in the hands of the most influential townspeople and landowners from the constituent hamlets of Coates, Sudeley, Greet, Gretton and Naunton, whose principal concern was to minimise their rates burden. Nevertheless, this form of local government could claim that it was economically administered and provided decision-making by the people most familiar with local circumstances. In a borough with a declining population and no prospect of rapid growth or industrialisation, this parish pump administration probably suited the parishioners' needs better than a more bureaucratic system.

1   Alicia C. Percival: 'Gloucestershire Grammar Schools from the 16th to the 19th Centuries', Trans BGAS, 1970, Volume 89, page 117

2   Anthea E. Jones: 'Protestant Dissent in Gloucestershire: A Comparison between 1676 and 1735', Trans BGAS, 1983, Volume CI, page 142

3   Emma Dent: 'Annals of Winchcombe and Sudeley', page 317

4   GRO, P368 MI 1/4, Doc. No. 29

5   GRO, P368 MI 1/4, Doc. No. 35

6   GRO, P368 MI 1/6

7   W. E. Tate: 'The Parish Chest', Cambridge, 1951, page 14

8   GRO, P368 OV 7/2

9   GRO, P368 VE 2/3

10   GRO, P368/1 VE 2/4

11   J. R. S. Whiting: 'Prison Reform in Gloucestershire, 1776-1820', Phillimore, 1975, page 101

12   Gloucestershire Notes and Queries, Volume II, page 474

13   Basil Williams: 'The Whig Supremacy, 1714-1760', The Oxford History of England, 1962, page 392

14   The Winchcombe and Sudeley Record, Volume 4, No 37, January 1893

15   W. E. Tate, op cit, pages 105-106

CHAPTER 19

THE GROWTH OF NONCONFORMIST RELIGIOUS BELIEF

During the latter part of the eighteenth century the practice of nonconformist belief began to develop vigorously in the Winchcombe district. One of the earliest extant dissenting certificates (in which a nonconformist religious group could register their existence with the bishop of the diocese) dates from 1764. It refers to a room in Benjamin Wood's possession, situated near the George inn, suggesting that the premises were in High Street. It was probably used by a small group of independents, including James Dobbins, William Durdfield, William Becket and William Tovey.

Although the earliest surviving dissenting certificate relating to premises used by Methodists in Winchcombe dates from 1786, followers of John Wesley had been active in the district well before then. Wesley was an inveterate traveller on evangelising journeys throughout England. He visited the north Cotswolds several times between 1739 and 1779 and was friendly with the Parker family, at Stanley Pontlarge, whose farm house he even referred to in his journal as home.[1] On Tuesday, 16 March 1779, Wesley preached at Gloucester in the morning and intended to preach in the open air at Stanley, in the afternoon, before going on to Tewkesbury that evening. But the vicar of Winchcombe, who was the Rev. Richard Roberts from 1778 to 1793, sent word that Wesley could preach in the Anglican church at Gretton; and the afternoon service was therefore rescheduled for six o'clock in the evening. When Wesley arrived in Gretton he was informed that the vicar had changed his mind; and he therefore held the service in an orchard situated close to the fountain in the village.[2] Perhaps the vicar's second thoughts about allowing Wesley to preach in the church had suggested he might incur a reprimand from the bishop of Gloucester.

One of the leading Methodists in Winchcombe at that time was John Staite, who is described in the muster roll of May 1798 for the Winchcombe and Sudeley Volunteers as a staymaker.[3] Wesley probably stayed overnight on 16 March 1779 at John Staite's house in Winchcombe. This visit was later commemorated by a plaque displayed on the wall, on Mrs. Emma Dent's initiative, inside what is now Wesley House in High Street. The plaque recorded that 'In one of his Evangelistic Journeys

the Rev. John Wesley, A. M. lodged here'; but it was removed at a change of ownership in the late 1980s. There is also a tradition that Wesley preached in the area
outside Great House, at the foot of what is now Castle Street, early in the morning
on 17 March 1779, before leaving for Tewkesbury.[4] (There is no doubt that Great
House existed in 1779: it probably dates from the first decade of the eighteenth century
and may have been built by Thomas Williams, a mason who was possibly also
responsible for building Wadfield House on the Sudeley estate.[5]) At that time, Great
House was inhabited by Joseph Smith, a maltster, and may have been used for private
Methodist worship. The previously mentioned dissenting certificate of 1786 is dated
3 January. It relates to a group of Methodists comprising John Staite, Samuel
Chadborn (a tailor) and William Burrows (a woolcomber), meeting in the dwelling
house formerly owned by John Heavens (one of Winchcombe's bakers), then in John
Staite's possession, which was to be used for public worship. The whereabouts of this
house is uncertain.

A major step forward was taken in November 1794 when John Staite concluded
an agreement with Thomas White, a Winchcombe soap-boiler, to pay £60 and the
legal costs, by 5 April 1795, for a property in Cowl Lane, comprising two houses, a
malting, a barn and a stable with a yard or garden. On 30 April 1795 this property was
conveyed to John Staite and other members of Winchcombe's Methodist group, who
were constituted as a trust on 30 November.[6] The dissenting certificate for this property is dated 29 October 1795 and is in the names of William Fisher (grocer), John
Fisher (mercer), John Staite and Thomas Slatter (shopkeeper). The date shows that
John Staite and his fellow Methodists had taken only six months to adapt the property for use as a meeting house accommodating about a hundred worshippers.

Only fifteen years later, Winchcombe's Methodists were ready to provide themselves with a purpose-built chapel. They had decided to build it on the same site in
Cowl Lane as the existing meeting house. When completed in 1810, the new chapel
was about 40 feet in depth from the carriageway and some 27 feet wide, with a singers'
gallery and space for an orchestra. It was capable of seating more than two hundred
worshippers, probably on benches at first but in pews in 1829.[7] This building
remains on the same site, on the eastern side of Cowl Lane, having been subsequently
extended and adapted to provide, among other uses, an infants' school, a Women's
Institute hall and, most recently, Winchcombe parish hall.

Winchcombe Methodist circuit was founded in 1812. It included Gretton, Stanley
Pontlarge, Gotherington and, initially, Cheltenham.[8] However, following the building
of the fine Ebenezer chapel in King Street, Cheltenham in 1812, Methodists in
Winchcombe began to yield precedence to Cheltenham and had probably done so
completely by 1816.

Some of Winchcombe's early Methodists were remarkably long lived. John Staite
had attained the age of eighty-four at his death on 26 February 1838. Towards the end
of his life, he continued to serve as a class-leader; and, when bedridden, the members
of his class would gather round his bedside.[9] Joseph Smith died in 1836, aged eighty.
William Tovey, who became master of Townsend's school (as mentioned in Chapter

25), died on 17 April 1855, aged ninety-five. And Thomas Howman, who was at various times a fellmonger and a parchment maker, was ninety when he died on 16 June 1860.

Baptists were also active in the Winchcombe district in the early-nineteenth century. Winchcombe's Baptist chapel was built in 1810 and opened on 1 January 1811. It could accommodate some 120 worshippers, suggesting a considerable membership at that time. The chapel survives as a building, off High Street on the north-western side, behind current building society premises, and is now used as the Winchcombe Guide hall. The most celebrated figure among early Baptists was the Rev. John Foster, who fulfilled the role of evangelising preacher and published a number of religious essays. He was apparently not impressed by Winchcombe's religious condition in the early-nineteenth century.[11]

There were probably other dissenting groups or individuals whose existence cannot now be reliably established. For example, bishop Benson's diocesan survey of 1735 records that there were then four Quakers living in the town, of whom one was a woman teaching in an unnamed school (probably a dame's school kept in a private house). But the pupils in this school were reported to be 'all of the church', presumably meaning that they were Anglicans.[12]

As members of the nation's established church, Anglican worshippers inevitably maintained a dominant position in Winchcombe during the early-nineteenth century. In addition to their natural inclination to worship in the parish church, some of these parishioners were probably encouraged by the prospect of receiving an occasional gift from one of the local charities administered by the vicar and churchwardens. But, alongside the established church, the members of the Methodist and Baptist chapels showed their spiritual independence in words of praise and provision of new buildings.

1   G. H. Bancroft Judge: 'John Wesley's Visits to Stanley and Winchcombe', Proceedings of Wesley Historical Society, Volume XIII, 1922, pages 63-68

2   G. H. B. Judge, op cit, page 65

3   The Winchcombe and Sudeley Record, Volume 5, No 50, February 1894, page 226

4   G. H. B. Judge, op cit, page 66

5   Arthur Oswald: 'The Wadfield, Sudeley, Gloucestershire', article in Country Life, Volume XCIX, No. 2565, 15 March 1946, pages 486-489

6   Frank C. Adey: 'A Cotswold Methodist Heritage', Winchcombe Methodist Church, 1979, page 13

7   F. C. Adey, op cit, page 19

8   G. H. B. Judge, op cit, page 67

9   F. C. Adey, op cit, page 28

10   F. C. Adey, op cit, page 31

11   Ralph Bigland: 'Historical, Monumental and Genealogical Collections relative to the County of Gloucester', Part 4, edited by Brian Frith, BGAS, 1995, page 1478.

12   Anthea E. Jones: 'Protestant Dissent in Gloucestershire: A Comparison between 1676 and 1735', Trans BGAS, Volume CI, 1983, page 142

CHAPTER 20

EARLY NINETEENTH-CENTURY SELF-HELP

Towards the close of the eighteenth century Winchcombe appeared to visitors a dismal town. In 1781 the Hon. John Byng visited the Sudeley estate from Cheltenham, where he was staying in the early days as a spa resort. In the Torrington diaries he described Winchcombe as 'a mean dirty Market Town'.[1] Some fifteen years later an American papermaker was touring Britain, to acquire knowledge of paper-making processes, and stayed briefly in Cheltenham, recording his impressions in a series of notebooks. On 28 July 1796 he joined a party of visitors wishing to see Winchcombe and Sudeley castle. The impression Winchcombe made on him is recorded as follows:

'Descended the hill and came to the valley where Winchcombe lies. Several paper mills here, but did not appear of much importance. Entered Winchcombe; mean little village formerly of great note having been a county of itself. After the introduction of Tobacco it raised a great deal and grew opulent [with it]. This being prohibited it became noticeably decayed. There being no good house in the village, the church, however, is large and has been a neat structure; formerly there was an abbey here.'[2]

No doubt these very critical views of the town's condition at that time were influenced by comparisons with Cheltenham's rapid growth and fine domestic buildings.

The population at the turn of the eighteenth century

In 1801 Winchcombe's estimated population was 1,888, having fallen from an estimated 1,960 in 1779. Some indication of how the male population earned a living can be obtained from the occupations of the force known as the Winchcombe and Sudeley Volunteers who were formed in May 1798. Although these volunteers were only a proportion of the Winchcombe area's male population, they probably represent most of the occupations and trades then being followed. Of the 115 listed volunteers (two names appear twice), only one man had no recorded occupation. As would be expected, the largest occupational group were 36 farmers, some of whom would have employed farm labourers who do not appear among the volunteers. The second largest group consisted of seven butchers. In the wool and cloth trades, there were two mercers, two woolcombers, two tailors, three breechesmakers and one weaver. At a time when most people still had to walk everywhere, the five cordwainers (shoe-makers) presumably met the local demand for stoutly made footwear. A surgeon (or doctor) and an apothecary provided health care. Perhaps the most unusual occupation was the one peruke (or wig) maker. Surprisingly, the building trades comprise only two masons, one slatter, one glazier, one plumber and two carpenters.[3]

The impact of the Napoleonic Wars

The Winchcombe and Sudeley Volunteers were formed because the entire country lived under threat of invasion by Napoleon's armies. In April 1798 the government authorised the raising of a volunteer corps in all the maritime counties, including Gloucestershire which was regarded as at risk of attack through the Severn estuary. Volunteers, consisting of 'known respectable householders' were to be recruited, drilled and armed immediately. In Winchcombe a meeting was held in the town hall, on Saturday 5 May 1798, under the chairmanship of Thomas Ashmore, a tanner, at which the town's leading inhabitants adopted the following resolutions:

'That an Association should be formed to consist of inhabitants of Winchcombe and Sudeley and the vicinity, and styled the Winchcombe and Sudeley Loyal Volunteer Infantry, and should be composed of respectable householders and such other inhabitants of the said parishes as might be recommended by two householders.

That an uniform, to be approved by a committee, be provided by each member at his own expense or otherwise.

That an application be made to Government for arms.

That the members will be ready to serve on any occasion which the necessities of the country may require, within seven miles of the Borough. And, finally, to provide for the necessary expenses, subscriptions were invited.'[4]

A committee was appointed to implement these resolutions. At a meeting on 8 May the committee decided to extend membership of the Association to inhabitants of any parish within three miles of Winchcombe; and, when the government had accepted their services, to provide a uniform. As originally envisaged, the design of the uniform was to be as follows:

' ... a dark blue jacket, with red facings, cuff, and collar, with a plain round yellow button; a plain white waistcoat of kerseymere or cloth, or leather with white metal buttons; black gaiters to reach to the calf of the leg, and white stockings; a small black cap with a red feather therein, and a black neckerchief.'

Although it is not known whether any infantryman was actually equipped in this uniform, the committee appointed officers and NCOs on 13 May and, on 5 June, appears to have held a muster parade on land belonging to Thomas Ashmore, near the turnpike gate at the northern end of North Street. Subsequently, the force's members were to attend the drill ground every Sunday and proceed to divine service in the parish church where their chaplain, the Rev. John Lates, was also the vicar. Infantry training was to be given on the drill ground at five o'clock on Sunday afternoons.

How active this volunteer force was is not recorded, although there is evidence of a muster of 51 members on 5 September 1803. Perhaps to the volunteers' relief, Nelson's brilliant naval victory at Trafalgar and Wellington's successful Peninsular campaign sufficiently reduced the threat of invasion to enable the government to disband these emergency forces.

The Napoleonic Wars caused severe hardship throughout the country. The threat of French invasion resulted in a financial crisis in February 1797, when the Bank of England was compelled to suspend cash payments, and in 1790 the outdated land tax was replaced by income tax in order to help pay for the war. The harvest in 1799 was very poor and scarce bread was also dear.[5] Further bad harvests between 1809 and 1811 brought some parts of the country close to famine and Napoleon's effective naval blockade produced a trade crisis in 1811.[6]

The proposed Winchcombe canal

Although there appears to be no evidence of severe hardship in Winchcombe during the wars, the town's isolation on the edge of the Cotswold escarpment was an obstacle to trade and the introduction of new industries. Travel to Cheltenham had been improved in 1792 when what was little better than a trackway over Cleeve Hill was replaced by the present line of the road, some 300 feet lower down. But the town's commercial leaders believed that improved transport would provide the key to increased prosperity. In about 1800 a group of businessmen, probably including William Durham, the owner of the paper mills at Postlip, and Thomas Fisher, a prominent Methodist and mercer, commissioned a feasibility study for the construction of a new canal to link Winchcombe with Tewkesbury. The study was carried out by James Barnes who produced a detailed prospectus explaining the advantages of cutting a canal just over eleven miles long, at an estimated cost of £21,665 2s. 2½d.[7]

James Barnes estimated that the annual weight of coal, salt and grocery goods transported to Winchcombe from Tewkesbury, Evesham and Gloucester, together with corn exported from the Winchcombe district to Tewkesbury, was 6,729 tons. He priced the transport cost at four shillings per ton, thus producing an annual income of £1,345 which would enable a sum of £26,916 to be borrowed at five per cent interest. On this calculation, the proposed canal must have seemed financially feasible.

The prospectus contains considerable detail about the likely advantages to Winchcombe and presents a clear picture of its topographical and commercial situation at the start of the nineteenth century. The following extracts are particularly informative:

' ... The Situation of Winchcomb is allowed by most People, who have a knowledge of it, to be a desirable one for Trade, if the completion of a Canal should take place; the Country round it, for many miles, shewing a Verdure of most excellent Land, producing great abundance of every necessary of Life.

By means of the Canal, the reduction in the Price of Carriage will be considerable; besides the great convenience that will accrue by a Water-Conveyance to the different Markets of Glocester, Bristol, Worcester, Birmingham, & c. in short, every Place where the Severn toucheth.-The Supply, from this Part of the Country, of Corn, Meal, and all sorts of Grain, will be immensely great.-There are several Stacks of Mills in and near this place, which are regularly supply'd with Water, and are deprived of making the best advantage of them, on account of the great inconveniency and expence of carriage to the Severn at Tewkesbury.

The Proprietors and Occupiers of Estates, upon and near the line of the Canal, will participate very largely in the Benefits resulting from it, as it will give the advantage of Water-carriage to a large tract of very productive Inland country, and some of the Land thro' which the Canal will immediately pass, being marshy, such land will be drained by it.

A saving of 50 per cent. will be obtained upon the Carriage of Corn and other commodities, which lie upon the borders of the Canal, and upon the carriage of such as lie at a greater distance, a greater saving in proportion. Land-carriage being lessened, the Farmers will have little occasion for Horses, and may substitute Oxen in their places.

The Canal will likewise operate greatly to the improvement of the Roads in its Vicinity, by taking off the heavy carriage during great part of the Winter, which is the Season for the Farmers to convey their Corn and other Product of their Lands to Market : the Bye-Roads being then impassable, and the Turnpike-Roads little better.'

Two commodities particularly interested James Barnes, namely imported coal and exported building stone. His assessment of the advantages of transporting coal by the canal is as follows:

' ... At present the Inhabitants of Winchcomb and its Environs, experience very great Inconveniences from the want of a regular and cheap supply of Coals : This Article, of which 1000 Tons a Year are consumed at Winchcomb, is at no time to be procured there, but by a very uncertain Land-carriage, at less Price than 23s per Ton, the Price is often 27s and 30s per Ton ; Prices which operate nearly to the exclusion of the Use of this most necessary Article amongst the Poor, and causeth them to commit Depredations upon the Fences of different Inclosures, in a manner nearly laid waste.

Upon a just and impartial calculation, Coals, by the Canal, will be delivered at Winchcomb, more than one-third cheaper than the present Prices, besides the conveniency of having Coals at any time when wanting ; consequently a considerable quantity more will be consumed when they are to be had with conveniency, and at such reduced Prices.'

As the destruction of hedges and fences for fuel was particularly troublesome to farmers and landowners in the Winchcombe area, cheaper coal was emphasised as bringing them indirect, as well as direct, benefits.

On building materials, the canal was expected to produce the following advantages:
' ... There is an excellent Free-stone Quarry at Postlip-Hill, about two miles from Winchcomb, supposed to be equal in size and quality to any in the Kingdom. Also, a remarkable good Slate Quarry at Harts-all, which is about four miles from Winchcomb : These Slate are exceeding light and durable. It is apprehended, that if a Canal be made from Winchcomb to Tewkesbury, there will be a great demand for those Articles, which of course must very considerably augment the Tonnage ... '

Despite James Barnes's thorough assessment of the costs and benefits of cutting the canal and his persuasive advocacy of the additional advantages accruing from it, the Winchcombe canal was not built. It is unclear why the decision not to proceed was taken: most probably, the uncertainty and financial strain resulting from the Napoleonic Wars forced the project's backers to conclude that it was too risky.

Establishment of a bank in Winchcombe

If a decision had been taken to proceed with the proposed canal, the financial arrangements would probably have been made through a recently established bank in the town. The two most prominent figures in this enterprise were Thomas Fisher and Thomas Ashmore, the tanner who took the initiative in setting up the Winchcombe and Sudeley Volunteer Corps. The bank's premises were in Thomas Fisher's mercer's shop in Hailes Street. The house at 11 Hailes Street, in which Thomas Fisher lived, is still known as Bank House. Other partners were William Durham and, probably, another Methodist, Joseph Smith of Great House.[8]

Fisher and Ashmore's bank was known as the Winchcombe Bank and there are surviving examples of banknotes signed by Thomas Fisher in 1816. Although the bank operated in conjunction with a bank in Cheltenham, the Winchcombe branch failed in 1819. Subsequently, the Cheltenham and Winchcombe Bank continued trading until the national banking crisis of November 1825 when over sixty country banks and six London houses failed.

Industrial enterprise

Winchcombe's comparative remoteness explains why there was little manufacturing industry in the district during the early nineteenth century. The main enterprise was paper-manufacturing at Postlip mills, where John Durham had been engaged as early as 1725 in water-marking and finishing paper manufactured in Holland.[9] By 1734 John Durham was paying rates on Upper Mill and Lower Mill; and, in 1745, on Middle Mill also. Durham must have prospered in this paper manufacture because, at his death in 1759, he left his substantial dwelling house at the corner of Gloucester Street and Malthouse Lane (which is now the Corner Cupboard inn) to his daughter Mary, who married Winchcombe's apothecary, William Reynolds.[10] This house was probably built in about 1550, using some stone from the former abbey

buildings, and would have provided the Durham family with a suitable residence for successful businessmen.

John Durham's son, William, took over the business and ran it until his death in February 1803.[11] Well before then, paper-manufacturing started at the three mills: writing paper at Upper Mill, brown or packing paper at Middle Mill, and blue or sugar paper at Lower Mill. Paper-making was then a laborious process, largely carried out by hand. Linen or cotton rags were the main source of raw materials which had to be sorted, cut into small pieces, and converted into pulp. The pulp was produced by beating the rags on an iron platen with an iron-shod wooden mallet – a process which might take all day. Before steam-powered machinery was introduced in 1854 work at Postlip mills consisted of unrelenting physical toil.

After William Durham's death the mills were leased by a partnership of the brothers Nathaniel, Edward and Thomas Lloyd who ran the business until 1824, when the owner, Lord Coventry, sold the mills to William Searle Evans, who had been a surgeon in Tewkesbury for many years. Nathaniel Lloyd was a commanding figure in Winchcombe, where he served as high bailiff and believed that part of his role was to clean up the town by preventing the inhabitants from tipping rubbish and filth in the gutter outside the houses.[12] The Lloyd brothers appear to have run the business in a spirit of stern but patriarchal benevolence which some of their employees may not have appreciated. The issue of *The Gloucester Journal* for 17 February 1812 reported what seems to have been an attempt at industrial sabotage, as follows:

'On the night of Tuesday last a most villainous attempt was made to destroy by fire the paper manufactory of Messrs. Lloyd at Postlip in this County. A piece of timber close to the Mills was set on fire but fortunately was discovered in time to prevent its communication with the buildings. A reward of fifty pounds has been offered for the conviction of the offenders, but they have as yet eluded detection.'[13]

Although the paper-manufacturing at Postlip mills provided vital employment for some of Winchcombe's inhabitants, its sometimes harmful effects on the river Isbourne, down stream of the town, were noticed. Charles Hanbury Tracy, later Lord Sudeley, had a fine new mansion built for himself at Toddington in the mid-1830s. Ralph Bigland, the Gloucestershire antiquarian, gives the following description of its situation:

'The new House is situate on the opposite Bank of the Isbourn Brook a tributary to the Warwickshire Avon. A branch of this Brook comes from Postlip, on the other side of Winchcomb, and the Water is much affected by the operations at the Postlip Paper Mills, from the effect of which it has not recovered at Todington.'[14]

Nathaniel Lloyd also operated the smaller Sudeley paper mill, at the southern end of Castle Street, which used water from the Beesmoor Brook. This establishment produced a fine quality, hand-made writing paper; but it does not seem to have survived as a producer of paper after Nathaniel Lloyd's death in 1845.[15] The mill buildings remain in their re-adapted use as the Sudeley castle holiday cottages and courtyard, situated on the eastern side of Castle Street.

Rather more employment, although mainly for women and young girls, was provided by the newly established silk mill (from which Silk Mill Lane is now named). In the mid-1820s Edward Banbury, coincidentally a native of Banbury, converted a three-storey building on the north bank of the river Isbourne from a corn mill to a silk mill. The 1834 register of electors shows the mill situated then in Bleby's Lane. By 1850 this enterprise employed more than one hundred women and children in the process of silk throwing, in which the hanks of white silk were first washed and then wound on small engines while children stood ready to take the bobbins off.[16] This was a potentially dangerous operation. *The Gloucester Journal* of 29 May 1858 reported an accident at the mill in which a little girl was badly bruised when her clothes caught in one of the wheels and she was taken round several times before it could be stopped. The mill was closed for a time in 1855 and subsequently reopened, before closing down completely in about 1872. Although work at the silk mill provided a means for women and young girls to augment a family's income, it failed to provide the jobs for men which were most needed. Eleanor Adlard's opinion of its unhappy legacy is as follows:

' ... the malodorous name of Silk Mill Lane, a country slum, and an unhappy memory of tired little girls woken up to go to work at 6 o'clock in the morning ... ' [17]

Tanneries provided a long-established source of work in Winchcombe, relying on plentiful local supplies of sheepskins and tree bark. The Sexty family maintained a flourishing tannery at the foot of Castle Street (sometimes known in the past as Tanyard bank or Tanyard pitch) on the northern side of the river Isbourne, in a former corn mill. There was also a tanyard at the foot of what is now Vineyard Street, maintained by Thomas Hunt, although the period during which this tannery operated is uncertain.[18]

Agricultural change

Agricultural enclosure was a comparatively late development in the Winchcombe district. The first General Enclosure Act of 1801 simplified the procedure, which had previously relied on private agreement or privately promoted Acts; and this may have prompted the enclosure award which was recorded in the Greet and Sudeley Tenements Map of 1815.[19] Among the largest landholdings were those of Thomas Ashmore, John Heavens and Susannah Wood. But there were also numerous smaller holdings, suggesting that yeomen farmers were still trying to gain a living from small-scale cultivation. The overall effect of formalising what may well have been previously informal arrangements was probably to make it more difficult for the cottager to eke out an existence on a reduced area of common fields. Some cottagers probably became merely agricultural labourers.

Livestock farming was still an important activity and the vestry was called upon to deal with the problem of straying animals. On 19 October 1813 a vestry meeting ordered that 'a parish pound be forthwith erected … at the back of the new Turnpike house at the end of the North Street in Winchcombe.' Samuel Roberts was given the contract for building the pound, which remained on the same site until its removal in 1891.

Early nineteenth-century social conditions

The limited available evidence makes a balanced view of social conditions in Winchcombe in the early nineteenth century hard to obtain. Some features can help to convey an impression.

The vestry records indicate that the leading townspeople were concerned to maintain law and order more effectively. Notice was given on 7 October 1810 that a Vestry meeting would be held for the following purpose:

' … to consult and advise as to the several depredations nightly committed by ill-disposed persons in and near this Town and particularly the mischief done in the night of Friday last to the new gates in the churchyard and other places, and also to conclude whether any, and what, steps shall be taken for the punishment of the offenders.'

When this notified meeting was held on 9 October 1810 it emerged that three main culprits had been identified, namely, Edmund Harker, Thomas Yardington and Thomas Moyall. This information had been given to the parish officers by Anthony Gilder. The vestry therefore authorised the churchwardens and overseers of the poor to apprehend and punish the suspected offenders and any accomplices, and to support and protect the informant 'against any injury he may sustain by reason of giving such information aforesaid'. The eventual outcome of this pursuit is not entirely clear. However, on 14 January 1811, the vestry resolved not to prosecute Thomas Yardington at quarter sessions, provided he paid two guineas in compensation for damaging the churchyard gates, publicly confessed his offence in *The Gloucester Herald*, and promised not to re-offend.

Whether this incident was merely random vandalism, possibly prompted by over-indulgence in one of the town's alehouses, or part of a consistent pattern of generalised criminal activity, is hard to assess. However, the vestry's reference to 'the several depredations nightly committed by ill-disposed persons' suggests a good deal of minor crime was then commonplace.

This impression is strongly confirmed by the formation of the 'Winchcomb Society for the Protection of Persons and Property and Punishing Felony'. It is uncertain when this society was founded and by whom. However, it is evident from a handbill notifying its annual meeting, on 14 August 1813, that it had already appointed Samuel Sadler as its solicitor and Thomas Fisher, the leading Methodist and banker, as its treasurer. The society's main purpose was to pay a reward to anyone providing infor-mation leading to the arrest and conviction of offenders who were guilty of any one of nine separate classes of offence. The specified offences were carefully defined and the promised rewards were graduated in descending order of the offence's seriousness. Thus, for example, information resulting in a conviction for murder attracted the maximum reward of £20, whereas burglary and highway or footpad robbery were rated at £10. The interests of farmers are clearly represented in the reward of two guineas for information relating to 'robbing any orchard or garden, barking or cutting trees, breaking or stealing any gates, stiles, or hedges, or posts, pales, or rails, or any ironwork belonging thereto'. The society's sixth article was clearly intended to convey an uncompromising message to any local person contemplating an offence, as follows:

'That these Orders be printed, and that each Subscriber shall be furnished with at least three copies thereof, that the same may be made public, in order to convince those who may be daring enough to violate the Laws of their Country, that no Compromise will be made with any Offender, but that all and every person who shall be guilty as aforesaid, will be prosecuted to the utmost Rigour of the Law.'

The society's membership was to be limited to forty; and it appears to have included such leading townsmen as John Heavens, William Staite, John Staite and Charles Poyner.[20] There is apparently no surviving record of how long it lasted or how many rewards it gave to informants.

Another example of self-help is the formation of the Winchcombe Amicable Society, originally set up in 1790, but re-founded in 1810 when some of its previous rules had proved defective. This organisation was a form of friendly society whose main purpose was to provide members with payments during sickness, a funeral benefit of forty shillings and a widow's lump-sum of £5. Membership of the Society was restricted to men aged between eighteen and thirty-five. On joining, members were required to pay a sum of 5s. 6d. and a monthly subscription afterwards. Full membership of the Society was only achieved after three years, when the benefits stated in one of the Articles of Agreement became available as follows:

' ... if any Member ... at the end of 3 years after his admission to the Society, shall by sickness, lameness or any other affliction (except such affliction shall be occasioned by drunkenness, fighting, cudgel-playing or from the venereal disease) be incapable of working for his livelihood … the Stewards shall pay him, during his inability to work, 8s. 6d. a week, until the fund of the said Society shall amount to £1,000; and when the fund shall amount to £1,000, then such Member shall receive 9s. a week until he hath received one year's pay at that rate … And after that 5s. a week until the fund is £1,000 and 5s. 6d. a week when it exceeds £1,000, though the same [sickness] should continue until his death.'[21]

The Society was to meet at four-weekly intervals 'at some reputable inn or public house in Winchcombe on a Tuesday night'; and every member was required to attend an annual divine service in Whitsun week, before proceeding to a dinner at his own expense. To safeguard the Society against paying benefit for what would probably have been a frequent cause of sickness, the rules provided that no member should be elected 'who hath not had the small-pox or cow-pox'. At one stage the Society is said to have had 336 members, of whom 152 were labourers.

Problems with Winchcombe's workhouse

How to provide for Winchcombe's poorest inhabitants was one of the vestry's continuing preoccupations during the nineteenth century's first two decades. Administration of poor relief cost the ratepayers £1,792 in 1815-1816 and £2,506 in 1818-1819.[22] These were substantial sums for a community of Winchcombe's size at that time. The financial burden was almost certainly increased by successive crises in the management of the town's workhouse, for which the former abbot's house was still used until 1815.

In 1814 Abbey House was jointly owned by Thomas Williams (described in the muster list of the Winchcombe and Sudeley Volunteers as an attorney), Charles Poyner (a mercer) and Richard James. In November of that year these owners decided to serve an eviction order, for the removal of the workhouse inhabitants, on the ground that Abbey House was dilapidated beyond repair and must be demolished. Thomas Williams and Charles Poyner, between them, owned the various parcels of land on the western side of Cowl Lane comprising the abbey's former curtilage: the claim of excessive dilapidation may therefore have been a useful pretext for getting rid of a building and its occupants which they saw as undesirable. The vestry was initially undecided how to respond to this threat. However, despite the undoubted historical value of the building, the owners went ahead with its demolition in 1815; and it was once again left to the antiquary Edmund Thomas Browne (then aged 36) to record the external appearance of the building in his two sketches of it.[23]

The vestry belatedly initiated legal proceedings against Williams and Poyner, but the litigation appears to have been unsuccessful and was only settled, at considerable cost to the ratepayers, two years later. In 1817 the vestry ordered payments of £210 to the former workhouse owners in settlement of all outstanding disputes and claims; £90 10s. 10d. to their clerk, John Chadborn, for his expenses in conducting the parish's case; and £114 to James Ross to settle his outstanding account for the cost of 'farming the poor'. As a final gesture of presumed defiance, Thomas Williams appropriated the borough's ceremonial maces as a lien on a debt allegedly owed to him by the town corporation; and they were only returned at his death.[24]

Meanwhile, the vestry was compelled to re-establish the workhouse in a former malthouse at the foot of what is now Bicks Lane, near the junction with Silk Mill Lane. The workhouse remained in these premises until 1836 when responsibility for poor relief was transferred, by the Poor Law Amendment Act of 1834, from the vestry to the newly established Board of Guardians for the Winchcombe Poor Law Union.

Dealing with illegitimacy

The birth of an illegitimate child inevitably concerned the parish officers, not primarily on grounds of moral disapproval, but because, without a legally recognised place of settlement, the unfortunate child would usually become a charge on the parish. One way of dealing with this problem was to obtain a justices' order compelling the father to pay a regular sum for the child's upkeep. The Winchcombe vestry's records include twenty 'orders of filiation in bastardy' made between April 1813 and February 1822. All the orders are for payment of a weekly allowance, ranging in amount from 1s. 6d. to 3s., presumably depending on an assessment of the reputed father's ability to pay. None of the fathers appears more than once in this record, but two mothers' names appear twice. Obtaining a filiation order was not the only means of dealing with this problem. Some overseers of the poor brought pressure to bear on the father to marry the mother before the child's birth. The comparatively low number of filiation orders made during this nine-year period may suggest that Winchcombe's parish officers were adept at applying such pressure.

The borough's situation in 1820

No surviving account describes Winchcombe's condition between 1800 and 1820. The overall impression is of an isolated market town where little new building had recently taken place, either in public buildings or for private housing. Despite the presence of a bank and some employment in the paper mills and silk mill, agriculture remained the dominant source of work. With the Sudeley estate still in an absentee owner's hands, there was no wealthy patron to take a lead in initiating physical improvements, such as modernised cottages or additional almshouses. The borough's corporation had insufficient income from market tolls to improve the town's fabric; and the vestry was concerned to minimise rate demands, particularly for maintaining the poor. In the aftermath of the Napoleonic Wars the primary concern among the leading townspeople was probably to ensure their own survival; but self-help was wearing thin.

1   Gwen Hart: 'A History of Cheltenham', Alan Sutton, second edition, 1981, page 126
2   A. P. Woolrich: 'An American in Gloucestershire and Bristol – diary of Joshua Gilpin, 1796-7', Trans BGAS, Volume XCII, 1973, page 176
3   The Winchcombe and Sudeley Record, Nos 50 to 52, February to April 1894, pages 221-227
4   The Winchcombe and Sudeley Record, loc cit, page 222

5   J. Steven Watson: 'The Reign of George III, 1760-1815', The Oxford History of England, 1960, pages 372-376 and 407

6   J. Steven Watson, op cit, page 470

7   'Reasons in favour of the intended Winchcomb Canal', GRO, P 368 MI 3/12

8   F. C. Adey: 'A Cotswold Methodist Heritage', 1979, page 30

9   F. J. T. Harris and J. L. Angel: 'History of Papermaking in and near Winchcombe', GSIA Journal, 1975, page 11

10   Philip Styles Collection: GRO, D 3530/5

11   Harris and Angel, op cit, page 13

12   Eleanor Adlard: 'A Short History of the Postlip Mill, Winchcombe', Frederick Muller Ltd, 1949, page 9

13   E. Adlard, op cit, page 10

14   Ralph Bigland: ' Historical, Monumental and Genealogical Collections relative to the County of Gloucester', Part 3, edited by Brian Frith, BGAS 1992, CCLXIX, page 1334

15   E. Adlard, op cit, page 19

16   Eleanor Adlard: 'Winchcombe Cavalcade', page 75

17   E. Adlard, op cit, page 75

18   J. A. Oakey: 'Reminiscences of Winchcombe, 1936', page 8

19   GRO, Q/RI 159 (copy also held in Winchcombe Museum)

20   Notice concerning 'Winchcomb Society for the Protection of Persons and Property, and Punishing Felony', copy held in Winchcombe Museum

21   'Articles of Agreement of an Amicable Society', instituted and held in the Borough of Winchcombe (1810), copy held in Winchcombe Museum

22   D. H. Aldred: 'Poor relief in Winchcombe, 1800-1851', University of Leicester MA dissertation, 1972; GRO, D 2947

23   Emma Dent: 'Annals of Winchcombe and Sudeley', page 149

24   Landboc, Volume I, page lxxxv, footnote 8

CHAPTER 21

AT THE START OF THE VICTORIAN AGE

Four years after Victoria became queen the 1841 census recorded the population of the parish of Winchcombe (including the various outlying hamlets of Greet, Gretton and Sudeley Tenements) as 2,613. This was an increase of 725 over the parish's population of 1,888 in 1801. Although families comprising five to eight children were then quite numerous, some of this increase was probably due to inward migration, putting considerable pressure on the existing housing stock. The census records for 1841 show frequent instances of shared accommodation, although some of those sharing were male or female servants.

The town's fabric

The town's central core had remained largely unchanged during the previous century. At The Cross, the booth hall and town hall needed major repairs which the corporation could not afford. The borough's whipping post, which had stood outside the town hall as late as 1800, had probably been removed, or at least ceased to be used for public floggings; but the stocks remained and were used until 1860, when a man was put in them to punish drunkenness.[1]

John Oakey's invaluable booklet, 'Reminiscences' of Winchcombe, gives an excellent account of numerous features which were lost in the twenty years or so after his birth in 1847.[2] Water was still obtained from the town's two water pumps and the numerous wells in yards and houses, which the occupiers shared. One of the town pumps was situated almost in the middle of North Street, approximately opposite the building now accommodating the post office. In the 1840s, there were three old cottages on the western side of North Street, set back behind the building line of the adjacent properties (one of which was John Oakey's father's house), so that the road was considerably wider than at present at that point, and the pump stood in an area lined with cobbles. The town's other pump was situated at the north-eastern corner of Jacobean House in Queen Square.[3]

Although some stone-built houses had been constructed in the late-eighteenth and early-nineteenth centuries, many dwellings dated from much earlier and were probably beyond their owners' means to refurbish and face in stone. A typical example was the house in North Street, belonging to John Oakey's father, which is shown in the photograph at Plate 4: this dwelling remained in residential use by the Oakey family until its demolition in 1857.[4]

Improving the roads

After the Winchcombe canal project had been abandoned, effort turned to improved roads. The Rev. F.E.Witts recorded the following observation in his diary for 23 December 1823:

'The road to Winchcombe [from Stanway] is better than it used to be, and a great alteration has been made between Winchcombe and Southam by which the road is carried round the tremendous hill, which it formerly ascended only to sink again into the vale by a precipitous descent. By thus skirting Cleeve Cloud there is no very heavy draught.'[5]

On 29 March 1833 an Act was passed for improvement of a number of roads in north-west Gloucestershire, including provision ' ... for the making, maintaining, and repairing the new branch of road from or near the end of Duck Street [now Vineyard Street], in the Town of Winchcomb aforesaid, to the turnpike road leading from Cheltenham to London at or near to a place called Andoversford ... '[6]

The most noticeable highway improvement was in the centre of the town where the length of road between the eastern end of Gloucester Street and the western end of High Street, then apparently known as Birporte Street, still had a carriageway width of only 10 feet 3 inches in places, with a sharp double-bend at the junction with Cowl Lane. On 9 February 1835 Dennis Trenfield, then owner of the property known as the Abbey Grounds, agreed with Nathaniel Lloyd and John Mann, on behalf of the Winchcombe Road Trustees and Surveyors of the Highways, 'for sale and purchase of part of the Abbey Ground for widening the Public Road'. The basis of the agreement was as follows:

'Mr. Trenfield sells and the Trustees buy so much of the Abbey Ground as this day stated and lying between the Road leading to the Church and the present Road running through the Town of Winchcomb, ... which is intended for a Turnpike Road in lieu of the present Road. The price of such land to be 200 guineas. Mr. Trenfield to take down and remove the Building called Small-bread Hall, to be entitled to the materials thereof and of the turretted Hall adjoining thereto ... '[7]

The surveyor's plan mentioned in this agreement is reproduced at Plan 6.

Although the highway surveyors seemingly required Dennis Trenfield to demolish two comparatively small former abbey buildings, they probably regarded this arrangement as an inevitable part of the price for creating the spacious expanse of Abbey Terrace and the visually important high stone wall, running westwards from Cowl

Plate 4

Lane to the south-east corner of the churchyard, which successive generations of townspeople continue to enjoy. The parties appointed the ubiquitous Edmund Thomas Browne as arbitrator, but he appears not to have recorded the two lost abbey buildings in one of his celebrated sketches.

The postal service

Local businessmen also sought a better postal service. On 5 March 1824 an anonymous Winchcombe resident wrote to the Post Office's London headquarters pointing out that the town had a postal service only on three days per week and suggesting some improvements. The following extract from the letter explains how the post was brought to Winchcombe in the 1820s:

' ... This post is conveyed by a man on horseback from Moreton-in-the-Marsh, distant about thirteen miles, and across a country somewhat barren and thinly inhabited; and I believe that, with the exception of Mr. Talbot's at Temple Guiting, and the few houses in that small village, the postman passes scarcely a single house between Bourton-on-the-Hill (one mile from Moreton) and Winchcomb; and in the winter season it is not an unfrequent circumstance that, by reason of snow, he cannot pass this road at all ... upon the whole I think it cannot be doubted, that a daily post from Broadway to Cheltenham through Winchcomb would prove no less profitable to the government than beneficial and accommodating to the people interested in it ... '[8]

In the 1820s Winchcombe's post office was kept in the back kitchen of the house in the south-western corner of Queen Square, now known as The Hermitage, where Mr. Wynn was the postmaster. In 1829 William Simmons took over as postmaster; and, by 1841 when he died and his wife Rebecca became postmistress, the Simmons family had moved to a house on the western side of North Street, where Mrs. Simmons also had a grocer's shop.[9] The letter pleading for improvements seemingly achieved a better service. As a first step, Winchcombe became a sub-post office of Cheltenham, with mail brought by a walking messenger who arrived at 11am and departed for Cheltenham at 4pm. When this arrangement proved inadequate a mail cart was introduced, arriving in Winchcombe at 4am and going on to Evesham, with the return journey calling at Winchcombe at 8pm and reaching Cheltenham at 9pm. But it was not until the 1850s that Anthony Trollope, better known as a novelist, was given the task of substantially improving rural postal services.

Relief of the poor

Major changes in the system for relieving Winchcombe's poorest inhabitants were made by the Poor Law Amendment Act of 1834. In place of the previous system of parish relief, which had caused the vestry so much concern at its rising cost, the 1834 Act enabled three nationally appointed commissioners to group parishes together in unions administered by an elected local board of guardians. The Poor Law commissioners appointed a high-powered bureaucrat, Edwin Chadwick, as their secretary. He set about the task of local reorganisation so zealously that the commissioners soon earned the title 'the three bashaws [that is, tyrants] of Somerset House'.[10]

In Winchcombe the Board of Guardians for the Winchcombe Poor Law Union was established on 18 January 1836. By 28 September of that year, the Guardians had completed their first task, namely the construction of a new, purpose-built workhouse for the town and surrounding parishes. This building was set back from Gloucester Street, to the west of Malthouse Lane, where it stood in extensive grounds facing on to Gloucester Street. Like so many of the commissioners' newly-provided work-houses, soon known to inmates as 'Bastilles', the Winchcombe workhouse remained until after World War II when it was still in use as a youth centre. The former site is now occupied partly by the Winchcombe day centre; but the Winchcombe Poor Law Union is recalled by the name of the dwelling on the western side of Malthouse Lane at the junction with Langley Road, Union Cottage.

The workhouse regime was intentionally harsh; but local conditions probably depended partly on how an individual master and matron managed the institution. In Winchcombe, William Fluck and his wife Sarah were appointed in 1836 as the first master and matron. William Fluck was then aged about forty: one of four brothers born in Hawling, he was a convert to Methodism and subsequently a prominent Methodist in Winchcombe until his death in October 1873. How he managed the workhouse is recorded in his obituary notice in the local Methodist journal as follows:

' ... For some years Mr. Fluck was governor of the union workhouse, a position in which, whilst he was exact and faithful in his duties, his kindly nature found ample exercise. Supplementary aid from his own not abundant means was often afforded in addition to the relief it was his duty to administer: and better still, along with these kindnesses were given such words of friendly, good advice about the best things, as made deep and lasting impressions on many hearts ... He was buried in the cemetery, Winchcombe, amid the almost universal testimony that the "best man in the town was gone".'[11]

Of 51 men, women and children accommodated in the workhouse in 1841, 39 were categorised as labourers, including two five-year-old girls and a six-year-old boy. Twenty-one of the residents were aged sixty or over, comprising twelve men and nine women. Although they are not classified in the 1841 census, some of the residents would have been accommodated during a spell of sickness and some of the younger women would have been 'lying in'.

In addition to accommodation in the workhouse, the Guardians also provided cash relief to poor people in their homes. The relieving officer in 1841 was John Mason.

Dealing with lawlessness

Throughout the 1830s the vestry was preoccupied with maintaining law and order in the town. The main concerns were drunkenness, vandalism, endemic poaching (to provide the meat which poor families could not afford to buy) and minor criminal acts. In October 1834 the vicar, the Rev. John Harvey, and sixty-one ratepayers petitioned the churchwardens and overseers to convene a vestry meeting for the following purpose:

'...to take into consideration the present state of the Police of the Parish, and to make such an Order or Orders respecting the same as may be deemed necessary for the due observance of the Sabbath, as well as to the prevention of Disorder, Drunkenness, and other Irregularity.'

The petitioners naturally comprised many of the foremost citizens, including the high bailiff Nathaniel Lloyd; Charles Lapworth, stern master of Chandos grammar school; the solicitor, Dennis Trenfield; the attorney, Giles Carter, then living in Queen Square; John Heavens, the baker who owned the fine early eighteenth-century house at the western corner of High Street and Castle Street; Caleb Grizzell, the draper living in the house now known as St Kenelm's; and, unsurprisingly, Edmund Thomas Browne.

The vestry's meeting was duly held on 31 October 1834, in the parish church, with the vicar in the chair. The following seven resolutions were approved, giving a clear picture of the town's experience of disorderly behaviour and how it should be remedied:

'1st.   That it is notorious that the Sabbath day Morning has been recently ushered in with scenes of regular pitched battles when nearly one hundred persons have assembled together.

2nd.   The beer houses have been opened and noise and disorder therein during divine service.

3rd.   That groups of persons meet in various parts of the town, obstruct the footpaths, make use of disgusting language which, to persons attending their usual places of worship, as well as to others, is a very great grievance.

4th.   That drunkenness has prevailed to an extent which is horrible to contemplate, common decency frequently outraged, and riot, disorder, and crime have often been the consequence.

5th.   That it is far from our wish to interfere with the liberty of the subject, but that it behoves us as heads of Families having Wives and Daughters to protect, to take care that common decency is not outraged by any Class of Society, and that we are determined, as far as in our power lies, both individually and collectively to use every means in our power to put down those scenes of disgrace which of late have been of common occurrence in this parish.

6th.   That for this most desirable purpose we call in aid the constabulary force of the parish to take their rounds frequently on the Sabbath day as likewise every other day in the week for the winter months, that is from the 1st November to the 1st of March, or such time and times as may be deemed necessary, and that they be paid the sum of 10s. per week for their services.

7th.   That a Committee be now appointed to carry into effect the aforegoing Resolutions.'

Although the approved weekly payment of ten shillings to the constables was probably an increase, only two of the ten constables then serving in the parish were allocated to the town. It therefore seems unlikely that they would have been able, without reinforcements, to ensure the reduction in lawlessness the leading citizens desired.

In any event, matters seem to have worsened during the following two years. At a meeting in the town hall on 22 October 1836 the vestry members deplored recent outrages at two of the turnpike gates in the parish, which led them to pass the following resolution:

'That these with the very recent occurrence of Highway Robbery committed in the Vicinity of the Town, and the apparently systematic plan of sheep stealing almost nightly committed on the farms in the neighbourhood render it highly expedient that prompt and vigorous measures be taken to check this system of midnight plunder, and if possible detect the offenders.'

Despite the harsh punishment then usual on conviction of what now seem comparatively minor offences, the probability of being arrested and brought before the justices must have appeared sufficiently remote to encourage the town's poorest people in criminal acts.

The Sudeley estate

Successive owners of the Sudeley estate had not made their presence felt in Winchcombe for nearly two hundred years. In the early-nineteenth century the habitable portion of some of the buildings was occupied by a tenant farmer and another portion was used as a public house, known as the Castle inn. The unexpected revival of the estate was due entirely to the Dent family, whose influence moulded Winchcombe's development throughout the Victorian age. The brothers John and William Dent had made their substantial fortune in the glove-making industry in Worcester and were looking for an estate where they could settle as landowning gentlemen. They accomplished the first part of the estate's purchase from Lord Rivers in 1830; and the remaining land and the castle itself were bought from the Duke of Buckingham in 1837. The Dent brothers' significance for Winchcombe is that they had the energy and financial resources to undertake the huge task of having the castle rebuilt, regenerating the run-down estate, and contributing, directly and indirectly, to improvements in the town.

1   Emma Dent: 'Annals of Winchcombe and Sudeley', page 147
2   J. A. Oakey: 'Reminiscences', privately printed, 1936
3   J. A. Oakey, op cit, pages 5 and 8
4   J. A. Oakey, op cit, page 3
5   F. E. Witts: 'The Diary of a Cotswold Parson', edited by David Verey, Alan Sutton, 1978, page 35
6   GRO, D2079/1/82
7   GRO, D2218/3/40 and Q/SRh 1835 B/3
8   GRO, P368 MI 3/12
9   The Winchcombe and Sudeley Record, No 10, October 1890
10   E. L. Woodward: 'The Age of Reform, 1815-1870', The Oxford History of England, 1954, pages 433-435
11   obituary notice supplied by Frank C. Adey, former Methodist circuit archivist, Cheltenham circuit

CHAPTER 22

THE HIGH BAILIFF'S ACHIEVEMENT

By 1850 Edmund Thomas Browne had been the town's high bailiff for about five years. As the corporation's leader, and probably the borough's most knowledgeable citizen, he was asked to reply to a series of queries intended to elicit information on the topography and social condition of Winchcombe at about that time. His answers provide a valuable record and personal assessment of the town he loved and in which he probably spent most of his life.[1]

Two answers describe the town's main buildings (but omitting any reference to the town hall and booth hall, for reasons which will appear later) as follows:

'There are many respectable houses; but being an Anglo-Saxon town others are old and irregular. The material generally used is stone, as extensive quarries abound in the surrounding hills.' [reply to Q3]

' … an interesting old house of Elizabethan character near the church [this is clearly Jacobean House], belonging to the bailiffs and burgesses, now used for attorney's offices, savings bank, Sunday school & etc, and a newly erected senior poor-house.' [reply to Q6]

Dealing with a question about the town's industries, the following answer appears:

' … a silk throwing factory employed about 32 adults and 100 children; 60 at Postlip Mills; a tannery on a moderate scale.' [reply to Q10]

The reply to a question about the existence of churches and chapels is very brief:

'One very fine old parish church dedicated to St Peter, erected about middle fifteenth century; and two chapels for Wesleyan Methodists and Baptists.' [reply to Q5]

With his customary discretion, the high bailiff omitted to mention that the parish church then needed major repair and the interior was extremely uncomfortable.

A potentially interesting question asked how the townspeople were chiefly employed and what was their social condition, to which the following succinct and somewhat ambivalent answer is given:

'The adult part of the poorer inhabitants of both sexes are chiefly employed in agricultural operations on the [blank space] acres of land which form the area of the parish. Their social condition may perhaps be deemed quite equal to that of most similar districts and superior to many.' [reply to Q12]

In his concluding general remarks Edmund Thomas Browne provided this additional information:

'It is a borough by prescription, with two bailiffs and ten burgesses ... The market is on Saturday and there are five fairs: the last Saturday in March, May 6, July 28 and two at Michaelmas [these two were the mop fairs or hiring fairs]. The March and July fairs are celebrated for the sale of horses, and are much frequented by many from distant parts of the kingdom. There is a mineral spring in the town, said to resemble the Harrowgate [sic] water.'

No further detail is given about the 'mineral spring in the town'. It is possibly a reference to St Kenelm's well on the Sudeley estate.

Improving the town's facilities

Despite his generally optimistic assessment of the town's condition at the time of this survey, Edmund Thomas Browne would have known that many improvements were urgently required. His public office enabled him to take the initiative.

In March 1846 he called a meeting to consider whether the town's fire engine should be kept in the booth hall (next to the town hall at The Cross), rather than remain in its traditional parking place in the parish church. The meeting held on 14 March agreed to prepare part of the booth hall for keeping the fire engine and for its removal from the parish church as soon as the alternative accommodation was available.[2] How effective the fire engine was in fighting fires, when no piped water supply existed in the town, is not mentioned.

In Winchcombe, as in many other towns throughout the country, the absence of a piped water supply and a sewage disposal system undoubtedly contributed to the spread of disease. During the national outbreak of cholera in 1849 Gloucester was afflicted, but Cheltenham – and perhaps Winchcombe also – seem to have escaped. Nevertheless, a public notice now in Winchcombe Museum's archive states that a 'day of fast and humiliation' would be observed on 25 September 1849 to help purge the country of cholera.

An obvious consequence of an increasing population living in unsatisfactory sanitary conditions was the need to provide more space for burials. The parish church itself was insanitary. In July 1846 the sexton showed the church's interior to a visitor, who included in his record of the visit the following observation: ' ... The ground beneath the pavement of the church is said to be full of dead bodies, and the effluvia is [sic] occasionally most offensive ...'[3] The matter was brought to a head in 1855 when a Privy Council order forbade burial in parish churches and, from 1 January 1856, in parish churchyards.

In response to this order, a vestry meeting chaired by Edmund Thomas Browne (not the vicar on this occasion), on 16 June 1855, resolved that the two churchwardens and seven of the town's foremost citizens be constituted a Burial Board which, in the first instance, should 'view the present state of the parochial churchyard ... and report ... what room for interments yet remain [sic] and as to the necessity of immediate steps being taken to carry out the directions of the Privy Council in providing a new burial ground for this parish'. The Burial Board set about their task purposefully: as well as Edmund Thomas Browne, the members included William Smith of The Farm and the solicitor Dennis Trenfield. Their initial report of 23 June 1855 indicated that sufficient space remained in the parish churchyard for burials to take place for one more year; and, thereafter, another site would be needed. On 19 June 1856 the vestry considered the Burial Board's recommendation that a new burial site, immediately adjoining the churchyard and within the Abbey grounds, should be bought for use as a burial ground. Additionally, Edmund Thomas Browne himself proposed that a quarter of an acre of land forming part of Spittle Leys Orchard alongside Greet Road should be acquired 'for the purpose of a parochial burial ground for nonconformists'. Both these proposals were unanimously approved; but the financial strain they were expected to impose on the ratepayers was probably reflected in the concluding words of the resolution that 'the repayment of the sum borrowed be made by yearly instalments extending over the longest period allowed by law.' The burials crisis was averted for the time being and the vestry's decision in 1856 resulted in establishing the Greet Road cemetery which still exists, although considerably extended.

A probable contributory factor to the public disorder of the 1830s was the absence of street lighting in the town. Exactly when street lighting was first introduced is uncertain. A vestry meeting on 9 December 1853 appointed a committee 'to receive tenders from persons willing to contract for lighting the lamps in the borough, including the finding of oil, wicks and cleaning the lamps from Monday the 19th of December instant until the 25th of March 1854'. The terms of this resolution suggest that a system of oil-lighting already existed in some parts of the town by mid-1853. The matter was again considered on 21 October 1854 when it was unanimously agreed that 'the cost of lighting the public highways within the Borough and attendant thereon shall be defrayed out of the rates made for … the repairs of the highways'. This may imply no more than a transfer of the cost of lighting from a specific rate demand for that purpose to the highways budget.

In any event, oil-lighting probably did not last much longer. A supply of town gas became available during the 1850s when a gas works was established at the foot of Hailes Street on the southern side, to the east of the junction with Silk Mill Lane.[4] This supply relied on extracting gas from coal which was brought from Tewkesbury. It seems likely that oil soon yielded to gas for street lighting.

Rebuilding the town hall

Probably the most onerous task Edmund Thomas Browne accomplished as high bailiff was rebuilding the town hall. During the first half of the nineteenth century the previous building had become steadily more dilapidated because the corporation's income, consisting mainly of market tolls and stallage (namely, the rent payable by stallholders for occupying a pitch on market days), was wholly inadequate to meet the cost of major repairs, still less of rebuilding. By 1850 it was generally agreed that the town hall was beyond repair, as was the adjacent building in High Street, immediately to the west of the town hall. This neighbouring building had previously been the booth hall; but, according to its description in a mortgage agreement of 3 October 1853, it had latterly been used partly as the borough lock-up and partly as the depository for the fire engine.[5] In response to a request from five of the town's leading citizens, including the vicar John Harvey and the ever-present solicitor Dennis Trenfield, Edmund Thomas Browne convened a public meeting in the former town hall, on 26 September 1851, 'to consider with the bailiff and burgesses the best means of repairing, or rebuilding and enlarging the Town Hall of Winchcomb, and providing the requisite funds for that purpose'.[6]

Although this public meeting agreed that rebuilding the town hall was essential, the difficulty of financing such a major operation meant that progress was inevitably slow. However, by August 1853, a very lengthy rebuilding specification had been drawn up; the architect, William Lane of Sudeley, had produced an approved design; and the brothers Richard and John Davis of Prestbury had been selected as builders, after the corporation had advertised for tenders in *The Gloucestershire Chronicle and Gloucestershire Journal.*[7] On 12 August 1853 the Davis brothers signed the following agreement with the corporation:

'We the undersigned do agree to execute the said works strictly in accordance with the foregoing particulars, and to complete the same, on or before 5 November 1853 for the sum of £283, weather permitting.'[8]

Despite the carefully drawn up specification, extra costs of £84 were incurred during the building operations, so that the corporation – perhaps after some argument over the 'extras' – eventually paid a total of £367 on 20 October 1855.

Although the corporation had authorised the Davis brothers to start the rebuilding in August 1853, it seems probable that arrangements for meeting the cost had not then been finalised. It was not until 3 October 1853 that they completed an agreement with the brothers John and William Dent, by then firmly established as owners of the Sudeley estate, for a loan of £225, repayable at a minimum of £10 per year over a thirty-year period, with interest at the rate of £4 per cent annually. In return for this loan the Dent brothers required substantial security, comprising the town hall itself and the immediately adjacent site, Jacobean House (then tenanted, as an office, by the solicitor Dennis Trenfield), and all the tolls and dues to which the corporation was entitled.[9]

The opening of the rebuilt town hall provided the occasion for a celebration of the borough's achievement early in 1854, although the precise date is uncertain. The brothers John and William Dent, as lords of the manor of Winchcombe and Sudeley, provided an excellent dinner in the new building, served by John Baylis of the White Hart inn. Before the meal, the courts leet for Winchcombe and Sudeley were held and the borough's officers for the coming year were appointed. They were Dennis Trenfield as steward; Edmund Thomas Browne as high bailiff; Thomas Haslum and Francis Merrell as constables; and Thomas Newman (surgeon), Charles Cooper (innkeeper), George Roberts (ironmonger) and Charles Lapworth (schoolmaster) as burgesses.

As both his uncles were not well enough to attend, John Coucher Dent presided as chairman on this occasion. He opened the proceedings by congratulating the townspeople on their achievement and wishing them well. As high bailiff, Edmund Thomas Browne replied in the following characteristically self-deprecatory way:

'He would just remark that his services, such as they were, would always be at the command of his fellow-townsmen. He would congratulate them on the fact that he thought they were really advancing in Winchcombe. They found that the surveyors were doing their duty, and keeping the roads in good repair. The sewerage of the town had been well looked to, and perhaps but few places in the kingdom could boast of being more salubrious than the town of Winchcombe. Then they had new public lamps, so that their darkness had been lightened, and last, though not least, they had their new Town Hall. But how was the last improvement obtained? Why, the old pile had been struck by a magic wand, and a new one had been raised; and he thought the enchanters would be found within the precincts of Sudeley Castle. Had it not been for the kind interference of the Messrs. Dent, the present Town Hall would not have been in existence. Trusting that they might have many friendly gatherings within its walls, and hoping that their successors might enjoy the same privileges as they did, he would conclude by drinking all their good healths, and wishing them every prosperity and happiness. (Applause)'[10]

Happily, Winchcombe's town hall remains on its historic site at the heart of the borough, where its red-brick structure and mock-Tudor design impart a sense of municipal dignity. (So great is the site's importance that the sum of £148,000, including £65,000 from the National Heritage Lottery Fund, was spent on refurbishing the town hall in 1999.) Although the high bailiff justifiably displayed his civic pride on that day in 1854, Edmund Thomas Browne may well have reflected ruefully, in private, on the time and effort he had devoted to the project and wondered how the corporation would ever repay the Dent brothers' loan.

Improving the postal service

In the early 1850s Anthony Trollope, the novelist, was given the task of improving English rural postal services, following his successful reorganisation of the letter post in Ireland. Gloucestershire was in the area to which his attention first turned and Mary Anne Simmons (appointed as Winchcombe's postmistress in 1869) recalled a visit Trollope paid to Winchcombe in 1851 to instruct the post office on issuing and paying money orders. Because he was passionate about hunting, Trollope went on his rounds dressed in hunting pink which, on his own admission, surprised many local postmasters. But he took his task seriously, claiming to visit every house in rural areas and trying to devise short cuts for the letter carriers, so that they would not be able to obtain the one-penny surcharge they were entitled to make for departing from their regular route. Trollope's own description of how he went about improving rural postal deliveries probably applies equally to some of Winchcombe's outlying farmsteads, as follows:

' ... I was perhaps a little in a hurry to get on, and did not allow as much time as was necessary to explain to the wondering mistress of the house, or to an open-mouthed farmer, why it was that a man arrayed for hunting asked so many questions which might be considered impertinent, as applying to his or her private affairs ... I was altogether in earnest; and I believe that many a farmer now has his letters brought daily to his house free of charge [that is, without a surcharge], who, but for me, would still have had to send to the post-town for them twice a week, or to pay a man for bringing them irregularly to his door.'[11]

Despite Trollope's efforts, mail delivery continued to depend on foot-slogging carriers who trod the miry lanes and steep hill country around Winchcombe. James Agg was appointed a rural messenger in 1856 and served continuously for thirty years. He vividly remembered having to trudge 'nigh up to the knees in mud' during the winter in the suitably named Dirty Lane in Gretton.

Re-roofing the parish church

The town hall was not Winchcombe's only public building needing major repair in the mid-nineteenth century. Successive vicars and churchwardens were concerned about the parish church's deteriorating state. Their concern culminated in six years of debate, between 1843 and 1849, by the vestry about the 'urgent necessity of taking immediate steps for repairing the roof of the parish church'. Finally, on 18 August 1849, a vestry meeting chaired by the vicar, the Rev. John Harvey, in the town hall (perhaps because the church's roof was too unsafe), decided to have the necessary repairs carried out 'without further delay' and to borrow £500, on the security of the church rate, to meet the cost. The roof must then have been repaired with remarkable speed and efficiency because the vestry received a report in the following year that the work had been completed at a total cost of £538 6s. 6¼d. The meeting recorded its cordial thanks to the vicar, the churchwardens and the two superintendents of the building work, Stephen Pryce and William Lane, for the very satisfactory manner in which the repairs had been carried out.

The high bailiff's memorial

Edmund Thomas Browne played a major part in the life of the borough, from his service in the Winchcombe and Sudeley Loyal Volunteer Infantry during the Napoleonic Wars to his final years as high bailiff. Although his death in 1859 deprived him of experiencing the major improvements to the town which occurred from 1860 onwards, his energy and determination perhaps encouraged his successors to emulate his firm resolve to restore some of the borough's former glory. The high bailiff's character was memorably recorded in the following obituary notice in a local journal:

'In our obituary of last week we recorded the death of Edmund Thomas Browne Esq, who for upwards of fourteen years has held the ancient and honourable office of High Bailiff of this Borough, and during that period has won for himself the universal admiration, gratitude and respect of his fellow townsmen. His character was a rare union of the sincere and unostentatious piety of the Christian, the education and learning of the scholar, the courtesy and polished manners of the gentleman, with the zeal, activity and tact of the man of business ... He was warmly attached to his native town, well versed in its ancient history and traditions, and quite an authority on all matters of an antiquarian nature; whilst to his exertions and public spirit the town is deeply indebted for many an important improvement. To the poor he was ever a kind and truly benevolent friend. In his death Winchcomb has indeed sustained a public loss.'[12]

On this occasion the obituarist did his subject justice.

1   'Answers to Queries – Topography and history of Winchcomb', signed at end: E. T. Browne; GRO, D2218/ 3/22
2   The Winchcombe and Sudeley Record, Volume 4, No. 37, January 1893, page 184
3   'Stray notes by a Rambler', miscellaneous newspaper cuttings, GRO, D2218/ 3/20
4   J. A. Oakey: 'Reminiscences', 1936, page 6
5   Mortgage agreement of 3 October 1853; GRO, D1675/ 1/4
6   Notice exhibited in Winchcombe Museum
7   GRO, D1675/ 1/4
8   GRO, D1675/ 1/5
9   GRO, D1675/ 1/4
10   report of town hall opening ceremony, 1854: GRO, D2218/3/20
11   The Winchcombe and Sudeley Record, No 10, October 1890
12   GRO, D2218/3/20

CHAPTER 23

THE VICTORIAN SOCIAL HIERARCHY

Although the second half of the nineteenth century saw remarkable changes in many of Winchcombe's buildings and public facilities, the townspeople experienced a largely unchanging social order throughout the Victorian age and the years before 'the Great War' started in 1914. As with the other north-Cotswold market towns, a sociologist might describe Winchcombe as a highly stratified society: put simply, there was a place for everyone and everyone was expected to know it. And, apart from such notable exceptions as Emma Dent at Sudeley and Lady Wemyss at Stanway, women were expected to fulfil a subordinate role. This long-term stability was helped by two factors: the district's continuing reliance on agriculture and most people's limited mobility.

Between 1840 and 1914 more than half the working population in and around Winchcombe were employed in agriculture or in trades associated with agriculture. Despite the severe agricultural depression of the 1870s, there was little drift from the land before 1914. Agriculture's dominance in the local economy meant that shopkeepers' and tradesmen's livelihoods in Winchcombe depended heavily on farming prosperity.

Limited mobility was an equally important factor in sustaining an ordered society. The borough had always been isolated from most of the county: even after Cheltenham's rapid expansion in the Regency period, Winchcombe tended to look outwards to Broadway, Evesham and Tewkesbury which were more accessible by road. John Oakey describes the first public vehicle he could remember, probably from the 1850s, as a horse-drawn coach driven from one of the inns in Broadway by Thomas Stephens, who changed the horses at the George inn in Winchcombe before continuing to Cheltenham. But the availability of a coach twice a week did not mean that travel to Cheltenham became much easier, as John Oakey explains:

' … Owing to the terrible state of the roads, this coach took some pulling. This was the only means of getting to Cheltenham, except by walking, and at that time to walk to Cheltenham and back was considered just a stroll … Two women, Mrs Pearson and Mrs Richardson, walked every other day, and sometimes three or four days together, to Cheltenham, each carrying two baskets loaded with eggs and butter, etc., returning loaded with things required for themselves and others. This was no easy task considering the roads. At this time some of the Winchcombe bakers took bread to Cheltenham on trucks or donkeys. Two huge baskets were strapped one on each side ...' [1]

And even when passenger transport improved and became more frequent, later in the nineteenth century, travel to Cheltenham still involved some vigorous walking. John Oakey again explains why, as follows:

'Later on were other conveyances, Tom Jones with his two horse bus, and Will Jackson with a covered spring waggon. No matter what the weather, passengers had to alight at the foot of the hill and often walked on to Southam, before they were caught up by the conveyance. It was a case of walking up the hill to save the horses, and down the hill to save your necks ... ' [2]

Although people were much more accustomed to travel on foot, their limited range gave little opportunity to compare life in Winchcombe with conditions elsewhere in the county, still less in the country. The result was generally to accept that what was would continue to be.

The poorest inhabitants

The inmates of the town's workhouse were probably seen, and regarded themselves, as being at the lowest level in Winchcombe's social hierarchy. The following extract from a report in the *Tewkesbury Weekly Record* for 29 March 1856, by a visitor to Winchcombe, provides a typically patronising view of their situation after the Poor Law reforms of 1836:

'The little, old, inconvenient Workhouse and its little, old, inconvenient system have passed away and are succeeded by a place and a plan far more beneficial to the pauper and more just to the rate-payer ... ' [3]

The labouring classes

A little above the workhouse inmates in social status were the 'labouring classes', as their social superiors described them. These people comprised the largest occupational group in and around Winchcombe: they sought work on the farms and great estates (including the revived Sudeley estate in the Dent family's hands), at the Postlip paper mills, in the silk mill while it survived until about 1872, in smaller enterprises such as the Winchcombe Brick and Tile Company at Greet, and in neighbouring stone quarries. Some of their sons and daughters obtained employment in full-time domestic service, which helped to ease the intolerable overcrowding in the homes of large families.

The greatest virtue for people in the labouring classes was struggling to maintain a spirit of sturdy independence, bringing up a family on low but carefully managed wages, and avoiding at almost any cost the shame of admittance to the workhouse. Luxuries did not exist for such people, who were probably grateful for any help the town's various charities could provide. But the spirit of independence is exemplified by the formation of the Winchcombe clubs, or friendly societies, which provided sick pay during ill health. The main societies were the Oddfellows, Foresters and Tradesmen's Benefit Societies: they were a focus for community self-help, particularly when they paraded on special occasions in their sashes and Sunday best clothes, led by the town band to the parish church with each club's elaborately embroidered banner carried proudly before them.

The Agricultural Association

The Winchcomb Agricultural Association was formed 'to encourage and reward the exertions of agricultural labourers and to give premiums to meritorious household and other servants'. The Association's rules for 1855 indicate that Edward Holland M.P. was the chairman of the management committee and the ever-present Dennis Trenfield combined the posts of treasurer and secretary. There appears to have been a branch within the wider Association known as Winchcomb Union Association, which 'the clergy, gentry and yeomanry, resident within the Winchcomb Union' were encouraged to support. This Association's patron was the Earl of Ellenborough; among the vice-presidents were the Earl of Wemyss, Lord Sudeley and John Dent.

The Association's purpose was to enable each member subscribing a sum of not less than ten shillings annually to recommend labourers and servants for an award at the rate of two recommendations for each ten-shilling subscription. The list of subscribers for 1854 names ninety-one members, of whom four were women. The subscriptions appear to be closely related to the member's social status. Thus seventy-one members each subscribed ten shillings, including the Winchcombe borough members, the Rev. John Harvey the vicar, Edmund Thomas Browne, William Smith of The Farm, and Dennis Trenfield. Subscriptions of £5 each were paid by the Earl of Ellenborough, John Dent, Samuel Gist of Wormington Grange, Edward Holland of Dumbleton, Lord Sudeley and the Earl of Wemyss. Total subscriptions for 1854 were £85 10s.

The rewards given in 1854 provide a fleeting glimpse of how some of the recipients lived. Class 1 was intended to reward 'labourers and labourers' widows who have brought up, or are now bringing up, the largest family without receiving parochial relief (except in cases of illness)': the sum of £4 was awarded to James Dean of Guiting Power for bringing up nine children. Class 2 rewarded labourers 'who have placed out the greatest number of their family in respectable service': the sum of £3 was awarded, as second prize, to Charles Lovesey of Kineton for placing his six children in service. Class 6 was for labourers 'who have worked, as daily or weekly servants, the greatest number of years for the same master or mistress, or on the same farm with successive masters or mistresses, and who shall receive a good character': the sum of £3 was awarded to John Pulley of Dumbleton for 31 years' service on one of Edward Holland's farms. Class 10 was for non-agricultural long service: the sum of £3 was awarded to John Kerry of Winchcombe for fifteen years' service with John Willis, and £2 to Thomas Merryman of Winchcombe for twelve years' service with the Dent brothers at Sudeley castle.[4] How truly are these men described as deserving members of 'the labouring classes'.

Public holidays and games

Working lives of unrelenting drudgery were occasionally relieved by brief, but intensive, respites. The town's main holiday was the Whit-Monday festival, which usually lasted three days. It began at 6 am, with ringing the parish church's bells, and included a procession to the church by as many as four hundred members of the Winchcombe clubs, starting to make their way through the town at 10 am. There were organised sports and games in the afternoon. The games included shin-kicking and cudgel-playing (or backsword) which were popular well into the nineteenth century. Stand-up fighting was a frequent spectacle in the town, as John Oakey explains in the following account:

'In Winchcombe in my early days there was seldom a Saturday night without seeing a small knot of young fellows marching off with two fighters to the battle-ground, more often for sport than for settling any real difference or dispute. The battle ground for lower Winchcombe was the Hill Croft, while the Enfield served for the top end of the town.'[5]

Some men sought relief in the temporary oblivion of hard drinking, for which the town's numerous beer houses provided ample opportunity.

The shopkeepers and tradesmen

Independent shopkeepers and tradesmen in Winchcombe regarded themselves as a higher stratum than the labouring classes in the Victorian social structure. During the 1840s this group included men such as George Timbrell, ironmonger living in High Street; William Hall, slater and plasterer, who occupied the premises in Abbey Terrace now the Plaisterers' Arms inn; Nathaniel Phillips, fellmonger, who then operated the Vineyard Street tannery; George Sexty, who ran the other tannery and lived in Hailes Street; and John Castle, a saddler in North Street. As buyers and sellers of materials and products, social and financial stability were highly valued by this group. As ratepayers, they took a close interest in the vestry's affairs; and John Castle was one of the two churchwardens during the 1850s. They might also be elected as burgesses in the corporation, although they would not expect to attain the dignity of a bailiff's office.

Shopkeeping provided a rare commercial opportunity for women. In the 1840s, as already mentioned in Chapter 21, Rebecca Simmons ran a grocery business and post office in North Street; and Sarah Major was a shopkeeper in Gloucester Street. More unusually, Ann Chadborn kept the Old Gate inn in North Street, and Jane Howman had a business as 'spirit dealer' at the Sun inn there.

There was also some scope for highly skilled craftsmen in the town. The 1841 census records William Johnson as a sixty-five-year-old clockmaker living in High Street. His son, Edwin Johnson, who presumably took over the business, is known to have made an English dial clock as late as 1878, when he was still working in Winchcombe.[6]

The farmers

A number of substantial farmers (or yeomen) lived in and around the borough throughout this period. They included men such as Thomas Greening at Langley, John Staite at Sudeley Lodge, William Morse at Corndean, James Finch at Almsbury Farm, Charles Summers at Wadfield, William Hyatt at Waterhatch and George Ireland. Because they were generally able to dictate wage rates and agricultural labourers' working conditions, these yeomen farmers were well respected and, in some cases, probably feared. They were primarily interested in employing thrifty labourers and maintaining a well-ordered system of poor relief. Cash payments for relief of agricultural labourers were important to them in helping to maintain an available pool of labour at times when men were not needed on the farm, and as representing a subsistence level with which agricultural wages were compared.

The professional class

A small group of independent and professional people, mainly men, appear to have lived relatively comfortable lives during the Victorian period. There were a number of solicitors, including Giles Carter, Dennis Trenfield and, much later, Edmund Smith Wood, the town's last high bailiff. In the 1840s the doctors were Clement Bancks and Thomas Newman, both living in High Street; and James Parker practised as a 'horse and cattle doctor' in Bull Lane. Between about 1870 and 1920 Dr. William Cox lived in the substantial house at the eastern end of Abbey Terrace (now occupied by Lloyds-TSB bank): he was the borough's last low bailiff and, for a time, organist at the parish church. The main local industry at Postlip paper mills was represented by the Lloyd brothers, of whom Nathaniel Lloyd lived in High Street until his death in 1845; and, subsequently, William Gates Adlard who lived at Postlip Hall until the 1870s. This group included a number of men and women of independent means, the men usually being described simply as 'gentleman'. Among such people in the 1840s were William Trotman and Edmund Thomas Browne, both living in High Street; Edmund Browne's cousins Susanna and Anna Maria Wood; and Mary Lates, widow of the former vicar the Rev. John Lates, and her nieces, Sarah Francis and Elizabeth Maggs, occupying Church Cottage, opposite the parish church.

Many of these people were charitably disposed to their less fortunate neighbours and provided practical help. Typical examples are the charities established by the respective wills of Hester Ann Durham and Mary Durham, the unmarried daughters of William Durham. In her will of 10 July 1849 Hester Ann Durham left the sum of £500 to be invested so that four-fifths of the annual interest be devoted to 'the purchase of clothing for ten poor men and ten poor women, being inhabitants of the town or borough of Winchcomb, not being each less than fifty years of age, such poor persons and clothing to be annually fixed upon by the minister, churchwardens and principal inhabitants of the said borough, in vestry assembled, and the clothing to be delivered to such poor persons on Christmas day.' The remaining one-fifth of the interest was to go to repair of the Chandos almshouses and providing clothes or fuel for the almshouse residents.[7] Mary Durham's will of 8 August 1854 bequeathed the sum of £300 to provide an annual investment income for 'the purchase of blankets, to be distributed annually, on the first Monday in November, amongst such poor and deserving persons resident within the parishes of Winchcomb and Sudeley ... as the minister, churchwardens and principal inhabitants of the said parish of Winchcomb, in vestry assembled, shall select ... '[8]

Provided inflation did not erode the value of their investments and other income, people of independent means were able to live relatively comfortable and self-fulfilling lives in Winchcombe throughout the Victorian age. An example of one such life is that of Anna Maria Wood who was born in 1782 and died on 27 May 1864. Her life and character were described (probably by Emma Dent) as follows:

'Miss Wood was a native of Winchcombe and lived for many years in the old-fashioned, comfortable family residence in High Street, with her cousin Edmund T. Browne Esq., to whom she was devotedly attached. Miss Wood was a gentlewoman in the strictest sense of the word, of that good old type which unfortunately is too rapidly disappearing from among us; an artist, according to the fashion of her day, painting portraits in miniature; a poet, loving every thing that was beautiful in nature and art ... Above all, Miss Wood, in life, was known and beloved for her many Christian virtues, and at her death for her loving remembrance of the poor, so that now and for ever, many will there be "to rise up and call her blessed".'[9]

Miss Wood's 'loving remembrance of the poor' was practically expressed by her bequest of a sufficient sum to produce investment income which would provide 'one shilling each to twenty poor widows and two shillings each to twenty poor old men' in the parish, together with warm cloaks for the women and warm stockings for the men.[10] The continuing value of this bequest was sufficient for twenty widows and twenty men to receive the appointed shillings, and for six shawls to be distributed to women and twenty pairs of stockings to men, at Christmas 1889.

People with substantial incomes or independent means were also able to commission some of the fine nineteenth-century dwellinghouses which greatly improved the town's appearance, as well as providing comfortable homes for the occupiers. Two outstanding examples in Gloucester Street are Cotswold House (No. 48) dating from the early nineteenth century, with its Greek doric portico; and the Gothic-style villa, originally built as the vicarage in the mid-nineteenth century (now known as the Old Vicarage, at No. 60).

The vicars

Successive Anglican vicars occupied a position of considerable importance in Winchcombe. As chairman of the vestry, the vicar had a substantial role in the town's government until the reforms of the 1880s replaced parochial control. The vicar also had important educational responsibilities, although teaching duties were mainly delegated to schoolmasters.

Two very different men served as vicar between 1834 and 1888. John Ridout Harvey was vicar for thirty-seven years from 1834. While he was clearly influential as the vestry's chairman, his relative poverty must have caused him acute embarrassment at times, as will emerge later in this chapter. John Harvey was succeeded in 1871 by the formidable Robert Noble Jackson, who had previously been curate at Sudeley where he was initially on friendly terms with Emma Dent and her husband, John Coucher Dent. The Rev. Noble Jackson was a retired naval chaplain: he commissioned the building for himself of the substantial dwellinghouse, known as Rathmore, in generous grounds on the western side of Gretton Road. Unfortunately it was demolished in 1976 to make way for later housing development on the site. After introduction as vicar, he attempted to assume personal responsibility for the town's moral welfare which resulted in conflict with Emma Dent who regarded it as very much her concern. Perhaps Noble Jackson's most lasting memorial is the parish church's superb chancel window, provided by voluntary subscription in 1872, portraying St Peter's attempt to walk across the waves to Christ. This choice of subject is reportedly an expression of the vicar's life-long love of the sea.[11]

The manorial lords

At the apex of Winchcombe's social structure from 1837 onwards were the Dent family. After the two brothers John and William Dent had established themselves in the substantially rebuilt Sudeley castle they attempted to revive the virtually defunct manorial jurisdiction of the borough and manor of Winchcombe. When they died within a year of each other – William on 11 October 1854, aged seventy-one, and John on 8 October 1855, aged seventy-eight – their nephew John Coucher Dent (the son of their brother Thomas Dent) inherited the Sudeley estate and the Dent fortune. He and his wife, Emma, moved to Sudeley castle in 1857 and immediately exerted a strong influence on Winchcombe, which continued until her death in 1900. As late as 4 October 1882, John Coucher Dent issued a summons for a manorial court to be held in the town hall on 18 October.[12]

Lord Ellenborough

However, even the Dent family had to assume a subordinate role in a titled person's presence. Such a person was Lord Ellenborough, whose country seat was Southam House, bought from the Delabere family. Ellenborough was nationally prominent as president of the board of control in Wellington's cabinet from 1829 to 1830 and subsequently held the same post in Robert Peel's first and second cabinets.[13] He had also gained the unwelcome distinction, at that time, of having his divorce proceedings in April 1830 reported on the front page of *The Times*, in place of the usual classified advertisements, following Lady Jane Ellenborough's infatuation with an Austrian diplomat, Prince Felix Schwarzenberg.[14]

Ellenborough also played a prominent part in local affairs. He was a justice of the peace and, following its establishment in 1836, chairman of the Board of Guardians for the Winchcombe Poor Law Union. In October 1841 Ellenborough resigned from his cabinet post to take up the appointment of governor-general of India, where he arrived in February 1842. Although his administration of India was characterised by absence of nepotism and seemingly genuine concern for the peoples of the sub-continent, he did not see eye to eye with some of the most senior army officers over his expansionist policy (which included the seizure of Sind province) and the cabinet recalled him in 1844.[15]

While Ellenborough was officially censured for his conduct of affairs as governor-general, he was rewarded with an earldom on return to England and was given a place in the cabinet in December 1845 as first lord of the admiralty.[16] The Earl's return to Gloucestershire in 1844 was a splendid occasion. In Winchcombe it was decided to combine a welcoming ceremony with a musical performance to raise money for major repairs then needed to the parish church organ. The following extracts from the lengthy contemporary report in *The Gloucestershire Chronicle* eloquently convey the pomp and circumstance of Ellenborough's arrival in Winchcombe on 6 November 1844:

'The arrangements for the reception of the noble Earl were confided to the able management of D. Trenfield Esq.

... it was arranged that a procession of the gentry and yeomanry of the neighbourhood should meet him at Cockbury, a mile and a half from Winchcomb, at half past nine on the Wednesday morning. On arriving at the rendezvous at about that time, we found the road lined on each side for a considerable distance, with carriages and other vehicles, and a number of horsemen drawn up in procession with banners, and a van containing a band of music, the whole headed by Mr. Trenfield. ... Shortly before ten o'clock his Lordship was seen descending the hill ... On nearing his escort he was received with repeated cheers, the band saluting him with "See the conquering hero comes". He appeared much gratified with his reception, and spoke very affably to many of the members of the cavalcade; and the procession having formed, processed to Winchcomb, where the cheers and other tokens of respect were redoubled; banners were suspended from many of the houses and across the road, and a little distance beyond the Abbey was erected a triumphal arch of evergreens and laurel. His Lordship entered the town still on horseback, exchanging greetings with many of the crowd whom he recognised ... '

Presumably in his capacity as manorial lord, John Dent then welcomed the distinguished visitor as follows:

' ... Welcome! thrice welcome! Earl of Ellenborough, (cheers) and may we hope that your Lordship, while valuing the Earldom, the mark of your Sovereign's approval, will not undervalue the humble gift which we have to bestow – the respect, and love, and heartfelt welcome of your old neighbours of Winchcomb (cheers).'

This welcome was followed by an elaborately formal, congratulatory address, on behalf of the bailiffs, burgesses and inhabitants of the borough and neighbourhood of Winchcombe, read by the town's low bailiff Edmund Thomas Browne (who was also suspected of being the author of this document). The ceremony ended with Ellenborough's grateful response, including the following shrewd analysis of how the existing social order would best be sustained:

' … I shall have great pleasure in renewing my friendly acquaintance with you all, and in co-operating with you in measures for assisting our poorer neighbours in their honest endeavours to maintain their families in independence and in comfort.

In this favoured district we have before us the bright example of the poor themselves in their constant kindness towards each other …

Thus encouraged we will proceed in our accustomed course, and endeavour to draw yet closer the bonds of mutual goodwill, which, happily, here unite the proprietor, the tenant, and the labourer.'[17]

Dennis Trenfield's downfall

The 'principal inhabitants of the borough', as they are so often called in the Winchcombe vestry's minutes, probably valued financial probity and social decorum as highly as the virtues enjoined by the ten commandments (which the vestry's meeting on 19 May 1778 had authorised the two churchwardens and their successors to display in gold lettering on a board beside the parish church altar). Any departure from these virtues would be frowned upon, possibly to the extent of social exclusion, in a close-knit community where a gentleman's word was his bond. The events which overwhelmed the ubiquitous and highly respected solicitor, Dennis Trenfield, in 1858 must therefore have seemed cataclysmic to his friends and clients.

Dennis Trenfield's name first appears in the vestry's records in December 1833. By that time, he had probably acquired the dwellings and other property on the former Winchcombe abbey site and was practising as a solicitor in the town. He held numerous influential positions: for example, in 1844 he is described as 'steward of the manor of Sudeley', and in the 1850s he was treasurer and secretary of the Winchcomb Agricultural Association. He was undoubtedly a trusted legal and financial adviser to many clients, with some of whom he was on intimate terms. However, by early-1854, matters had begun to go seriously wrong. In September 1853 Robert Timbrill, son of Dr. Timbrill of Beckford, sought a loan from Trenfield to enable him to pay off debts he had accumulated as a Cambridge undergraduate and was apparently told that as much as £400 might possibly be advanced. To find this sum Trenfield himself needed to raise money, presumably because he was by then in some financial difficulty. He did so partly by borrowing £200 from John Edwards, a farmer of Toddington. Because he could provide no security for this loan, Trenfield gave John Edwards a bond dated 17 February 1854 for the borrowed sum, purportedly signed by Robert Timbrill and the Rev. Edward Dupre, then vicar of Temple Guiting: disastrously, he had forged both signatures on this bond.

Some time elapsed before this transaction became public, but Trenfield was eventually indicted for forging and uttering the bond and was due to appear at Gloucester crown court during the 1858 spring assizes. Presumably anticipating the shame of a guilty verdict, he fled to London before the trial date where he attempted suicide by shooting himself. In the event, he sustained serious head wounds; a warrant was issued for his arrest; and police constable Smith, who escorted him back from

London, described at the subsequent trial how his jaw was so severely broken that he had to have medical attention on arrival at Cheltenham.

A detailed report of Dennis Trenfield's trial appeared in *The Gloucester Journal* for 10 April 1858. His counsel's defence was that he was on such intimate terms with the Rev. Edward Dupre and Robert Timbrill that putting their names to the bond was justifiable in the circumstances; but the judge did not accept this defence and, 'after a five-minute consultation', the jury returned a guilty verdict. Despite a recommendation for mercy by counsel on behalf of John Edwards, the judge passed sentence of ten years' penal servitude, which at that time meant transportation.[18]

The inevitable sequel was the disposal of Trenfield's property. A notice in *The Gloucester Journal* for 24 April 1858 announced that an auction of his real estate would be held at the White Hart inn, Winchcombe, on 8 May. Lot 2 in the auction comprised 'that most desirable freehold estate known as The Abbey', including 'two good dwellinghouses fitted up with every convenience for families of respectability, ...' The description of Lot 6 is particularly interesting: it comprised a dwellinghouse on the north side of Gloucester Street (then occupied by William Hall) 'with a large garden behind, called The Kingsmoor', thus apparently confirming that at least a residual part of the medieval 'Kyngesmoor' remained extant in 1858. A one-line notice in the same paper for 29 May 1858 announced that the property known as Winchcombe Abbey had been sold for £2,350 to Mr. C. Fawdry (this may well have been Cornelius Fawdry who appears in the 1841 census as a 30-year old farmer in Gretton). What happened to the rest of the estate is not mentioned.

The vicar's financial embarrassment

It is unclear how many of the town's inhabitants were entangled in Dennis Trenfield's financial web. The hapless vicar, John Ridout Harvey, was certainly one of them. His turn to appear at Gloucester county court came on 16 September 1858, when the same John Edwards and Mr. Slatter sought to show that the vicar, while himself insolvent, had joined with Dennis Trenfield in issuing two promissory notes, namely one for £200 to Mr. Edwards on 21 November 1856 and the other for £300 to Mr. Slatter in January 1858. During these proceedings it emerged that the vicar had been insolvent since May 1855; and it was apparently well known in the town that he had assigned the proceeds of his living, except for an allowance of £100 per year to support his wife, seven children and himself, for his creditors' benefit in September 1857. Despite a plea on the vicar's behalf that Trenfield had taken advantage of his friendship and misled him, and the prosecution's recommendation of leniency, John Harvey was sentenced to nine months' imprisonment (running from 4 May 1858) for having contracted debts without probable means of payment.[19] After his imprisonment John Harvey served his Winchcombe parishioners for another twelve years, becoming the third longest-serving vicar.

Dennis Trenfield's legacy

There is no evidence that Dennis Trenfield returned to the town after 1858. Nevertheless, despite his downfall, his participation in the agreement which created Abbey Terrace, twenty-three years previously, provides an unexpected memorial to him. It will probably never be established how many other 'principal inhabitants of the borough' were involved in these affairs, or suffered financially, as Trenfield's creditors. But the events of 1858 undoubtedly left some of the leading citizens less well off than they had anticipated and probably raised the question whether, in this closely knit community, one man should have so much trust placed in him.

1   J. A. Oakey: 'Reminiscences', 1936, pages 12-13
2   J. A. Oakey, op cit, page 14
3   GRO, D2218/3/20
4   Pamphlet entitled 'Rules and Regulations of the Winchcomb Agricultural Association for the Year 1855', printed by G. Norman, Cheltenham, 1855
5   J. A. Oakey, op cit, pages 17-19
6   Graham Dowler: 'Gloucestershire Clock and Watch Makers', Phillimore, 1984, page 136
7   The Winchcombe and Sudeley Record, No 5, May 1890, page 23
8   The Winchcombe and Sudeley Record, No 5, May 1890, page 24
9   The Winchcombe and Sudeley Record, No 5, May 1890, page 22
10   The Winchcombe and Sudeley Record, No 5, May 1890, page 21
11   Eleanor Adlard: 'Winchcombe Cavalcade', page 38
12   copy of summons received by Rev. R. N. Jackson, previously held in Winchcombe parish chest
13   E. L. Woodward: 'The Age of Reform, 1815-1870', The Oxford History of England, 1954, pages 634-637
14   Mary S. Lovell: 'A Scandalous Life, the biography of Jane Digby', Richard Cohen Books, 1995, pages 63-70
15   E. L. Woodward, op cit, pages 403-407
16   E. L. Woodward, op cit, page 638
17   extracts from *Gloucestershire Chronicle*; GRO, D2218/3/20
18   *Gloucester Journal*, 10 April 1858; microfilm copy in Gloucester Local Studies Library's archive
19   *Gloucester Journal*, 18 September 1858; microfilm copy in Gloucester Local Studies Library's archive

CHAPTER 24

THE BOROUGH'S VICTORIAN RENEWAL

In 1861 the total population of the parish of Winchcombe (including the neighbouring hamlets) was 2,937. Ten years later, a slight increase had taken the population to 2,993, the nineteenth century's peak. The numbers then declined slightly to 2,951 by 1901. A fairly stable population meant that available resources could be devoted to renewal of existing facilities, rather than providing for incomers to the town.

The town in the 1850s

A reporter in the *Tewkesbury Weekly Record* for 29 March 1856 had already been impressed by the recent development, described (in part) as follows:

' … Twenty years have made a considerable alteration for the better in the appearance of the streets. The alterations about the Abbey and the Churchyard [the creation of Abbey Terrace], are visible and great improvements … The old and unsightly Town Hall has given place to a structure which, if not of great architectural pretensions, is in point of utility and convenience, a great advance on its predecessor. Some spacious and handsome shops have been erected, and in others many progressive alterations and improvements have been carried out …

But there are two distinct signs of progress in Winchcomb which seem to stand out in advance of those already enumerated. At the north side of the town quite a suburb of nice, new, comfortable-looking cottages are in the course of erection, and they appear so superior in accommodation and taste to the generality of such buildings, as to lead to the hope that they may become the examples of a better style of dwellings for the working people of the district around, and we earnestly hope that the prosperity of the town may justify the erection of many more of the same class … [The report then praised the newly built infants' school in Abbey Terrace.]'[1]

Despite these signs of improvement, Winchcombe still retained many eighteenth century features. The new cottages that so impressed the reporter in 1856 were almost certainly the stone- and brick-built houses on either side of Gretton Road at the southern end. Just to the south of these cottages was the toll gate at the northern access to the town, with a similar toll gate on Greet Road, both operated by the same toll keeper. The eastern approach was gated at what was known as 'Footbridge Gate': one gate was on the Broadway Road and the other at the foot of what is now Stancombe Lane.[2] On the western entry to the town the highway sloped steeply down to the junction with Corndean Lane where the toll gate and the toll keeper's cottage (later named Gate House) were situated.[3] At the foot of steeply sloping Vineyard Street the river Isbourne still had to be crossed through a ford. However, towards the northern end of North Street, the Tarrant Brook was culverted in the 1850s; and the consequently reduced risk of flooding in that area made possible the construction of the property now known as Anchor House, the adjacent dwelling and Barebones Farm. The public weighbridge was established at The Anchor, conveniently situated near the toll gates.[4]

Emma Dent's arrival in Winchcombe

Following the death of the Dent brothers, John Coucher Dent (their nephew) and his wife Emma moved from their home in Worcester to Sudeley castle in 1857. Emma Dent was one of the daughters of John Brocklehurst, a wealthy manufacturer in Macclesfield and, for a time, a Member of Parliament for that Cheshire constituency. She was an intelligent, cultured and industrious Victorian lady who cared deeply for the Sudeley estate and neighbouring Winchcombe. Following her husband's death in 1885, much of her energy was devoted to the improvement and continuing welfare of the estate and the townspeople.[5]

Dent's almshouses

The Dents lavished new buildings and facilities on the town and helped to restore or improve existing buildings. The first new building was the almshouses on the southern side of Abbey Terrace, on the site immediately to the west of the Plaisterers' Arms previously occupied by Thomas Pittaway's old cottage and the former Bell inn (before the innkeeper transferred the business to the existing premises in Gretton Road).[6] John Oakey recalled starting work on the site in March 1863. By April 1865 the almshouses were completed, at a cost of about £4,000, of which £2,000 came from a legacy by John Dent while John Coucher Dent provided at least £500.[7] The distinctive design of the almshouses is due to Emma Dent's choice of the London architects Sir (as he later became) Gilbert Scott and J. Drayton Wyatt, although much of the detailed work and supervision of the building were the latter's responsibility. Consequently, like some of the Sudeley castle rebuilding, the Dent's almshouses' design reflects the Gothic style these architects favoured, although the building work was carried out by local masons.

Dent's school and school house

The almshouses were followed by the newly built infants' school and school house, immediately to the west of the parish church, completed in 1867. For this purpose, the land occupied by the former Beech cottage had to be acquired,

bringing the total cost of the work to about £2,000. Although these buildings are no longer used for school purposes, the architects' distinctive design has been largely retained in the residential conver- sion. It is evident that the sympathetic design and careful choice of materials were intended to provide a building subordinate to, but in keeping with, the parish church, as well as echoing the Dent's almshouses' external appearance.

Extension to the town hall

Although the town hall had been rebuilt as recently as 1853, its accommodation proved inadequate by the late-1860s. The positioning of the original building had left an area along the eastern flank which provided a wide entrance into North Street at The Cross. In 1871 the corporation decided to use this parcel of land to provide a new wing to the building for the purpose of 'a Magistrates' Retiring Room and Waiting Room Under', as the magistrates' court was then held in the town hall. The bailiffs and burgesses contracted with Henry Pearson, the local builder, to add the new wing at a cost of £413.

However, by that time, the corporation had paid off only £65 of the original loan of £225 from the Dent brothers for the rebuilding in 1853. The corporation's high bailiff and treasurer, Dr. Thomas Newman, therefore sought a further mortgage of £300 from John Coucher Dent, bringing the total debt to £460. The mortgage agree- ment of 14 February 1872 provided for the corporation to repay the loan at the rate of £10 per year and annual interest at the rate of £4 per cent.[8] The corporation evidently experienced difficulty in meeting repayments because they were obliged to convey 'The King's School House' (that is, Jacobean House in Queen Square) to John Coucher Dent on 28 June 1876 for the sum of £200, which was applied to reducing the mortgage debt from £460 to £260. This debt was not finally paid off until 9 April 1891. Although the agreement transferred Jacobean House to private ownership for the first time in the building's history, it enabled John Coucher Dent to instruct Drayton Wyatt to carry out essential restoration, which the corporation had been unable to afford, and some enlargement, in 1879. The property then remained in the Sudeley estate's ownership until it was sold to a private buyer in 2000.

THE PARISH CHURCH, WINCHCOMBE,
(AS PROPOSED TO BE RESTORED)

J. DRAYTON WYATT, ARCH?

LONDON, — SEPT? 1870.

The parish church's restoration in 1872

While it had seemed to the Winchcombe churchwardens of 1849 a major and costly operation, the roof repair to the parish church, completed in 1850, was little more than patching up. In the early 1870s the barn-shaped, stone-slated roof over the chancel remained in place, with heavy roof timbers and cross members on the underside. The church's interior was still furnished with box-pews, allocated to named occupiers (including the Dents), and a ladies' gallery with rows of seating at the east end; the organ occupied the tower arch at the west end; and two unsightly stoves, with long metal chimneys rising to a clerestory window, stood in the central aisle. These features can be seen in the photographs at Plates 5, 6 and 7. The Rev. Robert Noble Jackson's induction as vicar in 1871 provided the essential stimulus for a complete refurbishment of the interior and, on the exterior, the reinstatement of the clerestory carrying through to the east end of the chancel. Once again, probably at Emma Dent's behest, the architect was Drayton Wyatt. While his approach has sometimes been criticised for what can be seen as excessive removal of some remaining medieval features, notably the original, stone-built, octagonal pulpit, those responsible for the restoration undoubtedly regarded the result as a superb achievement. The total cost of the work was £3,311 19s. 11d.: this very considerable sum was met entirely by voluntary subscriptions, including £500 each from the Dents and Lord Sudeley, implying that the vicar was an accomplished fund-raiser as well as contributing £100 himself.

The restored parish church was reopened on 6 March 1873, but a small financial problem remained. The total subscriptions plus interest on the amount invested fell short of the cost by £59 13s. 6d. It was therefore decided to issue a further subscrip-

Plate 5

tion list at the rate of five per cent of each initial subscription. The response to this invitation proved sufficient to pay off the outstanding amount.

Emma Dent's generosity to the parish church continued after her husband's death. In 1895 she arranged for the wooden pulpit to be replaced by a Painswick stone pulpit (which remains in use), replicating on a larger scale the stone pulpit removed in 1873.

Plate 6

Additionally, she gave the stone screen which now stands in the belfry arch at the church's west end. The detailing of the screen, which bears the coats of arms of Mercia, Gloucester Abbey, Queen Victoria, Winchcombe abbey, the borough of Winchcombe and Lord Ralph Boteler, exemplifies Emma Dent's sense of historical continuity. This sense is also evident in her placing of a Saxon, stone-built cross in the garden land of the property now known as Abbey Old House, following an archaeological excavation that established the position of the central tower of the demolished Winchcombe abbey church.[9]

Coffee taverns

As part of her concern for Winchcombe's moral welfare, Emma Dent was determined to tackle the problem of excessive drinking by substituting coffee consumption for beer drinking. It is difficult to be certain how many inns and beer houses existed in the town in the latter part of Victoria's reign: there may have been as many as nineteen simultaneously. In High Street the George inn and the White Hart inn each occupied their present site, with the Craven Arms situated opposite the White Hart. In North Street there was the Marquis of Granby (immediately north of the town hall and now Granby House), the Sun, the Bull (at the corner of Bull Lane), the Grape Vine (on the site of the present post office), the White Lion and The Gate (now No. 80). Contrary to the traditional belief, the Anchor was not an inn or beer house in Victorian times: its name derived from the maker's name or trade mark of the public weighbridge on the premises.[10] In Chandos Street, the Dog and Gun occupied the brick-built private house subsequently known as Hodnett House and now renamed

Plate 7

Jasmine Cottage. In Hailes Street there were the Sudeley Arms (now Nos. 21 and 23) and the Wheatsheaf (now part of the private house, Mercia). The imposing property known as Tudor House provided accommodation for The Plough at some time. The Plaisterers' Arms occupied its present site in Abbey Terrace; and, after 1863, The Bell inn traded from Gretton Road following demolition of its premises on the site

acquired for Dent's almshouses. In Gloucester Street, the Unicorn stood almost opposite the parish church (on the present Cotteswold Dairy site); the Crown was at the corner of Mill Lane; the Original (or alternatively, Lower) Packhorse (later West End stores) occupied what are now the dwellings at Nos. 79 and 79A; and the Upper Packhorse was at the house later known as The Guelders (No. 83). The Corner Cupboard did not become an inn until 1872 when the first licence for the premises was granted to William Richardson.[11]

Plate 8

Because of its central position at The Cross, Mrs. Dent would have preferred to establish a coffee house at the George inn; but this was strongly opposed in the town and she had to settle for the premises at The Gate, towards the northern end of North Street (now No. 80). When the coffee tavern, as Mrs. Dent called it, was established there she provided coffee free of charge for members of the working men's institute.[12] However, the George inn did not escape Emma Dent's attention: in 1884 she arranged for Drayton Wyatt to renovate the external pilgrims' gallery, which had become extremely dilapidated.[13] She also arranged for the New inn, in Hailes Street, to be transformed into a coffee tavern in 1882 when she was able to acquire the free-hold of the property for £355.[14]

A piped water supply

The Ordnance Survey sheet for central Winchcombe in 1884 shows that numerous houses in the central area had a well in their garden, from which the occupiers obtained their water supply for all purposes. Families who had no access to a well still had to rely on the two town pumps. It was not until 1887, the year of queen Victoria's golden jubilee, that a piped water supply was provided. To commemorate the jubilee Emma Dent met the cost of bringing a water supply from St Kenelm's well on the Sudeley estate to a town main, from which it was distributed by the Winchcombe Union Rural Sanitary Authority, who met the cost of installing mains for a domestic supply throughout much of the town by borrowing £1,000 from the Public Works Loan Board.[15]

It was decided to combine celebration of the queen's jubilee with inauguration of the water supply on the same day, Tuesday 21 June 1887. At that time William Charles Belcher, who had installed the first printing press in Winchcombe and ran a stationer's business, also reported the town's events for *The Evesham Journal and Four Shires Advertiser*. He was probably the reporter who described the day's events at great length in that newspaper, from which the following extracts are taken:

' ... The day was ushered in with a peal of 1,887 changes on the Parish Church bells, commencing at six o'clock in the morning ... As the morning advanced the entire population seemed astir, clothed in their Sunday best, the glorious summer sunshine infusing a feeling of warmth and happiness into every heart. The streets, too, presented a gayer appearance than they had worn for many a year. Strings of coloured streamers crossed the thoroughfares, and from the windows of numerous houses hung flags of all sizes and descriptions ... '

A thanksgiving service for the jubilee was held in the parish church, at which the vicar preached a sermon of gratitude for the queen's virtues and benign rule. The cere-monies then continued as follows:

' ... On leaving Church, the members [of the Winchcombe Clubs] re-formed in processional order, and accompanied by school children, with various flags and devices marched off to the Abbey Terrace, where a semi-circle was formed around the temporary fountain, erected for the ceremony of opening the Winchcombe Water Supply. The Square by this time had become thronged with people, and

Plate 9

presented quite a gay and holiday appearance …

Addressing the large assemblage present, Mr. E. S. Wood [the last high bailiff] said he had now the honour to offer for Mrs. Dent's acceptance the address which had recently been signed by the householders in the town as a slight acknowledgement of the noble gift that day completed …

Turning to Mrs. Dent, Mr. Wood, in the name of the town, then presented to her the address, which was engrossed in old English on vellum, and beautifully illuminated, with the impression of the ancient seal of the borough in colours …

At this point, the Vicar's little daughter, Miss Ada Balfour Noble Jackson, presented Mrs. Dent with a very handsome bouquet of choice white flowers, composed of arum lilies, orchids and maiden-hair ferns, adding at the same time the simple but impressive words: "Thank you very much for the water" … '

Mrs. Dent's response to this display of heartfelt gratitude dwelt partly on the virtues of her uncles and late husband, whose absence affected her deeply on such a public occasion, in the following words:

' … I hope you all believe what a really sincere pleasure it has always been to me and mine to take a part in anything relating to the good of Winchcombe, how for 40 years you and your interesting old town have ever been in my best thoughts, and how it was the great wish of those who are gone to leave an influence for good and not for evil among you. I seem to stand here today as their representative, and in their name, and to their memory, present you with what I know you all value, and which I hope both now, and in years to come, will remind you of good men and true – loyal to their Queen and country – and who would indeed have rejoiced in this day of Jubilee. (Loud Cheers).'

The reporter then described the ceremony's climax:

'Mrs. Dent then touched a small spring near at hand, instantly a stream of water, pure as crystal, leaped high into the air, amid loud clapping of hands. The band then played the National Anthem, which was taken up by all present, and so the ceremony ended ... '[16]

This moment is recorded in the photograph, unfortunately now rather faded, at Plate 9, showing Mrs. Dent and the assembled townspeople outside the house now known as St Kenelm's (then the home of Edmund Smith Wood, solicitor and last high bailiff) in Abbey Terrace. Later in the day, 500 of Winchcombe's inhabitants sat down to one of Emma Dent's generously provided meat teas; and the girls attending the day and Sunday schools each received a jubilee medal and new shilling.

Emma Dent was not the sole benefactress on this splendid day. The vicar and leading parishioners gave beef, plum pudding, tea and tobacco to eighty-four 'aged and infirm poor folks'. Edward Adlard and his wife provided the residents of Chandos almshouses with 'an excellent hot dinner'. Tea was provided at the Abbey for 120 children of the Baptist Union chapel and their teachers; and the Wesleyan Methodists laid on a substantial tea for their Sunday school. Finally, the workhouse inmates had beef and plum pudding, presumably with the blessing of the Board of Guardians.[17]

A modern fire engine

With the installation of a public water supply, the townspeople decided to equip the borough with a modern fire engine. The 1789 appliance had lasted over a hundred years and was hopelessly antiquated. In 1891 a list of 101 subscribers was compiled from amongst the town's leading citizens; a new fire engine was bought from Shand, Mason and company; and the old appliance was given to Mrs. Dent for display as a museum piece at Sudeley castle.[18] Acquisition of the fire engine was naturally followed by formation of a fire brigade, comprising a sergeant in charge (paid £5 annually) and five assistants (each receiving 10s. per year).[19]

The railway fails to connect

One benefit of Victorian progress that did not reach Winchcombe during the queen's reign was a connection to the fast-growing railway network. Although the difficult Cotswold terrain probably deterred some would-be railway speculators, an attempt was made in 1866 to promote a scheme for a branch-line from Beckford to Winchcombe. The proposal was set out in detail in The Winchcomb and Midland Railway Act 1866, which was enacted on 16 July 1866.[20] Section 5 of this Act describes the authorised length of railway as follows:

Plate 10

'A Railway, Five Miles and Six Furlongs or thereabouts in Length, commencing in the Parish of Beckford in the County of Gloucester by a Junction with the Ashchurch and Evesham Railway, and terminating in the Parish of Winchcomb in the said County of Gloucester near the Toll House at the North Street, at Gretton Turnpike Gates at Winchcomb.'

The Act names the railway's promoters as John Coucher Dent, William Smith, William Montagu Baillie, Francis Edwards and John Charles Handfield, who were authorised to form, with other subscribers, the corporate body to be known as the Winchcomb and Midland Railway Company. The major railway operator, then simply known as the Midland Railway Company, was authorised to subscribe to this new undertaking provided three-quarters of its shareholders approved. Section 6 of the 1866 Act provided for the new company's share capital to be £42,000 in £10 shares; and section 10 enabled it to borrow £14,000 on mortgage, once the capital was fully subscribed. Plans and sections of the proposed line were deposited as part of the statutory procedure; and the estimated cost of constructing the line was £40,595. The Act required the proposed railway to be completed within three years from 16 July 1866; and, if it were not, the company's powers lapsed for any uncompleted section.

The new company's first directors were nominated as John Coucher Dent, William Smith and John James Sexty, together with two others to be appointed at the first meeting. The directors had no discretion about the tolls and charges to be levied for passengers and freight that were specified in great detail in sections 27 to 32 of the Act. For example, the maximum charge for first-class travel was to be threepence per mile;

for second-class, twopence per mile; and for third-class, one penny farthing per mile.

Despite the considerable effort that must have been involved in producing detailed plans and financial estimates, and the substantial cost of promoting a railway act in parliament, the proposed railway was not built. It is unclear what brought about the promoters' decision not to proceed with the scheme. As the sum of £40,595 must have seemed very costly, at that time, to provide less than six miles of railway on a branch line terminating in Winchcombe, it presumably failed for lack of financial support. In the event, it was almost another forty years before the railway reached Winchcombe.

The Victorian era's achievement

The Victorian era was a time of hugely increasing self-confidence as British financiers and engineers helped to create an empire governed from Westminster and Whitehall; and the royal navy safeguarded trade routes across the oceans. Evidence of this national pride (sometimes misdescribed as jingoism) can be seen in the queen's jubilee celebrations in Winchcombe, one of which is recorded in the photograph at Plate 10. But the Victorian era's enduring legacy in the town was a profusion of fine buildings and new facilities, which then brought about its renewal and still delight the discerning eye.

1   *Tewkesbury Weekly Record*, 29 March 1856; GRO, D2218/3/20
2   Plan of Thomas Pardington's estate, 15 April 1865; GRO, D2579
3   J. A. Oakey: 'Reminiscences', page 9
4   information about The Anchor provided by Mr. Graham Stephenson of Anchor House, Winchcombe
5   Jean Bray: 'The Lady of Sudeley', Long Barn Books, 2000, is the biography of Emma Dent
6   J. A. Oakey, op cit, page 7
7   costs provided by Jean Bray for this and other buildings financed by the Dent family
8   Mortgage agreement dated 14 February 1872, GRO, D1675/ 1/4
9   Gloucestershire Notes & Queries, April-June 1895, Volume VI, Part VI, pages 133-134, contributed by Rev. John Taylor, then vicar of Winchcombe
10 further information provided by Mr G. Stephenson of Anchor House
11 Philip Styles collection; GRO, D3530/5
12 Jean Bray: 'The Lady of Sudeley', pages 100-101
13 The Winchcombe and Sudeley Record, Volume 2, No. 15, March 1891, page 64
14 information provided by Jean Bray
15 The Winchcombe and Sudeley Record, Volume 4, No 38, February 1893, page 197
16 The Winchcombe and Sudeley Record, Volume 4, No 38, February 1893, pages 191-195
17 The Winchcombe and Sudeley Record, Volume 4, No 38, February 1893, page 195
18 The Winchcombe and Sudeley Record, Volume 4, No 37, January 1893, pages 185-186
19 The Winchcombe and Sudeley Record, Volume 4, No 38, February 1893, page 198
20 The Winchcomb and Midland Railway Act, 1866, 29 & 30 Victoria, Cap. cxcvi, archived in House of Lords Record Office

CHAPTER 25

FURTHER STEPS IN FORMAL EDUCATION

After Townsend's school (established by the terms of George Townsend's charity) started in 1683, there was provision for three boys' schools: the other two were the King's school and Chandos grammar school. How these three separate establishments functioned independently is uncertain. The minutes of the borough corporation's meeting, on 3 February 1865, to consider how the King's school's master should be accommodated, indicate how that institution had operated since the early 1670s, as follows:

'Mr. Lapworth [master of the school] produced a copy of an agreement dated 5 January 1671 entered into between the then Bailiffs and Rev. Henry Thorn[e] of Oxford who had been elected Master of the School therein designated Her Majesty's [sic] Free School at Winchcomb and which is supposed to be that now known as the King's School whereby the said Henry Thorn[e] was to have possession of the said School House rent free provided he kept the premises in good and proper repair.'[1]

It emerges from this record and other sources that successive vicars of Winchcombe were responsible for educating boys attending the King's school, although the actual teaching may well have been undertaken by a paid assistant whom the vicar appointed.

At some stage, possibly as early as the 1690s, the King's school and Chandos grammar school were merged, with the vicar responsible for the boys' education. This arrangement seems to have continued until about 1832 when, following the death of the Rev. John Lates, it was considered too demanding for the vicar also to undertake educational responsibilities; and the two schools resumed their separate existence. In 1834 they were said to be in 'a ruinous and dilapidated state'.

In 1829 the charity commissioners reported that Townsend's school comprised a master and some twenty to thirty children of the parish who were being taught to read. The master was paid £20 per year and the school was described as 'well conducted'.[2] John Oakey attended this school in about 1853 or 1854, when the master was William Tovey, then aged over ninety, and described it as follows:

'My first school was the back kitchen of a cottage in Gloucester Street, … The schoolmaster was William Tovey, over 90 years of age. He died just after I was removed, aged 95. He sat on a high stool, for he was unable to get about very well.

He had a long stick however, with which he could reach us all, the room being not more than ten feet by ten, and we often got a rap on the head, I can tell you. If we were very refractory his daughter Rebecca took us in hand. She was not much over 70 …'[3]

The Townsend's school's inadequate premises and William Tovey's death probably led to its merger with the King's school in about 1855.

Shortly after the separation from the Chandos grammar school, the town's corporation adopted strict rules for management of the King's school. As they clearly describe how it was intended to operate, the rules are worth stating in full, as follows:

'1st. The School hours to be from nine till twelve in the morning and from two till five in the afternoon.

2nd. No boy to be admitted under eight years of age, nor continued beyond twelve, and to be a native or inhabitant of Winchcomb.

3rd. The Master to keep a book in which to register the name and age of every candidate in the regular order in which application may be made for him, and during the course of the same week to furnish in writing the particulars to the Governors.

4th. As often as a vacancy may occur on the Foundation, the place to be supplied by the senior boy in point of entrance on the list, who may then be eligible; but nevertheless, in every instance, the boys who shall have been the private pupils of the Master in his School for the space of the last preceding twelve months, and paid for to him, if they should be eligible to the Foundation with respect to age, birth and residence, to be entitled to the precedence over such as shall not previously have been his pupils.

5th. Under no pretence whatsoever, except prevented by illness, is a boy to absent himself from school; and if, in defiance of the regulations, he should so do, he shall, for the first offence, be reprimanded by the Master, and a task imposed; and should he in like manner offend a second time, he shall be utterly excluded the School, and his place instantly supplied by the next eligible candidate in rotation.

6th. No holydays to be allowed except a fortnight at Christmas, and (instead of the usual Midsummer vacation) the last fortnight in August; it being deemed that the boys may during the harvest be best enabled to render some little service to their respective parents.'[4]

These rules were approved on 16 September 1841 by Nathaniel Lloyd and Edmund Thomas Browne (as, respectively, high and low bailiff) and by four of the burgesses, Dennis Trenfield, Thomas Howman, Thomas Brydges and John Castle.

In the 1830s Richard Turner was master of the King's school: he was described as 'an agricultural labourer, with a talent for elementary arithmetic, but innocent of grammar and composition'.[5] These qualities were presumably considered adequate for teaching the children of small farmers and artisans. Shortly after the King's and Townsend's schools were amalgamated, John Oakey described his experience of the school as follows:

'… We were then transferred to the Kings and Townsends School, held in an old cottage where Mr. Wood's office now stands. The school fee was 9d. a week for two years, after which period there was no charge. The Master was Mr. Clement Augustus Cunningham, a great swell, but as poor as a church mouse. He taught penmanship thoroughly and the first two or three rules of arithmetic …'[6]

Plate 11

Clement Cunningham's poverty is confirmed by Emma Dent's record of money lent to him.[7] Nevertheless, despite the inadequate salary, he remained master of the King's school (as it was still called) until 1874. He was succeeded by John Sheldon, whose more generous salary was guaranteed by John Coucher Dent after his appointment on 13 July 1874.

Although it was regarded as the town's leading school during the seventeenth and eighteenth centuries, little is known about Chandos grammar school until the early nineteenth century. It was presumably held continuously in the original building in Chandos Street which became known, in the early twentieth century, as The Presbytery (because of its subsequent use as the Roman Catholic priest's residence). This building is illustrated in the photograph at Plate 11. In the 1840s the school's trustees appointed Charles Lapworth as master. Unhappily, he gained national notoriety in 1844 in newspaper reports of involvement in a flogging which allegedly resulted in the death of one of the boys, Algernon Conrad Carter. But, despite the boy's parents' strong representations and the inquest jury's critical comments on the master's conduct, Lapworth remained master of the school until his own death in 1866. He was succeeded by Thomas C. Webb who was a true scholar and, subsequently as church-warden, a transcriber and cataloguer of the Winchcombe vestry's records.

Formation of Winchcombe school board (1875)

The Education Act of 1870, immortalising the name of W. E. Forster, was intended to provide every English child under the age of thirteen with elementary education, although free of charge only to parents who could not afford the fees.

However, there was an uneasy compromise in the Act between denominational and non-sectarian educational principles, enabling denominational schools to continue unchanged where they met local needs satisfactorily. Otherwise, the Act provided for locally elected school boards to be established, with the power to levy a rate, build schools, appoint teachers and, eventually, to compel school attendance.[8]

The Act caused an educational upheaval in Winchcombe, largely because the Chandos grammar school could only accommodate 45 pupils in its then overcrowded building and the King's school was catering for 66 boys in accommodation intended for 52, whereas the officially estimated requirement was accommodation for a total of 150 boys. The problem resulted in a vigorous, inter-denominational squabble, in February 1875, during the election for Winchcombe Union's first school board. The board was to consist of seven members: eleven candidates were initially nominated, each representing a denominational interest. The Churchmen (or Anglicans) comprised William Brain, a Greet farmer; John Coucher Dent; the Rev. Robert Noble Jackson; Dr. Thomas Newman; William Smith of The Farm; and William Warder, a Gretton farmer. The Nonconformist interest was represented by James Grist, a Winchcombe draper and Wesleyan Methodist; John James Sexty, Winchcombe farmer and Baptist; Samuel Smith, Winchcombe surgeon and Unitarian; Thomas Ward Swinburne, wealthy owner of Corndean Hall and Baptist; and Joseph Townsend, a Winchcombe banker and Wesleyan Methodist. Two of the Churchmen, Dr. Thomas Newman and William Warder, quickly withdrew from the contest, leaving their four colleagues to oppose the five Nonconformists for the seven-member board.[9]

An attempt was then made to avoid the divisiveness and expense of a contested election. Nonconformist electoral arithmetic showed that they could not achieve more than three members of the Board and it was apparently obvious that the Unitarian, Samuel Smith, had no chance of being elected. Although James Grist was willing to withdraw, Samuel Smith's refusal to do so made a poll inevitable.

The election's central issue was whether a new school building was needed in Winchcombe. Thomas Swinburne was then building a new schoolroom, to accommodate about ninety pupils, in association with the new chapel he had just provided in Gretton Road (still surviving as the Cotswold Christian centre). It was suggested that this school building should be leased to provide the required additional accommodation. However, John Sexty opposed this suggestion and favoured building a new schoolroom as a more economical course in the longer term. Although Sexty and Swinburne were both staunch Nonconformists, they then engaged in a pamphleteering battle in which John Sexty argued that educational issues should be decided on principle, not on personalities, and included the following clarion call to all nonconformist voters:

'If as Nonconformists, we have not quite forgotten the traditions of our past history; if the wrongs, the struggles, and sufferings of three hundred years are not blotted from our memories, then I am sure we may meet next Wednesday with perfect confidence.'

Thomas Swinburne's response regretted what he regarded as an excessively denominational attitude and sought to encourage leasing his new building in Gretton

Road, rather than financing an expensive new school. Not to be outdone, the Rev. Noble Jackson published an election address denying a report that he favoured a costly, new school building and asking the electors to vote for him, John Coucher Dent and William Smith as the candidates who had given most support to Winchcombe's existing schools.

Although the war of words continued until polling day, the event passed off quietly. *The Evesham Journal's* reporter noted that there was no disorder and very little drunkenness. In the event, after some misguided efforts by agents and canvassers to direct votes towards the weaker candidates on either side, the four Churchmen were elected, with William Brain (614 votes) topping the poll and the Rev. Noble Jackson (585 votes) coming second. As had been expected, three of the Nonconformists were returned. Thomas Swinburne's strong support brought him 575 votes, whereas John Sexty obtained 495 and Joseph Townsend 310. While James Grist (273 votes) and Samuel Smith (31 votes) were both unsuccessful, the election demonstrated the continuing vitality of nonconformist opinion in the town.

Merger of King's and Chandos grammar schools

In 1876 the King's school and Chandos grammar school were amalgamated, occupying a new building in Chandos Street (on the site of the present Roman Catholic church). Thomas C. Webb was appointed as schoolmaster, at the miserly salary of £80 per year and capitation fees. Despite his valiant efforts, the grammar school appears to have achieved an average attendance of only twenty-four boys until 1907, when poor health forced his resignation. The master and twenty-three pupils attending the school in 1905 are shown in the photograph at Plate 12. Shortly after Thomas Webb's resignation the school was closed. Following a brief period of use as a working men's club, the buildings were sold for £200 in 1915 to Mrs. Elizabeth Forster of Postlip Hall, who arranged for the new school building to be adapted as part of the Roman Catholic church she had been determined to provide, and for the original Chandos grammar school building of 1621 to be converted for use as The Presbytery.

Although Winchcombe lost Chandos grammar school, income from the endowment of Lady Frances Chandos was used, from 1910, to provide scholarships for Winchcombe boys who qualified for grammar school education in Cheltenham. The endowment now continues in the Chandos exhibition foundation, a charity providing financial help for educational purposes to individuals or schools in the Winchcombe district.

Boys' elementary school

Meantime, a new elementary school for 160 older boys was provided in 1883, costing £1,713, at the southern end of Gretton road, opposite Thomas Swinburne's Union chapel. This school continued as a boys' school until 1952 and the building remains in use as the Winchcombe youth club.

Plate 12

Schooling for infants and young children

The origins of a school for Winchcombe's infants are difficult to establish. *The Evesham Journal's* report on 27 February 1875 refers to an infant school being held in the 1830s at the Packhorse inn, in Gloucester Street, where the teacher's name was Craddock. This school was mainly supported by Lady Swinburne of Corndean Hall, grandmother of Thomas Swinburne.[10] The school apparently continued until 1858 when the first formally recognised infant school was provided by William Smith of The Farm (the house at the foot of Hailes Street, subsequently rather grandiosely titled Charingworth Court). John Oakey describes William Smith as follows:

'... He was popularly called "Billy Smith of the Farm". He was small in stature but very active, and everything he did was properly done. He employed all the aged and unfit, whom no one else would employ. He was a real benefactor to Winchcombe ... His portrait, painted, deservedly hangs in the Town Hall, and is one of the most perfect likenesses of a man I have ever seen. At one time he owned a great deal of property in Winchcombe. Never a drunkard or gambler, he died comparatively poor, respected and beloved by the people ...'[11] [This portrait can still be seen in the Winchcombe museum in the town hall.]

The school building William Smith provided was completed in 1857, costing him personally about £2,500, and still stands on the southern side of Abbey Terrace at the corner of Vineyard Street. (It is now occupied by the workingmen's club and

Plate 13

various commercial uses.) The building is shown in the photograph at Plate 13, probably taken between 1860 and 1865. This is possibly the oldest surviving photograph of Abbey Terrace. The expense of maintaining this school was initially borne by William Smith and John Coucher Dent, with some help from a government grant. The first master of the school was James Henry Wark; and Hannah Wark, his wife, was schoolmistress.

Dent's National School

Despite this infants' school's success, the Dents were keen to establish a National School in the town, for which a sum of £1,200 was available as a legacy in John Dent's will. As already described in Chapter 24, this intention was realised, ten years later, when Drayton Wyatt designed and supervised the building of the school immediately to the west of the parish church in Gloucester Street. The school was ready to open on 1 January 1868. The opening ceremony was naturally an occasion for Emma Dent to present an address to each child attending and to give an entertainment and speech to their parents in the evening.[12] Her address to the children carefully prepared boys and girls for later life as follows:

'... at the time when you leave the National School, we would particularly urge the boys *at once* to enrol their names as attendants of the night school ... because ... those who passed at once from the National to the Night-School, are now amongst the steadiest, the best, and the best informed of our young men in Winchcombe and its neighbourhood. For you, girls, no night school is provided; it being thought far better that you should be at home without anything to call you out of doors after dark, and I am certain of this, that each one of you must feel that home is the best place for you then.

Now, when you leave school, you have in general to go at once to service, or the paper mill, or take an active part in home duties, in any case, the real lesson of life and its trials for you will then begin ...'

Later in the day, Mrs. Dent explained her deeply felt purpose in providing the school, as follows:

'... I often feel a very great responsibility, living in the big castle – and having so many more of the good things of this life: and when I have heard the voice of God telling me to help these my sisters, it has always seemed to me as if you were most to be helped by helping your children, helping them to become good women, and good wives and mothers, when it will be their turn to take your places ...'

William Smith's infants' school continued to provide for the youngest children after Dent's National School opened on 13 January 1868, with the teaching duties divided between Miss Margaret Malins and Miss Elizabeth Freeman. Two surviving log-books, kept by successive schoolmistresses for the next forty years give an almost day-to-day account of the new school's progress. The opening entry on 13 January 1868 is:

'I – Elizabeth Freeman commenced my duties as School Mistress for the first time in this School, admitted 4 children, viz, Martin Oliver, Charles Hall, John Late and Laura Reeks.'

The number of children attending the new school grew quickly and had reached 111 after two months. At first Miss Freeman taught all the children single-handed in a schoolroom measuring 50 feet long and 24 feet wide. In June 1868, with more than 140 children attending, Margaret Corbitt was appointed as an assistant. But, as she was a pupil-teacher and may not have been aged more than fifteen, Elizabeth Freeman continued to bear the main responsibility for teaching the school's four classes. Later in the same month, Lucy Pardington was appointed as another assistant pupil-teacher.

When John Coucher Dent carried out the school's first inspection, on 3 July 1868, he recorded the following report in the log-book:

'The Infant School has made a good beginning under Miss Freeman. Those presented for examination have passed without a failure very creditably. The other classes are carefully taught. The Religious Instruction is satisfactory. The Marching, Singing and Exercises are as they should be. The children are tidy, cheerful and nicely behaved.'

Following his appointment as vicar, the Rev. Robert Noble Jackson took a keen interest in the school's progress and may well have encouraged Elizabeth Freeman to persevere in what must sometimes have been an onerous task. Some of the 140 children came to school from outside the town and all of them were aged under eight. Reports of sickness and epidemics appear frequently in the log-books; and, because small children could not walk the miry roads into the town, bad weather reduced the attendance, especially in winter. School holidays differed little from the present arrangements, except that the summer holiday, from mid-August to mid-September, was known as 'harvest vacation'. Small children were still expected to help in the fields where many of their parents worked during the harvest; and the vital task of gleaning, after the corn had been gathered, often provided an essential supplement to poor families' incomes.

In April 1875 the newly elected Winchcombe United District School Board became responsible for the infants' school. The only difference Elizabeth Freeman noticed was the requirement to keep an extra account book, which the Board's clerk, Edmund Smith Wood, regularly examined. But there was some financial benefit for parents: the Board reduced the weekly fee from 3d., or 2d. for 'tradesmen's children', to 1d. for all children. By 1885 the school comprised four classes and a kindergarten. The main subjects were reading, writing and arithmetic; but there was also needlework and music. Much attention was devoted to marching and drill, whether as a discipline or a form of physical training. On 28 May 1885 Elizabeth Freeman's entry in the school's log-book simply says: 'My duties as Mistress expire today'. Alice Malpass succeeded her on 6 July.

In 1886 the infants' school was moved to the Wesleyan Methodist chapel in Cowl Lane. Despite the fact that it had been situated next to the Pardington family's pigsty in Cowl Lane (with sales of pigs held on Sunday mornings), the chapel of 1810 had been improved internally in 1862 and had served the Methodists well. However, some of the leading Methodists wanted to move to a better site and to provide a permanent manse for the minister. Thus, when the former chapel was vacated in 1886, Emma Dent was able to buy the building for £195.[13] On her instructions, Drayton Wyatt extended and remodelled the building's face so that it stood level with the frontage of the adjacent cottage; and John Oakey undertook the building work to transform it into a school.[14] However, the stern inscription in stone above the newly-constructed entrance to the building is undoubtedly Emma Dent's personal inspiration: 'Inspector noster est Deus'. The renovated premises were described as 'good in themselves, and a very great improvement on the older ones'.

The year 1887 was queen Victoria's golden jubilee and the school's log-book records that 'Mrs. Dent visited and distributed Jubilee Medals to all the children' on 20 June. Entries for November 1888 indicate that pupils' health was not merely at risk from childhood's common ailments. On 2 November, 'Five children have been absent, smallpox being in the families'; and, on 9 November, 'Very poor attendance throughout the week and especially today. Parents are afraid to send their children owing to the smallpox'.

Alice Malpass ceased to be schoolmistress in May 1890. She was succeeded in the following month by Francis Hacker, who was helped by two assistant mistresses. The three teachers had to cope with as many as 160 children when there was full attendance. Precautions for the children's health were still very basic: as late as 18 March 1904, the schoolmistress reported:

'Mr. Gardner, the new correspondent, has been into School this morning. He has sent three buckets containing sawdust – he wished me to pour carbolic acid over it so as to disinfect the School as there are three cases of small pox in the town.'

However, there were happier moments in the lives of Winchcombe's youngest children, as the schoolmistress described in her own evocative record of the Empire Day celebrations, on 27 May 1907, as follows:

'Empire Day was celebrated this morning – Being a fine warm day, after the registers were marked and the flags distributed, the children were marched into the playground. The Union Jack was hoisted, the children then sang the National Anthem – after which Class I recited a piece entitled "The British Flag" – then they sang "Flag of Britain". After this the children marched past the flag, each saluting as they passed. The children made a very pretty picture with their little flags and happy faces – that the two gentlemen of the Committee present wished to have their photos taken. Mr. Hawley was sent for, and after the March past, the children were arranged in two groups and photographed. They were then marshalled into the School room where each child received a bun and a packet of sweets – the National Anthem was again sung and three cheers given for the King – after which the children were dismissed, a half holiday granted for the afternoon.'

But there were also tragic events, such as the following report made only four days later in 1907:

'The attendance has not been good this week. Several children have chicken pox. Received a note from Mrs. Jennings stating that her little girl Connie had a sore throat

(Monday). Doctor was sent for, he pronounced it diphtheria in a very bad form, she died yesterday.'

In 1897 the buildings the Dent family had provided for the National School (immediately to the west of the parish church) were enlarged so that they could accommodate up to 170 older girls, after they had left the infants' school. This arrangement continued until 1952.

Private schools

There was also some scope for private educational enterprise in Winchcombe during the nineteenth and early-twentieth centuries. Winchcombe trade directories for 1856 and 1866 show that Misses Elizabeth and Mary Tombs maintained a ladies' school in North Street (presumably in the house of their parents, Edward and Mary Tombs) during those years.[15] And Kelly's Directory for 1879 records that Miss Maria Lapworth (presumably Charles Lapworth's daughter) then ran a young ladies' boarding school in Queen Square. An example of a preparatory school is shown in David Aldred's book of photographs taken in Bishop's Cleeve and Winchcombe: Slatter's preparatory school was kept in the dwelling known as Fairview House (now No. 25) in Hailes Street from about 1870 until at least 1939.[16] This establishment had started as a young ladies' school and began to admit boys in the 1920s.

Although educational provision was still far from ideal in the early twentieth century, the Victorian age had seen great improvement, especially in girls' education. A foundation had been laid for the further development later generations would expect.

1   Borough of Winchcombe minute book from 1837 onwards, GRO, D 1675/1/1
2   Further Report of the Commissioners for Inquiring concerning Charities, County of Gloucester, 1829, No. xxi, page 165
3   J. A. Oakey: 'Reminiscences', 1936, page 15
4   GRO, D 1675/1/1
5   article in The Evesham Journal, 27 February 1875, archived on microfilm in Evesham Library
6   J. A. Oakey, op cit, page 15
7   Jean Bray: 'The Lady of Sudeley', page 49
8   E. L. Woodward: 'The Age of Reform, 1815-1870', page 464
9   A full account of the School Board election is given in The Evesham Journal, 27 February 1875
10   article in The Evesham Journal, 27 February 1875
11   J. A. Oakey, op cit, page 22
12   Emma Dent: 'A Few Words to the Mothers and Children of Winchcombe, January 1, 1868', GRO, D 2218/ 3/16
13   F. C. Adey: 'A Cotswold Methodist Heritage', 1979, page 59
14   J. A. Oakey, op cit, page 29
15   Kelly's Directory, 1856; Morris Directory, 1866
16   D. H. Aldred: 'Bishop's Cleeve to Winchcombe in Old Photographs', Alan Sutton, 1987, page 90

CHAPTER 26

THE VICTORIAN ERA ENDS

A t the start of the 1870s the only nation-wide system of local government was the administration, since 1836, of the Poor Law, represented in the Winchcombe district by the board of guardians for the Winchcombe Poor Law Union. Outside the major towns, control of the county was still effectively in the hands of the justices of the peace, meeting in quarter sessions. In Winchcombe, the borough's corporation retained certain residual functions, such as collection of market tolls, and owned the town hall; but it was unable, through lack of powers and adequate income, to fulfil the range of municipal functions needed in a developing community. By the end of the nineteenth century, considerable changes would have occurred in this rather haphazard system of providing local services.

The rural sanitary authority

As a result of central government's overdue reform of sanitary administration, the Winchcombe Union Rural Sanitary Authority was established in 1872 to be responsible for sanitation and water supply. As its title implies, the authority's administrative area was the same as that of the board of guardians. The authority was managed by a committee, which included the three members of the board of guardians for Winchcombe parish, seven 'gentlemen of the town', the medical officer of health, the sanitary inspector and the board's clerk (J. H. Stephens, who was later appointed clerk to Winchcombe rural district council and to the board of guardians).[1]

Abolition of Winchcombe corporation

The Municipal Corporations Act of 1835 had reformed the great majority of ancient corporations in England, but some boroughs were not affected by the Act because their population was considered too small. These places included Winchcombe and Chipping Campden. The smaller boroughs were eventually dealt with by the Municipal Corporations Act of 1883, which provided for the remaining self-elected corporations to be abolished, on 25 March 1886, and for their property to be devoted to the local inhabitants' benefit in accordance with a scheme to be formulated by the Charity Commissioners. The practical result of this legislation in Winchcombe was that an assistant charity commissioner, the Hon. T. H. W. Pelham, held a public inquiry at the town hall on Wednesday, 23 March 1887, to establish what the corporation's property and income had been at the date of abolition; what should be done with any surplus; and how the remaining property should be administered. This inquiry was well attended by the leading townspeople and fully reported in *The Evesham Journal* for 26 March 1887.[2]

Until its abolition, Winchcombe corporation had continued to consist of the two bailiffs and ten burgesses. The last holders of these historic offices were: Edmund Smith Wood, high bailiff (a solicitor); Dr. William Cox, low bailiff; and the following burgesses – the Rev. Noble Jackson, David Harvey (gentleman), Charles Austin (grocer), Richard Castle (saddler), James Grist (draper), Edward Adlard (described as gentleman of Postlip), George Smith junior (grocer), Joseph Hall (plasterer), Henry Pearson (carpenter) and Thomas A. Slatter (described as high bailiff of the county court). Despite Edmund Smith Wood's practical experience as high bailiff, the assistant commissioner had difficulty in establishing what the corporation owned: it was clear that they owned the town hall (although it was still mortgaged to the Dent family) and the borough's two silver maces; but there was doubt about the ownership of land left in trust for certain charities which the corporation had in practice administered. There was also some doubt about the corporation's income, although it was clearly small and intermittent: the income from letting the large room in the town hall for concerts and lectures was said to average £10 annually; there was some income from leasing to stallholders the market standings in the ground-floor area of the town hall; and there were also small sums (£3 3s. in 1885, for example) from tolls for fairs and shows allowed by custom in Abbey Terrace. Edmund Smith Wood was careful to point out that the shows were 'a great nuisance to the inhabitants of Abbey Terrace' and, as a resident there himself, he would like to see them stopped. The only assured income available to the corporation had been for letting the room used as a court by the justices at £10 annually and as the county court at £6 annually, together with the letting of a ground-floor store room at £8. From this sum of £24, such expenses as the hallkeeper's salary, rates and the cost of repairs had to be met.

When the inquiry turned to discussion about how any surplus corporation income might in future be spent for the townspeople's benefit, the assistant commissioner was presented with a variety of possibilities. J. H. Stephens urged that any funds should be used to pave the streets (by which he apparently meant the creation of pavements for pedestrian use); but Edmund Smith Wood maintained that the cost of the town's few existing pavements had been met from Townsend's charity and was now the highway board's responsibility, although the board had refused to accept it until they had been taken to quarter sessions and compelled (presumably by a court order) to repair the footways. The Rev. Noble Jackson was supported by others in his suggestion that any surplus income should be invested in a fund for the purpose of repairing and improving the town hall; and W. S. Smith said that income should be used to provide a free public library in the town hall. However, this suggestion did not appeal to one of the last burgesses, James Grist: he proposed selling the town hall to the brewing company which owned the adjacent Marquis of Granby public house (on the western side of North Street) and buying 'the Infant Schoolroom' (by which he presumably meant the infants' school William Smith had provided in Abbey Terrace) for use as a town hall. At this stage, the assistant commissioner attempted to shorten the proceedings by pointing out, rather unkindly in these circumstances, that Winchcombe no longer needed a town hall and its existence was the only excuse for maintaining it.

Despite the assistant commissioner's scepticism about retaining the town hall, the scheme subsequently approved by the Charity Commissioners for disposal of the borough corporation's property provided for the building to be vested in a newly established Town Trust, which was set up as a charity in February 1891 and still carries out its original functions. Thus, although the town hall was not needed by Winchcombe rural district council, when the council was instituted as part of further local government reform in 1894, the building itself, on the visually important site at The Cross, has survived to remind later generations of Winchcombe's former status as an ancient royal borough, proudly administered by its two bailiffs and ten burgesses. However, the townspeople's predominant view in the 1890s was probably satisfaction that the largely moribund corporation was at last being replaced by a directly-elected council.

Queen Victoria's golden jubilee

Although her name would eventually be synonymous with the era of British imperial power, queen Victoria was an unpopular monarch in 1870. Following the death of her beloved Albert, prince consort, she had become increasingly reclusive and neglected her public duties. However, 1871 proved to be the start of a revival in the queen's popularity, seemingly due to public sympathy for her, and subsequently for the prince of Wales, during illness each of them experienced in that year.[3] Subsequently, the monarchy's standing steadily improved until, by the golden jubilee year of 1887, there was a national expression of overwhelming loyalty and patriotism, with 21 June appointed as 'Jubilee Day'. On that evening bonfires were lit on hills throughout the land, with the starting signal being given by lighting a fire on the Malverns.

Winchcombe's leading inhabitants held a public meeting at the town hall on Friday, 18 March 1887, to consider how they might best celebrate the jubilee. The vicar, Robert Noble Jackson, was voted chairman for the occasion: in his opening remarks he was careful to emphasise that, despite his great loyalty to, and admiration for, the queen, 'the present depressed state of agriculture and business' required the assembly not to adopt any over-ambitious and costly proposal.[4] He then mentioned a number of schemes which were seemingly being discussed in the town, as follows: a new town hall; a better school house for the grammar school; a new clock for the parish church's tower; a portrait of the queen by a local artist to be placed in the town hall; a drinking fountain to be erected in Abbey Terrace; and a fete to be held in the town on Jubilee Day, with a free tea provided for every woman inhabitant of Winchcombe who was the same age as, or older than, the queen. The vicar then invited comments on these proposals or other ideas.

A lively discussion followed. William Short (town crier) suggested building new almshouses because he considered the existing Chandos almshouses 'a discredit to the town'; but Thomas C. Webb (master of Chandos grammar school and a church-warden) immediately opposed this suggestion, saying that much had recently been done to make the accommodation more comfortable and to ensure that the old people were cared for properly. James Grist then suggested that some public baths should be provided because 'it would tend to promote health and cleanliness among the youth of the town, besides affording them the opportunity of learning the art of swimming'. He pointed out that a good site for this purpose existed at the back of the old Sudeley mill, which could readily be adapted for a swimming bath if Mrs. Dent would permit it. Richard Castle seconded this suggestion; but, in later discussion, Dr. William Cox doubted whether there would be lasting enthusiasm for the project. Frank Bird (a partner in Postlip paper mills) then intervened to propose buying a new fire engine to replace the existing one, which 'was perfectly useless'. Thomas C. Webb seconded this proposal.

At this juncture a lengthy intervention by Edmund Smith Wood characterised most of these suggestions as over-ambitious and too costly for Winchcombe: he thought that 'a feast for the poor people' of the town should suffice and he reminded the meeting that, provided Mrs. Dent and the rural sanitary authority had completed the work, it was intended to inaugurate the town's new water supply on 24 June as part of the jubilee celebration. But this call for prudent expense did not impress Dr. Cox, who thought 'they should do that which would prove most beneficial to the working classes'. Unsurprisingly, he advocated providing a cottage hospital in the town which would involve converting an existing cottage for this purpose, costing about £100, with annual running costs of between £60 and £70.

The vicar then attempted to sum up the merits of the proposals and assess how much support each had obtained. On a show of hands, about forty people supported public baths; about twenty favoured a cottage hospital; and three were for a new parish church clock and two for a new fire engine. 'A forest of hands' was raised in favour of a feast for the poor and the young people of the town. The meeting concluded by appointing a committee of twenty-one of the leading townsmen to consider the merits of the proposals.

The Evesham Journal's issue of 26 March 1887 went on to report that, after a long discussion, this committee had decided to recommend that Winchcombe's jubilee celebration should take the form of 'a dinner to all the poor people over the age of fifty, and a tea to all the school children, and any others under the age of thirteen'. The committee had reportedly examined the possible provision of a public swimming bath, but had concluded that sufficient money could not be collected for the feast and the swimming bath. Consequently, they decided to recommend setting up a private company to establish the baths as a permanent jubilee memorial. The proposed company would have capital of £200, raised by issuing 400 ten-shilling shares, which was considered sufficient to provide a covered-in bath, measuring 50 feet by 24 feet, properly heated, and equipped with dressing rooms. A sub-committee was to be formed which would invite the public to subscribe for shares and carry the project forward.

At this early stage, James Grist and Richard Castle (the chief supporters of the proposed swimming bath) must have been pleased that it seemed likely to go ahead. If so, they would perhaps have been surprised by Dr. Cox's determination to ensure that Winchcombe was provided with a cottage hospital. Dr. Cox set about canvassing support for his own project with such energy and enthusiasm that, by 18 June 1887, *The Evesham Journal* was able to publish the first list of ninety-four subscribers to the project. The subscription list was headed by Emma Dent promising a donation of £10 and an annual subscription of £5, and Lord Sudeley promising a £10 donation and £3 3s. annual subscription. Lord Elcho, Edward Adlard and James Agg-Gardner M.P. each promised a donation of £5 and an annual subscription of £2 2s. Not all the subscriptions were sums of money: William Pardington promised a daily supply of milk from his farm dairy and one of the local chemists, A. Lee Hall whose shop was at The Cross, opposite The George, promised drugs for the hospital's patients.

Faced with such enthusiasm for the rival project, the supporters of a swimming bath company presumably accepted defeat on this occasion; although the project was subsequently revived, as this chapter explains later.

However, instead of converting an existing cottage, as Dr. Cox had originally suggested, a site was bought on the eastern side of North Street for £130 and work on a purpose-built cottage hospital started early in 1888. Lord Elcho again proved to be a most generous supporter, providing ready-worked stone for the frontage at his own cost.[5] The building work was carried out by John Oakey, then aged forty-one and well-established as an independent builder in the town.[6] The hospital was ready to admit the first patient on 27 October 1888 and Dr. Cox was appointed, appropriately,

as medical officer. The project's total cost of £473 (including about £100 for furnishing and fitments) proved considerably more than he had originally estimated for a converted building, but it was raised entirely from voluntary subscriptions and fund-raising events. Although this cottage hospital was superseded by the present Winchcombe hospital in 1928, the rock-faced building still stands at 23 North Street, now used as a private dwelling (previously known as Glanville and more recently as Bostock House). When the hospital use ceased, the first residential occupier was the grandson of the Victorian hymn writer Henry Francis Lyte, author of 'Abide with me'. The borough's coat of arms on the building's facade is its sole reminder of queen Victoria's golden jubilee.

The strength of nonconformity

Evangelical religious belief provided the moral foundation of the Victorian era. Regular church attendance, Sunday school and family Bible reading were interwoven in the nation's religious fabric to a nowadays-inconceivable extent.

Methodism continued to flourish in Winchcombe in this favourable climate and became more closely associated with Liberal political opinion, although not exclusively. At the start of the 1880s about a hundred children regularly attended the Methodist Sunday school. But the accommodation available to the minister and the congregation had become increasingly unsatisfactory. As there was no manse in the town, it was difficult to persuade a married man to remain as minister: although the Pearson family gave the Methodist church the exquisite, seventeenth-century stone-built house at the foot of Hailes Street (now known as The Follies) for the manse in 1869, it was subject to the existing occupier's life tenancy and did not become available to the minister until 1877.[7]

Successive ministers and leading Methodists had longed to provide a new chapel, to replace the building in Cowl Lane which was seventy years old in 1880; but finding a satisfactory site proved difficult. This problem appears to have been solved by the enterprise and initiative of James Grist and Henry Pearson, both of whom were prominent Methodists and (as already mentioned earlier in this chapter) sufficiently respected in the town to serve as corporation burgesses. In 1883 Henry Pearson succeeded in buying for the sum of £410 the comparatively large site on the southern side of High Street, then occupied by James Harding's bakery and an adjacent cottage, to the east of Dr. Cox's house in Abbey Terrace (the building now used by Lloyds-TSB bank). He used the rear portion of this site to build an attractive house for his family and sold the front part (including the existing buildings) to the Methodist building committee for £360.[8] As the site sloped quite appreciably downwards from High Street, building the new chapel involved demolition of the existing bakery and cottage and excavation of substantial foundations to support a building 70 feet long and 34 feet wide, set back from the highway at a higher floor level. However, the foundation stone was laid on 3 December 1884 and the new chapel was opened on 24 June 1885. The total cost, including the furnishings, amounted to £1,740, of which £1,222 had already been given or promised. Part of the outstanding balance came by way of £195 for the sale of the Cowl Lane chapel to Mrs. Dent; the remainder was cleared by voluntary giving within the year.[9]

Sadly, James Grist and Henry Pearson lived only for another two years, dying within a month of each other in November and December 1887. But Henry Pearson's daughters, Hester and Elizabeth, generously gave the family's house their father had built, to the rear of the chapel, for the manse in 1889.[10]

The leading Congregationalist in Winchcombe district was Thomas Swinburne of

Corndean Hall. He arranged for the imposing Congregational chapel to be built, on the western side of Gretton Road, between 1873 and 1878. This involved removing a large thatched barn previously on the site and bringing as much stone as was reusable from the former silk mill building (which had finally closed in 1872).[11] The manse, on the southern side of the chapel, was added in about 1880. Taking the title from the Congregationalist Union of England and Wales, this chapel was known as the Union Church. The building still dominates this visually important site at the southern end of Gretton Road, providing an evangelical church for the Winchcombe district, now known as Cotswold Christian centre.

An expression of patriotism

The patriotic feelings which had characterised the silver jubilee celebrations, and were repeated in 1897 at the queen's diamond jubilee, were closely allied to notions of British imperialism. It was widely believed that an effective imperial power required properly trained armed forces to uphold its interests, wherever they might be threatened. One expression of these views was the willingness of some young men to join volunteer army battalions.

In Winchcombe this feeling was exemplified by several requests to the War Office, between 1886 and 1889, to form a company of the First Gloucestershire Volunteer Royal Engineers. Eventually, the War Office agreed to these requests in June 1889 and a meeting was held in the town hall on 15 July at which some seventy men submitted themselves as candidates. By 31 July eighty-two men had been enrolled in G (Winchcombe) company, comprising four sergeants, four corporals, four second corporals and seventy sappers, under company sergeant-major Maurice Bailey. Another eighteen sappers joined the ranks towards the end of the year.[12]

G company's first important public engagement was a church parade on Sunday, 17 November 1889, when they assembled at 10.15 a.m. in the Abbey Field (approximately the area now on either side of Barnmeadow Road). Led by the battalion's commandant (a lieutenant-colonel of the Royal Engineers) and its full band, the company marched by way of Back Lane, The Anchor, North Street and The Cross to the parish church. A contemporary description of the scene is as follows:

'The morning, though cloudy, happily held fine, and as the Company, in their new scarlet uniforms and spiked helmets, reached The Cross, the scene presented was of the most animated character. The streets were literally packed. Natives and strangers were there; old men with hoary locks, and sprightly youths and maidens, all turned out to see the soldiers.'

The church service was conducted by the vicar, Frederick Binyon, who had succeeded Robert Noble Jackson the previous year, with Dr. William Cox in his other capacity as choirmaster, and Walter Haslum, himself one of the volunteer sappers, as organist. Appropriately, the service ended with a stirring rendering of 'Onward, Christian soldiers' and the national anthem. G company was then marched away to The Cross, where the commandant congratulated them on the turnout and warned that they still had a great deal to learn. Finally, their drill-instructor dismissed the parade.

At this distance from 1889 it is impossible to tell whether any of G company's volunteers seriously contemplated the reality of a soldier's life. But there appears to have been a tragic sequel for at least one of them. The parish church's memorial to seven men from Winchcombe who gave their lives in the Boer War (or the South African War as it was officially described) records that private Charles Knight of the Second Rifle Brigade died at Ladysmith on 6 April 1900. He was almost certainly sapper Charles Knight who had enrolled in G company in July 1889.

Emma Dent's last years

In addition to major building works she commissioned at Sudeley castle, Emma Dent continued to lavish improvements on the town. In 1884 she had arranged for John Oakey completely to rebuild the then very dilapidated house in Gloucester Street, to the west of Dent's school, known as Three Gables. Mrs. Dent wanted the rebuilt house to appear in keeping with its surroundings and therefore instructed John Oakey to use as much old building stone as was available. Much later, in the 1920s, he had to explain to two sightseers who thought it was a fifteenth-century building that he had built it.[13] The building, in its condition before the 1884 rebuilding, is illustrated in the photograph at Plate 14. Mrs. Dent also commissioned John Oakey to build the bridges needed to provide a new carriage drive to Sudeley castle from the foot of Vineyard Street in 1891. His memoirs describe how, during excavation of the foundations for Vineyard Street bridge over the river Isbourne, he found the stump of the town's ducking school which had been used for punishing scolding women.[14] The

Plate 14

siting of this punishment engine explains why the street had once been called Duck Street (sometimes also referred to as Duke Street, for no apparent reason).

Queen Victoria's diamond jubilee in 1897 was the occasion for Mrs. Dent to arrange for the parish church's clock to be substantially refurbished and for a new preacher's cross to be erected in the southern corner of the churchyard, where only the stump of the earlier cross then remained. With her typical concern for architectural detail, Mrs. Dent provided for the new cross to be a modified copy of what was considered to be a fifteenth-century cross in the parish churchyard at Wedmore in Somerset. The queen's diamond jubilee was commemorated in Winchcombe by a thanksgiving service in the parish church on Sunday, 20 June 1897, followed by a dedication of the restored cross.

James Grist's suggested provision of a swimming bath, during the public meeting in March 1887 to discuss how the queen's golden jubilee should be remembered, had not been overlooked. About ten years later, in what was perhaps her most imaginative gift to the town, Emma Dent enabled this proposal to be realised. At a cost of £400, she arranged for the Beesmoor Brook to be diverted, at a point to the north-east of Almsbury Farm, just above its confluence with the river Isbourne, to provide an attractive swimming bath equipped with a diving board and spring board. The bath was situated in the area originally suggested by James Grist, which was approximately the land now adjacent to gardens of the Sudeley estate holiday cottages, with an entrance to the bath from the foot of Castle Street. A bowling green was subsequently laid out in the same area.

Although Emma Dent's generosity continued into the 1890s, there were increasing signs of tension with some of the leading townspeople during her last years. Two main causes perhaps explain this tension. First, she fervently supported the Tory cause in national and local elections, which inevitably resulted in conflict with people in the district who held Liberal opinions. These disagreements were so serious that they even resulted in the temporary dismissal from building work at Sudeley of John Oakey, who was a strong admirer of Gladstone and did not attempt to conceal his Liberal views in her presence.[15] Secondly, there was some resentment that her influence over matters which were properly the townspeople's business had become too strong. This feeling was exemplified by some of the views expressed towards the end of the assistant charity commissioner's inquiry into the corporation's property on 23 March 1887.

On that occasion Edmund Smith Wood had suggested that the borough's maces should in future be kept in the museum Mrs. Dent had established at Sudeley castle; but Thomas Swinburne and J. H. Stephens opposed this suggestion and submitted the counter-proposal, supported by the vicar Robert Noble Jackson, that the parish stocks should be returned from the Sudeley castle museum to their former position at the town hall. George Troughton even asked rhetorically whether the stocks might have been stolen.[16] The sequel to this episode was a short report in *The Evesham Journal* for 2 April 1887, clearly inspired by information Mrs. Dent provided, pointing out that the stocks had been neglected in the past and were taken to Sudeley castle for safe keeping with the specific authority of Winchcombe's penultimate high bailiff, Dr. Thomas Newman.

Plate 15

The report offered the immediate restoration of the stocks to the town and also suggested that Jacobean House (which had been preserved and restored at the Dent family's expense) might be re-purchased by the town for possible use as a cottage hospital.[17] While this report may well have corrected factual misunderstandings in some townspeople's minds, what had been said at the inquiry was probably intended to harm Emma Dent's reputation and create resentment of her in the town.

Ill health and partial blindness clouded Emma Dent's last year, although she apparently remained lucid until the end on 22 February 1900, a few days before her seventy-seventh birthday. It is very difficult to assess exactly what the Dent family spent on new facilities and improvements in Winchcombe during the Victorian era. At the very least, it exceeded £8,000; but this estimate omits Emma Dent's numerous personal gifts to individuals and good causes in the town. Almost as important as her financial contribution to the town's welfare was the example of her unusual combination of strong religious belief, moral duty, antiquarian interest and scientific curiosity. In his memorial address in the parish church three days after her death the vicar, the Rev. Dr. John Taylor, caught something of her essence in the following passage:

'No one could come into contact with her without receiving the impression of a vigorous personality. A French archaeologist who happened to meet her in this church turned to me after she had gone and exclaimed enthusiastically, "But she is a queen". He was right. She was a queen, not only in bearing but in munificence.'

And, despite the resentments she had sometimes endured from certain townspeople, a public subscription to commemorate her life and recognise her generosity to the town and its people enabled three stained glass windows to be placed, in 1901, in the north aisle of the parish church she cherished. The figures portrayed in each window were carefully chosen to represent virtues exemplified in Emma Dent's life: St Barbara for concord and industry, St Mary of Bethany who was full of good works; and St Catherine whose guide was the truth.[18] Just as Jan van Eyck's medieval painting of St Barbara shows her usual emblem of a tower in the background, the tower held in St Barbara's left hand in this stained glass window is reputedly a model of the north tower Emma Dent commissioned at Sudeley castle in 1890. The symbolism would have appealed greatly to her.

Queen Victoria's death occurred exactly eleven months after Emma Dent's – on 22 January 1901. The sixty-four years of the Victorian era had seen much-needed improvements in Winchcombe's fabric and institutions, as well as a lessening in some workingmen's ingrained habits of hard drinking and rough pastimes. But certain characteristics were largely unchanged at the turn of the century: the district's economy was still essentially agricultural; poor transport, particularly towards Cheltenham, maintained a sense of isolation; educational opportunity was still very limited, despite the improvement in schools; and, perhaps above all, grinding poverty and fear of the Union workhouse, especially in old age, afflicted many families whose breadwinner was an agricultural labourer.

1   The Winchcombe and Sudeley Record, Volume 4, No. 38, February 1893, page 198
2   *The Evesham Journal*, 26 March 1887, archived on microfilm in Evesham Library
3   Sir Robert Ensor: 'England, 1870-1914', The Oxford History of England, 1936, page 26
4   *The Evesham Journal*, 26 March 1887, archived on microfilm in Evesham Library
5   The Winchcombe and Sudeley Record, Volume 1, No. 1, January 1890, page 4
6   J. A. Oakey: 'Reminiscences', 1936, page 29
7   F. C. Adey: 'A Cotswold Methodist Heritage', page 52
8   F. C. Adey: op cit, page 58
9   F. C. Adey: op cit, page 59
10   F. C. Adey: op cit, page 59
11   J. A. Oakey: op cit, page 5
12   The Winchcombe and Sudeley Record, Volume 1, No. 1, January 1890, pages 2-3
13   J. A. Oakey, op cit, page 9
14   J. A. Oakey, op cit, page 7
15   Jean Bray: 'The Lady of Sudeley', page 127
16   *The Evesham Journal*, 26 March 1887
17   *The Evesham Journal*, 2 April 1887
18   Although the central one of the three stained glass windows gives the figure's title as St Mary of Bethany, 'plena fructibus bonis', this is probably intended to represent St Martha of Bethany: see D. H. Farmer: 'The Oxford Dictionary of Saints', O. U. P., page 264

CHAPTER 27

THE GREAT WAR CRACKS THE EDWARDIAN MOULD

The Winchcombe district's population in 1901 was 2,951. The twentieth century's first decade saw the start of improved means of transport which eventually altered the town's character and its inhabitants' way of life irrevocably.

The railway's arrival

After the failure to build the railway line from Beckford proposed in 1866 no further attempt to link Winchcombe directly to the railway system was seriously envisaged until 1898. The Midland and South Western Junction Railway (MSWJR) then canvassed a proposed new line from Andoversford to Stratford-upon-Avon which would have served Winchcombe. Alarmed by this prospect of competition, the Great Western Railway (GWR) replied with a proposal for a double-track railway of just under twenty-two miles from Honeybourne junction to Cheltenham's Malvern Road station, with stations at Toddington and Winchcombe and halts at Hailes abbey and Gretton. The station at Toddington was intended as a depot for transporting fruit cultivated in the surrounding district and it was hoped that better access to markets would also encourage more vegetable growing.[1]

The construction of the line between Broadway and Gretton was a remarkable civil engineering achievement; tragically, it cost the lives of four workmen on 13 November 1903 when a section of the Stanway viaduct collapsed while it was being built. The line was progressively opened for freight and passengers as track was laid and stations built. Winchcombe station was opened on 1 February 1905, although there was no passenger service to Cheltenham's Malvern Road until August 1908. Until then, the GWR operated a motorised bus service (seen in the photograph at Plate 16) between Winchcombe station and Cheltenham, travelling by way of Bishop's Cleeve.[2] Although there was some disappointment that the station was in fact at Greet, the availability of additional land near the site enabled a market to be opened there. The market lasted for about twenty years, but was closed when improved road transport meant that farmers had ready access to markets at Gloucester and Andoversford. The railway's novelty encouraged many of the town's inhabitants to make the three-mile journey to Toddington on opening day and walk back to Winchcombe.

"Winchcombe's First Motor Bus." starting for maiden trip Feb. 1st. 1905. Station in background.

Photo J. P. Hawley, Chemist, Winchcombe.

Plate 16

Travel by motor bus and car

Although the GWR's motorised bus service showed how travel to Cheltenham by road could be speeded up, the service was withdrawn in 1906. The horse-drawn bus continued to provide a service into Cheltenham from The Gate coffee tavern in North Street until the outbreak of war in 1914. But it was already becoming clear that the petrol-driven engine would be the principal means of travel in future. The earliest privately owned motor cars were seen in the town in the late-1890s, probably in 1897 or 1898. Two local owners of vehicles were reputedly Dr. John Halliwell (whose car had the registration number FH 64) and Mr. Charles Lane of The Bays in Gretton Road (registration number FH 12).[3] At first, like the railway, the passing of a motor car was an event; but it would not be long before the number of cars meant that the town's roads were no longer a safe play area for children.

It was probably the condition of the roads in the Winchcombe district, as much as the cost of buying a motor car, which hindered the early growth in vehicle use. Until about 1916, the roads were surfaced with crushed, bluish-grey rock from the Malvern hills which made them unpleasantly dusty in dry weather or slippery with mud in the wet. Road maintenance consisted of employing men to scrape the surface clear with hoes and then to lay the recovered material on it again. But, after 1916, tarmacadam was progressively used for road surfacing.

Improved facilities in the town

In 1900 the county council commissioned the building of the new police station at the Anchor crossroads, which included accommodation for holding the county court and magistrates' court and cells for prisoners. The handsome, rock-faced building occupies a visually important site at the crossroads, where its slightly elevated position provides a timely reminder of the constabulary's presence in the town.

Although the Winchcombe cottage hospital still provided an essential service to the town's inhabitants, on the site in North Street, there was insufficient room to include isolation facilities for patients with extremely infectious diseases. To remedy this deficiency, Harriet Richardson (wife of William Richardson, licensee of the Corner Cupboard inn) agreed on 12 November 1904 to sell to Winchcombe rural district council about one acre of land in the arable field known as Giles Piece on the northern side of Langley Road.[4] The council then provided a single-storey wooden building on the plot for an isolation hospital.

In May 1910 Mrs. E. O. Waddingham presented a drinking fountain to the town, in memory of her husband John Waddingham of Guiting Grange, who had died two years previously. John Waddingham had been a justice of the peace and, for twenty years, chairman of the Winchcombe bench of magistrates. When Gloucestershire county council was established in 1888 he was one of the first aldermen to be elected and held that office until his death; his financial acumen had been greatly valued by council members. But John Waddingham was chiefly remembered in the Winchcombe district for his conscientiousness, devotion to public service for some forty years and kindness to his less fortunate neighbours.

The ceremonial presentation of the fountain to Winchcombe parish council (as it then was) had originally been scheduled for 17 May; but Edward VII's sudden death on 6 May was followed by a period of national mourning for the late king and the ceremony was re-arranged for 31 May. It was one of those grand occasions, combining formality with a genuine expression of feeling, so dear to the heart of provincial towns in Victorian and Edwardian England. The county council's chairman, M. W. Colchester-Wemyss, had been invited by Mrs. Waddingham to unveil the fountain, dedicate it to public use, and hand it over to the parish council's chairman, who was then Dr. William Cox.

The lengthy report of the event in *The Evesham Journal* for 4 June 1910 shows that everything, down to the last detail, went according to plan. The county council's chairman delivered a splendid eulogy to John Waddingham's virtues; Mrs. Waddingham turned on the water supply to the fountain 'with a key gaily decked with ribbons'; and William Cox accepted the gift, on the parish council's behalf, 'with very great pride and pleasure'. Dr. Cox's acceptance speech particularly emphasised John Waddingham's personal kindness and generosity to poor people in the neighbourhood.

The fountain was positioned in Abbey Terrace (with the county council's permission as landowner) in the area outside the property now know as St Kenelm's, where the house extends forward adjacent to Stone House. Like so many municipal drinking fountains and troughs at that time, it was supplied by the Metropolitan Drinking Fountain and Cattle Trough Association, at Mrs. Waddingham's expense. However, this fountain's design was especially elaborate, incorporating a gas-lit lantern at its apex. *The Evesham Journal's* reporter described it as follows:

'The fountain is a massive and very handsome one, and of a somewhat unusual design. The base is surrounded by double granite steps with a third small step for the children under each of the two drinking jets. On the base is a die supporting a large basin cut out of a solid block of granite into which the water runs. In the basin is a smaller die, supporting an ornamental pillar around which are four small red polished granite columns. Over this rises some ornamental bronze work, supporting a glass globe, in which are two incandescent gas burners. The total height is 13 feet 9 inches. On each of two sides at the foot are double troughs, the upper parts containing water for horses and cattle, and the lower portions water for dogs. The greatest width is 12 feet 6 inches. The erection is all of Aberdeen grey polished granite ... '[5]

The fountain was also suitably inscribed to the memory of John Waddingham of Guiting Grange. Unhappily, in the early 1950s, the motor car's seemingly inevitable despoliation of civilised living in Abbey Terrace resulted in the fountain's removal.

Self-help gains its reward

John Oakey's account of his life describes how it was possible, by virtue of hard work and skills acquired through practical experience, to leave school in 1860 with little formal education and eventually become a highly successful builder and a pillar of the community. A comparable achievement is exemplified in the life of George Greening, father of the late Harold Greening of 15 Gretton Road, who belonged to what was perhaps the last generation able to make good in Winchcombe largely by self-help.

Born in 1874, as one of ten children brought up in a cottage in Bull Lane, George Greening soon learnt the meaning of hard work by helping his father (Henry Greening) in the fields at harvest time and gleaning with his mother (Jane Greening) after the corn had been harvested. Henry Greening's full-time work was in Sexty's tanyard and he was allowed to go reaping during the harvest to supplement his low wages. Gleaning was also a vital family income supplement. After the harvest was over Jane Greening gave her son the collected gleanings to take to one of the local threshing floors in Giles Piece, where the corn was threshed and winnowed from the chaff. The corn then had to be taken to the town mill at the foot of Mill Lane, to be ground into flour. The final stage in the process was for Jane Greening to prepare the dough in flat loaves, as the family required, and for George Greening to take them for baking at George Smith's bakery in North Street.

By his own admission, George Greening hated school and was glad to leave before he was eleven years old to start work as odd-job boy in William Smith's small estate at The Farm, at the foot of Hailes Street. His first chance to learn practical skills came in 1890 when he started work in the saw mill and timber yard then operated by William McQueen at the southern end of Gretton Road, approximately on the site now occupied by Winchcombe fire station. The timber yard, like the tannery, was then a thriving business using locally produced raw materials which the proprietor had to travel around the district to buy. In the yard there were stables for the horses kept to haul the timber carriages, bringing in the tree trunks from wherever they were felled; a sawing shed, complete with a saw-pit for cutting the trunks into manageable lengths; stacking and drying sheds; and workshops where carpenters and wheel-wrights made the whole range of products local farmers needed, from waggons to hurdles and feed troughs.

When George Greening left the timber yard, on William McQueen's sudden death in 1897, he had already acquired a thorough knowledge of the timber business and practical carpentry skills. He then worked briefly for a local wheelwright, Joe Banks; but, appreciating that the motor car would soon put wheelwrights out of business, he decided in 1899 that his best prospect was employment as a carpenter in the building trade. During the next few years he worked on the new police station in Winchcombe, alterations to the accommodation at Sudeley castle, and highly specialised restoration of the parish church at Hailes. Between 1904 and 1915 he worked for a local builder, probably Arthur Yiend, who was then building some characteristically rock-faced houses with slate roofs, still to be seen on Cleeve Hill and in various places in Winchcombe. By this time George Greening had saved enough to arrange for his employer to build a pair of such houses in Gretton Road, just to the south of the timber yard: one house was for himself and his wife and the other for his parents.

After the Great War he established his own rural carpenter's business, in which his son, Harold Greening, also worked with him for a time. Perhaps his crowning achievement came in about 1930 when the former timber yard, which had meantime become a rural district council works depot, came on to the market and he was able to buy it for £330.[6]

George Greening's life is significant not only as illustrating what a determined individual could achieve from humble beginnings: it helps to show how profoundly Winchcombe was changing at that time. The timber yard finally closed just before the outbreak of the Great War, partly due to increased imports of foreign timber and partly through inability to compete with mass-produced agricultural equipment and tools made from more durable (but less aesthetically satisfying) materials. And the closure of the timber yard was inevitably accompanied by some loss of the range of skills which had enabled it to flourish, such as tree-fellers, sawyers, hurdle-makers, wheelwrights, waggon builders and general carpenters. The traditional rural economy was starting to change irrevocably as the products of the timber yard, the tannery and the smithy could no longer compete with the mass-produced article made elsewhere, or were superseded by new products turned out in purpose-designed factories. Similarly, the local brewing of beer and cider-making would soon cease as the brewing companies took over production and acquired licensed premises.

Forebodings of war

Despite Winchcombe's comparative isolation, events in the wider world were soon to have a dramatic impact on the town. Although he was a grandson of queen Victoria, Germany's kaiser William II alternated between displays of apparent friendship for England and military adventures which alarmed European politicians. In particular, the build-up of the German navy by admiral Tirpitz from 1897 onwards was seen by the British government as a direct threat to Britain's naval supremacy. By 1909 fear of German naval superiority was so great that the government was forced to undertake an accelerated programme of building dreadnoughts for the royal navy.[7]

In Winchcombe, despite forebodings of eventual conflict, life continued normally. The first Winchcombe carnival was held in the grounds of Sudeley castle on bank holiday Monday in August 1906. However, some young men were sufficiently patriotic to join the Gloucestershire Yeomanry during these years; and the Sudeley castle grounds were the scene of a very different activity in May 1908 when the Yeomanry held their annual training camp there. This was an occasion to display military fervour in Winchcombe: a welcoming ceremonial arch, with numerous flags and decorations, was erected at the top of Vineyard Street, where the Yeomanry marched past on their way to the camp site at Sudeley.[8]

Winchcombe rural district council and board of guardians

Throughout the Edwardian years Winchcombe rural district council and the board of guardians continued to fulfil their important local government role. Continuity in membership of both bodies was remarkable. When the Rev. William Darke Stanton retired as chairman of the council and the board on 9 April 1910 he had held office continuously since the council's formation at the end of 1894. This was an occasion for the vice-chairman, F. W. Hinton, to express their thanks for the chairman's long service and arrange for presentation to him of an illuminated address in the following terms:

'We, the members and officers of the Board of Guardians and Rural District Council (formerly the Winchcombe Highway Board and Sanitary Board), on the occasion of your resignation as our chairman, desire to place on record our appreciation of the valuable services you have for a long period, extending over nineteen years, rendered in connection with the work, devolving upon the Board and the Council, and we beg to assure you that we shall always cherish a happy recollection of your uniform courtesy and kindly consideration during your close association with us. We trust that the evening of your long life may be blest with health and happiness.'[9]

The Rev. William Stanton was naturally 'considerably affected' by this show of support, which he modestly declared that he did not deserve.

The board of guardians remained as preoccupied as ever with management of the workhouse, which averaged some sixty inmates in 1910, of whom about one-half were men. On average, about 300 vagrants were 'relieved' each fortnight, including some fifty women. At the board's meeting on 21 May 1910 the tramp master (supervisor of the vagrants) reported that the tramps had broken 12 tons 15 cwts. of stone during the previous fortnight as part of their 'task work'. When board member Albert Day observed that this quantity of stone breaking did not seem very much for 226 men, the clerk pointed out that the available space for this activity was limited and some men had done wood-chopping and gardening instead.[10]

Plate 17

The outbreak of war

The proclamation of a state of war with Germany was made at 11pm on 4 August 1914.[11] Enthusiasm for the war gripped the country and so many young men and 'time-expired men' (former regular soldiers who had served their term) volunteered for the armed forces that the existing War Office staff could not cope with them satisfactorily. In some places there were neither enough uniforms nor training facilities for the new recruits. Nevertheless, there was widespread belief that British forces would have taken Berlin by Christmas and the war would be over by the end of the year. To show Winchcombe's opinion of the German enemy, one of the parish church's ugliest grotesques was nicknamed 'Kaiser Bill'. When the expectations of an early victory were not realised, and the allied armies were in disarray by the end of 1914, the country was forced to acknowledge the reality of a protracted war of attrition.

Winchcombe during the war

From 1915 onwards Winchcombe's inhabitants adapted progressively to the requirements of the Great War (as contemporaries then described it). Twenty-four special constables were sworn in, including John Oakey, and proudly wore their armlets and lapel badges to show that their job was to support the local constabulary.[12] The local magistrates became responsible for swearing in recruits for the armed forces. In 1916 'daylight saving' (as British summer time was initially called) was introduced, resulting in farmers' complaints about disruption of daily routines on the farm.

As the numbers of wounded soldiers invalided back from the front-lines in France and Belgium grew rapidly in 1915, military and civilian hospitals were soon unable to cope with them. Additional staff and accommodation were urgently required. This need was met in Winchcombe by the Gloucestershire Voluntary Aid Detachment No. 6, familiarly called the VADs, under their redoubtable commandant Miss Wedgwood of Stanway. The detachment consisted of Henry Dent-Brocklehurst of Sudeley castle as assistant commandant, Dr. Halliwell as medical officer, Mrs. Halliwell as quarter-master, four trained nursing sisters, twelve women for general nursing duties, six probationers and six cooks. Dr. Halliwell also undertook the melancholy task of dealing with inquiries about missing soldiers. Accommodation was provided by using the assembly rooms (originally William Smith's infants' school) in Abbey Terrace and the former Wesleyan Methodist chapel in Cowl Lane. The commemorative plaque still to be seen on the front wall of the assembly rooms records that 809 sick (sometimes from the effects of gassing) and wounded soldiers were cared for in Winchcombe between 6 May 1915 and 30 November 1918.

Many of the soldiers were brought directly from field hospitals to this accommodation and became familiar figures in the town, dressed in their 'hospital blues' as the uniform was called. To show their appreciation of the care they received, some of the less severely wounded gave concert parties in the town hall for Winchcombe's children. Surviving photographs of these occasions show that colourful performances by minstrels and pierrots were especially popular.

However, no attempt at forced cheerfulness could overcome the war's grimmest reality for those with a loved-one serving in the forces. This was the ever-present dread that the telegraph boy's knock at the door heralded the arrival of an official telegram announcing that a relative had been killed in action, seriously wounded, taken prisoner, or – perhaps worst of all in some ways – had been reported missing on some remote battlefield, such as the Dardanelles where many men of the Seventh Gloucester Regiment were killed or wounded in July and August 1915. One of the first volunteers from Winchcombe to be killed in action, on 2 March 1915, was nineteen-year-old, second lieutenant Clifford Bird, serving in the King's Shropshire Light Infantry, at St Eloi in Flanders.[13] Two months later, on 9 May 1915, private W. Parker died 'in the glorious charge of the Gloucesters at Aubers Ridge', close to Festubert.[14] Eventually, seventy-eight men of Winchcombe and the immediately surrounding hamlets sacrificed their lives.

By early-1915 268 volunteers from the Winchcombe district had joined the armed forces; and a further 128 volunteered by the beginning of December, almost fifteen per cent of the total population. The volunteers' families looked upon their departing husbands and sons with immense pride. Thomas Green of Gloucester Street saw his four sons, Frederick, William, Charles and Walter, enlisted in the army by March 1915.[15] Mercifully, none is recorded as killed in action.

The armed forces' voracious demand for men to replace the casualties at the front-line soon could not be satisfied by volunteers alone. In January 1916 conscription was introduced for unmarried men aged between eighteen and forty-one, with exemption for munitions workers and coal miners, and was extended later in the year to married men.[16] The loss of men to the forces in the Winchcombe district resulted in a shortage of agricultural labourers, which was not overcome by hiring out German prisoners of war (of whom about sixty were stationed in Winchcombe) to some of the larger estates. This deficiency was met in two other ways. First, some women became full-time agricultural workers. Secondly, farming mechanisation was accelerated. In January 1917 a Cheltenham company held a motor ploughing demonstration at Uckington to show how a tractor and four-furrow plough could do the work of three or four teams of horses.[17] In July 1918 a Cirencester company organised a gathering of Cotswold farmers to demonstrate the operation of the 'Titan Tractor', manufactured by the International Harvester company of Milwaukee, coupled with the three-furrow, self-lifting Hamilton plough, which left the ploughed land ready for cultivation.[18] Only farmers' inability to invest in, or unwillingness to adopt, new methods could delay the widespread substitution of ploughmen and labourers by machines.

Despite the introduction of new methods and the efforts of government-sponsored county committees for agriculture, food production was insufficient to meet essential needs. Although rationing of food did not start until February 1918, the quality of available food deteriorated gradually during the war and a soup kitchen was established in Winchcombe to provide poorer families with at least one square meal a day.

However, following the declaration of war against Germany by the United States in April 1917, America's entry into the war ensured that an eventual German surrender was probable. Although British generals had advised their government that the war would last well into 1919, the German government sought terms for peace in October 1918. At this late stage in the war, private William Edgar Holmes of Winchcombe was awarded the Victoria Cross while serving with the Grenadier Guards at Cattenières on 9 October.[19] Finally, the armistice took effect on 11 November. The news was greeted in Winchcombe by celebratory peals of the parish church bells.

The Great War's aftermath

The end of the Great War was immediately followed by a different scourge. What appears to have been a virulent strain of influenza reached England from central Europe in October 1918 and spread rapidly, eventually affecting about three-quarters of the entire population.[20] In the worst cases complications resulted in pneumonia, which was almost always fatal, and local newspapers in November and December 1918 recorded numerous deaths.

Parishes throughout the country were determined to recognise publicly the sacrifice made by those who had died on active service. The Cheltenham firm of sculptors, R. L. Boulton & Son of Bath Road, advertised the availability of village war memorials and offered a range of designs to suit local circumstances.[21] When the parishes of Winchcombe and Sudeley decided to join in a combined memorial, it was this company who supplied the Cross which still stands so eloquently in Abbey Terrace, where general Sir Ian Hamilton unveiled it on 4 August 1920.[22] The memorial's upper plinth commemorates individually the seventy-eight men who gave their lives during the war.

The next-of-kin of every member of the armed forces killed in the war was sent a memorial scroll from king George V, bearing this message: 'He whom this scroll commemorates was numbered among those who, at the call of King and Country, left all that was dear to them, endured hardness, faced danger, and finally passed out of the sight of men by the path of duty and self-sacrifice, giving up their own lives that others might live in freedom. Let those who come after see to it that his name be not forgotten.'[23] This noble intention is fulfilled annually at Winchcombe's Remembrance Day service.

1   Colin Maggs: 'Railways of the Cotswolds', published by Peter Nicholson, 1981, pages 68-69
2   Stephen Mourton: 'Steam Routes around Cheltenham', Runpast Publishing, 1993, page 11
3   Memoirs of Arthur Shekell, from 1903 to 1980
4   indenture dated 12 November 1904, archived in a copy in Winchcombe museum
5   *The Evesham Journal*, 4 June 1910, archived on microfilm in Evesham Library
6   George Greening: 'A brief autobiography, with some reminiscences', deposited in Winchcombe museum in the Harold Greening bequest
7   Sir Robert Ensor: 'England, 1870-1914', The Oxford History of England, 1936, pages 412-413
8   *Cheltenham Chronicle and Gloucestershire Graphic*, 9 May 1908
9   *The Evesham Journal*, 16 April 1910
10   *The Evesham Journal*, 28 May 1910
11   A. J. P. Taylor: 'English History, 1914-1945', The Oxford History of England, 1965, page 2
12   J. A. Oakey: 'Reminiscences', page 30
13   memorial plaque to Francis Clifford Bird in Winchcombe parish church
14   *Cheltenham Chronicle and Gloucestershire Graphic*, 26 June 1915
15   *Cheltenham Chronicle and Gloucestershire Graphic*, 6 March 1915
16   A. J. P. Taylor, op cit, pages 52-55
17   *Cheltenham Chronicle and Gloucestershire Graphic*, 27 January 1917
18   *Cheltenham Chronicle and Gloucestershire Graphic*, 27 July 1918
19   *Cheltenham Chronicle and Gloucestershire Graphic*, 4 January 1919
20   A. J. P. Taylor, op cit, pages 112-113
21   *Cheltenham Chronicle and Gloucestershire Graphic*, 1 March 1919
22   D. Verey and A. Brooks: 'Gloucestershire I: The Cotswolds', page 731
23   *Cheltenham Chronicle and Gloucestershire Graphic*, 25 October 1919

CHAPTER 28

BETWEEN TWO WORLD WARS

The population of Winchcombe and Sudeley parishes in 1911 was 3,013, including eighty-one people accommodated in the workhouse. By 1921 it had declined to 2,814 (with eighty living in the workhouse); and there was a further fall to 2,634 (with fifty-four in the workhouse) by 1931. The 1914-1918 war probably contributed marginally to this reduction as some men who became munitions and engineering workers moved away and did not return. Later in the 1930s there was also a drift away from agricultural work during the farming depression of those years.

The early-1920s saw a gradual return to normality after men in the armed forces were demobilised. Normal working resumed on the large estates in the Winchcombe district and some additional forestry work became available in the area with the Forestry Commission, which had been established to increase the supply of home-grown timber. Nevertheless, some of the changes prompted by the war's demands were not reversed; and, together with gradual improvements in living conditions, the settled pattern of pre-war generations started to alter almost imperceptibly. The late Bert Butler described the 1920s in Winchcombe as 'the golden decade': in his experience, three factors justified this description.

The status of women

The first factor was the status of women which had begun to change during the war. Women's work had proved essential to the war effort, which had taken some of them outside the home for the first time. After the war they could not be expected to return to a largely subservient role: some sought full-time or part-time employment and greater opportunities for self-expression. Although this trend was more apparent in industrial towns, rural areas were not exempt, despite poorer employment prospects for women.

One practical result of this increasing public awareness of women's worth was the founding in Winchcombe of the Women's Institute (the W.I.) in 1919. This involved raising £500 to buy the former Wesleyan chapel (which was no longer needed as an infants' school) in Cowl Lane from the Dent-Brocklehurst family in 1929. The building thus started its fourth semi-public use, as a meeting place for W.I. members. Mrs. Marian Dent-Brocklehurst became the first president. The W.I.'s initial importance was in giving women an opportunity to show their varied practical skills, to have those skills appreciated more widely, and to gain new interests outside the confined scope of the tradesman's home or the agricultural worker's cottage. Winchcombe Women's Institute became firmly established and celebrated its eightieth anniversary in 1999.

Radio broadcasting

The second influential factor was the development during the 1920s of radio broadcasting, or the wireless as it was universally called. The first cumbersome loudspeaker set was reportedly used in Winchcombe in 1924 and the Daventry transmitter soon revolutionised the quality of broadcasting reception from the station known as 2LO. This national improvement in communications perhaps had its greatest effect on listeners in rural communities who gained instant access to news, opinion and entertainment previously obtainable mainly from newspapers, magazines and live performances. Although the radio's arrival was welcomed by most people, one result was the eventual decline of music-making which had been such a feature of the town's life in Victorian and Edwardian times, with inspiration from the musically talented Haslum family.[1]

The electricity supply

The third fundamental change was the arrival of the electricity supply in Winchcombe in 1928. Kelly's Gloucestershire directory of 1927 records that Winchcombe 'is lighted with gas by a company whose works are in Hailes Street'.[2] This was a reference to the Winchcombe Gas Light & Coke company which continued to operate the town's gas works on the site adjacent to the junction of Hailes Street and Silk Mill Lane. The availability of electricity enabled the streets and public buildings to be lit more adequately, although the George inn already had its own electricity supply (presumably using a privately operated generator). Just as importantly, electricity eventually lessened some of the drudgery involved in daily toil on the farm, at the mill or work bench, or in the home, although its immediate use was mainly for lighting.

However, despite these improvements, calling the 1920s 'the golden decade' must not hide the reality that times were far from golden for some of Winchcombe's inhabitants. As an agricultural labourer's weekly wage could still be as low as £2, and the workhouse continued to provide basic residential accommodation for those who could not maintain themselves in long-term sickness or old age, thrifty habits were an essential means of survival. The housekeeping burden fell heavily on many wives and mothers who used all their cooking and clothes-mending skills to make ends meet. Luxuries were not affordable. The Sunday school 'treat' provided the year's only special occasion for many children.

Winchcombe pottery's revival

A country pottery had existed at Greet since at least the 1840s. The 1841 census records that forty-five-year-old William Becket [sic] was then a brickmaker at Greet and George Richings worked as a potter, aged twenty-five. They presumably worked together at or near the site on the northern side of what was later to become known as Beckett's Lane. However, production of pottery ceased early during the 1914-1918 war and the last employee, Elijah Comfort, who was then apparently working on his own after the death of Richard Beckett, his employer, left to become an agricultural labourer.

The recovery began from 1926 onwards when an aspiring young potter began to rent the pottery buildings and produce the pots for which Michael Cardew later became nationally celebrated. From the outset, he re-employed Elijah Comfort; and, with the help of Sidney Tustin as fourteen-year-old potter's boy they eventually succeeded, after many practical problems of restoring the kiln to working condition, in turning out enough saleable products to make the pottery once more a going concern. As early as 1928, Michael Cardew was sufficiently confident to have what he described as 'a wooden hut' built on the site for his own, and subsequently his family's, living accommodation; and his first one-man show was held in London that autumn.[3]

By his own account, Cardew's purpose was to produce pottery which ordinary people would be able to afford and to use for everyday living. This approach meant that articles had to be priced so that they were not regarded as luxury items or ornaments; and, because everyday use would naturally result in breakages, regular lines had to be kept in production so that customers could rely on obtaining replacements. Both these requirements inevitably limited the development of the pottery and its profitability. However, Cardew's long-term achievement was to show how, by immense determination, a rural, craft-based workshop could succeed. This lesson was learned by his successors at the pottery and has been applied by other local craftsmen working at the pottery site and elsewhere in Winchcombe's neighbourhood.

Winchcombe's churches

Formal religious observance remained important for many of Winchcombe's older inhabitants. The full churches on Sundays which were normal before the war were not regained afterwards, probably because the younger generation no longer regarded outward religious observance as so important. Some habits were so deeply ingrained that even the war's upheaval left them unchanged. One was tolling the curfew every evening, between 24 October and 24 March, at 8 pm. The curfew bell in the parish church was rung for ten minutes, followed by as many tolls of the tenor bell as corresponded to the elapsed number of days in the month.[4]

The Rev. Frederick Wickham was appointed vicar of Winchcombe in 1920 and was succeeded thirteen years later by the Rev. T.E. Meurig-Davies, who was notable for his interest in the parish church's history. With improvements in public and private transport, the parish church was becoming a landmark for increasing numbers of visitors to the town. In 1927, one such visitor to the Cotswolds was Henry Ford who reputedly wished to have the church dismantled and then, following its transport to the United States, rebuilt at his Greenfield village museum at Dearborn, Michigan. In the event, the parish church was not for sale and he had to be content with acquiring a disused blacksmith's forge from Snowshill and a seventeenth-century cottage from near Chedworth.[5]

Methodism continued vigorously under the leadership of the Rev. George Crossland, who was appointed in 1922. He was reportedly a robust character and was known to conduct a Sunday evening service, accompanied by a pianist from the church, in a room at the Gardener's Arms (now the Harvest Home) in Greet. He also preached outdoors at the pilgrims' gallery in the George inn's courtyard.[6] The Baptist chapel and the Congregational Union church in Gretton Road usually maintained a full-time minister.

As already mentioned in Chapter 25, Mrs. Elizabeth Forster of Postlip Hall had made great efforts to establish a permanent place of Roman Catholic worship. When Postlip Hall was sold to W. E. Muir in about March 1915 Mrs. Forster arranged for the refurbished St James's chapel at Postlip to continue in use for Roman Catholic worship. However, on the advice of Father Wilfrid Palmer, she had acquired the former Winchcombe grammar school building in Chandos Street for adaptation to provide a church. The essential work was carried out by local builders and volunteers, among whom police sergeant J. G. O'Rourke was reputedly prominent; and the formal opening and dedication of the church were scheduled to take place on Easter Day, 4 April 1915. Unfortunately, Mrs. Forster had suffered for some time with a heart condition and she died just before Easter, so that the dedication eventually took place on 18 April 1915. After the war Wilfrid Palmer was appointed resident Roman Catholic priest at Winchcombe and lived in the building in Chandos Street known as The Presbytery, which had been the original Chandos grammar school. This building is shown in the photograph at Plate 11.

Winchcombe in 1927

A visitor to Winchcombe in 1927 would have been impressed by the variety of shops and services available to a resident population of some 2,700. As well as the usual shopkeepers found in a rural market town, James Clapton had a saddler's business in North Street and Samuel Bayliss's blacksmith's forge at Tythe Court in Back Lane was kept in business by his successors, the Pidgeon brothers. The post office on its present site in North Street was run by William Charles Belcher, who had introduced the first printing press in the town in the 1890s, and had been sub-postmaster since 1893. George Quant, whose postcards of local scenes were later much prized, ran a stationer's business near the post office; and George Tovey's well-stocked bookshop occupied 13 North Street.

Increasing use of motor cars and motor cycles had encouraged Leonard Pudell to establish the Cotswold garage in Queen Square. John Oakey (then living at Balloon House in Gloucester Street) was still in business as a builder, as was Amos Hall who also lived in Gloucester Street. Although it would not survive for much longer, Sexty's tannery continued working on the site at the foot of Castle Street, near the junction with Silk Mill Lane. The town's flour mill was operated in Mill Lane by Day & Sons. The paper mill at Postlip continued to provide much-needed local employment. By 1927 Frank Adlard managed it; but his father, Edward Adlard, who had commissioned the building of the row of almshouses for former employees in Brook Close and

Plate 18

converted a number of cottages in the town to accommodate mill workers, was still associated with the business.[7] In Greet Road William Gillett and George Williams each had a carrier's business.

For people who needed a solicitor, the choice was between Ernest Smith-Wood, who maintained his family's long-established practice and was also county court registrar and justices' clerk, and H. W. (Henry) Stephens who continued as clerk to the rural district council and the board of guardians. One of the town's three doctors was George Cox, son of Dr. William Cox, who had played such a large part in founding the cottage hospital. Wilfred Soden, who lived at the house called Irwell in Abbey Terrace (now Lloyds-TSB bank), and Douglas Pim were also practising doctors.

Local government was administered by Winchcombe rural district council, comprising twenty-nine surrounding parishes with a population of about 9,000. This area was the same as that of Winchcombe Union, including parishes as far afield as Beckford (until its transfer to Evesham rural district on 1 April 1933), Cutsdean, Hawling, Pinnock and Hyde, and Southam. Winchcombe was a registration district for births, marriages and deaths. Henry Stephens, who was also superintendent registrar, used the front portion of the house in High Street, next to the Methodist church, for a register office; and Walter Haslum was a registrar of marriages. The Town Trust continued in being, with George Tovey as clerk; and Raymond Lewis was town crier.

Leisure and sports facilities

With some increase in leisure time between the wars there was a growing demand for sports and leisure facilities other than the traditional pursuits of football and cricket, although both games had flourishing clubs in Winchcombe. The swimming bath Mrs. Dent had established at Sudeley meadow continued as a going concern, with James Major as honorary secretary: until it closed in the late-1930s, a season ticket still cost as little as three shillings. Within the grounds of the property known as Pigeon Close (now renamed Ashby) on the western side of Cowl Lane, people were able to enjoy a tea garden and play tennis on a hard court.

When Sexty's tannery finally closed in the early 1930s the buildings were quite quickly converted to use as a cinema and dance hall by the enterprising L. W. Barnard. The Old Tanneries cinema, as it was called, opened to the people of Winchcombe on Boxing day 1933.[8] Performances started at 6 pm each evening and prices for adults ranged from 6d. to 1s. 3d., or 1s. 6d. for a reserved seat. There was a matinee performance at 2.30 pm on Saturday afternoons. Winchcombe thus gained the benefit of what one historian has called 'the greatest educative force of the early twentieth century'.[9]

Formal education

During the 1920s publicly provided education was available at three schools in Winchcombe. The public elementary school for boys continued in the building at the southern end of Gretton Road, which could accommodate up to 160 boys. Charles Lewis was the school's master. Towards the western end of Back Lane a new building had been completed in 1911 to provide a more suitable infants' school, capable of taking as many as 180 girls and boys. The schoolmistress was Emily Catton in the 1920s. As explained in Chapter 25, girls' elementary education continued in the former Dent's National School (immediately to the west of the parish church) in Gloucester Street, where Miss Booker was schoolmistress. This school continued to receive the sum of £20 annually from George Townsend's 1683 charity during the 1920s. Winchcombe's few grammar school pupils were required to travel daily to Cheltenham.

Winchcombe hospital

By the mid-1920s the cottage hospital in North Street was proving inadequate for the town's needs. To replace it with more suitable accommodation, the private house off Cheltenham Road on the town's western outskirts, built in 1904 for Frank Bird and originally known as Cotswold, was adapted in 1927 for use as a hospital, which opened in 1928.[10] The building was subsequently extended in 1936. This was achieved entirely by voluntary subscriptions and fund-raising activities.

Winchcombe rural district council's abolition

Neville Chamberlain, minister of health in Stanley Baldwin's second (Conservative) government, was determined to reform what he regarded as the chaotic system of English local government. Legislation enacted in 1929 provided for boards of guardians to be replaced by public assistance committees; and for the pattern of local government to be substantially changed.[11] There was no room in Chamberlain's scheme of things for comparatively small rural district councils, such as Winchcombe. The consequent reorganisation's details took some time to implement; but, by 1 April 1935, Cheltenham rural district council was ready to assume the responsibilities, but not the entire administrative area, of Winchcombe council. The division of the twenty-eight former Winchcombe constituent parishes was complicated, with only fifteen merging into the extended Cheltenham rural district council area.

Winchcombe rural district council's last meeting was held on Tuesday, 26 March 1935, with Albert Day as chairman, George Hunt as vice-chairman and twenty-one members. Much of the meeting concerned routine matters; but time was found at the close to pay tribute to the longest-serving members and the clerk, Henry Stephens, who had held that office for some thirty-two years. Albert Day of Manor Farm, Greet, had been a council member for about twenty-five years and chairman since March 1928, as well as chairman of the board of guardians: members thanked him for his courtesy and kindness. Those members transferring to the extended Cheltenham rural district council looked forward to serving on it. It was left to Henry Stephens, who was about to retire as clerk, to express some regrets: ' ... he thought it was a very great pity that Winchcombe should lose its identity in this way. The town was right in the centre of a large agricultural area which comprised the rural district, but Cheltenham was not in the centre: in fact it was right outside'.[12]

The sequel to Winchcombe rural district council's abolition was the election, held on 1 April 1935, of four councillors for the Winchcombe ward of the newly extended Cheltenham rural district council. Initially there were seven candidates, of whom five had served on the abolished council. However, Albert Day and Charles Greening withdrew: of the remaining five, Amos Hall topped the poll with 287 votes and was closely followed by Mrs. Edith Carter (269), Charles Bentley (266) and Mrs. Edith Lishman (259).[13] As part of these local government changes, Winchcombe parish council was also re-organised and the newly elected council's twelve members held their first meeting on 8 April 1935. Although Albert Day and Charles Greening had withdrawn from the Cheltenham council election, they both secured a place on Winchcombe parish council – Charles Greening as elected chairman and Albert Day as a member. Other members included Charles Bentley, Charles Forty and Amos Hall. The council's clerk was J. L. E. (Jack) Smith-Wood, thus maintaining the family tradition as a Winchcombe solicitor and adviser to public bodies in the town.[14]

No extension of licensing hours

Alcohol consumption on the customary scale in mid-nineteenth-century Winchcombe had long since ceased, probably due partly to the severe restrictions imposed, in the interests of the war effort, on licensing hours during the 1914-1918 war. By 1935 the town's licensees found these restrictions irksome: consequently, the Cheltenham and District Licensed Victuallers' Association represented at Winchcombe police court, on 8 March 1935, that an additional half-hour be added to the normal evening opening hours of 5.30 pm to 10 pm during the summer months, as had already been permitted at Evesham and some towns in Gloucestershire.

The Association's advocate submitted a rather romanticised case to the licensing justices, part of which was as follows:

'A considerable number of the population of Winchcombe and district are engaged in agriculture and in summertime work until late in the evening. It is only reasonable that they should be given extra opportunity of receiving refreshment after they have finished their work ... There were hundreds of visitors who came into the neighbourhood during the summer months, and spent as much of the daylight as they could on the surrounding beautiful hills. Naturally, on their way back, they wanted some refreshment, but not necessarily alcoholic ... In this district there was a number of good cricket pitches, and throughout the summer these were visited by many teams, for the purpose of playing evening matches. These matches did not finish before nine o'clock, and surely it was reasonable to expect the players to desire some sort of refreshment after their games? ...'

Despite this eloquent submission, the Winchcombe magistrates were unimpressed by the supposed needs of agricultural workers, tourists and cricketers. The earl of Wemyss, as chairman of the bench, dismissed the application in one sentence: 'The Bench has always shown itself ready to give extensions when any good cause has been shown, and after careful consideration of the matter, we consider that no special cause has been shown why Winchcombe should be granted an extra half-hour which has not been granted to many other places.'[15]

Silver jubilee of King George V

Perhaps in an effort to unite British public opinion in the face of a deteriorating international security situation, the National government declared that George V's silver jubilee should be celebrated on 6 May 1935. Although an additional holiday was welcomed, public enthusiasm on this occasion was more muted than for queen Victoria's two jubilees, not least because some 1.5 million men of working age were unemployed and money was tight for many of those in work.

In Winchcombe the parish council was expected to take the lead in organising the jubilee celebration, but was very reluctant to incur extra expenditure resulting in an increased rates demand. The council decided to allocate £20 towards the cost of the celebration and indicated that any larger sum should be met voluntarily. On 15 March 1935 a public meeting was held in the town hall to discuss how the jubilee should be celebrated. Major J. H. Dent-Brocklehurst, as chairman for the occasion, proposed that the jubilee should be mainly a celebration for the town's children; and any remaining funds should be used to help Winchcombe hospital. He then mentioned the parish council's somewhat uninspiring suggestions, as follows: aluminium mugs to be presented to all the schoolchildren; a united church service at 11 am on jubilee day; a free tea to all children aged fourteen and under; hiring a radiogram for the day; a meat tea for everyone aged seventy or more; some entertainment for the children (either a patriotic film at the town's cinema or some form of sports); and a firework display. He favoured an executive committee to raise more funds and arrange the celebrations.

In the following discussion William Major, as the parish council's vice-chairman, sought to deflect responsibility for organising the celebrations from the council so as 'to relieve the ratepayers as much as possible'. As an enthusiast for a permanent jubilee memorial, Mrs. Edith Carter thought that the hospital should collect its own funds and suggested that a public convenience, which would be 'of great benefit to the town and tradespeople', be built. The chairman intervened to say that this suggestion was a matter for the parish council. After further discussion the chairman's suggestion of an executive committee was accepted and thirteen members were elected to it. Possibly to his consternation, William Major was elected chairman when this committee met and C. P. G. (Charles) Lewis became honorary secretary.[16]

At the executive committee's meeting on 28 March, captain Gerald Reynolds of Corndean Hall attempted to make the parish council responsible for the celebrations by suggesting that levying 'a twopenny or threepenny rate' was better than asking for subscriptions. William Major again resisted parish council involvement and added, conclusively, that it was then too late for the council to issue a precept. The committee decided that the main celebration should be a tea for all the town's children between the ages of three and fourteen (then the school-leaving age) and presentation of a jubilee mug to all the children. This would involve providing tea for about 300 children and buying some 400 mugs (to include about 100 children who were too young to qualify for the free tea). This event would take place in the W. I. hall (the former Methodist chapel in Cowl Lane) and the assembly rooms (William Smith's infants' school in Abbey Terrace). There would also be children's sports in the afternoon and a visit to the cinema after the tea.

In addition to the children's celebration, the committee decided to provide a meat tea for all men and women in the town aged seventy and over; and there would be a united church service at 10.30 am in the parish church on jubilee day. Some committee members still favoured a more permanent memorial: Victor Statham of Lloyds bank in the town, who had been appointed honorary treasurer, suggested that a set of jubilee chains be placed around the war memorial in Abbey Terrace. But William Major stood firm against any such extravagance, remarking that 'they must carry out the jubilee plans first of all and see how they stood regarding any surplus funds.'[17]

On jubilee day the celebrations began with a thanksgiving service in the parish church at 10.30 am, which included Walter Haslum's stirring rendering of Elgar's 'Pomp and Circumstance' march. The children's sports took place in the afternoon on the Almsbury field, after which the children paraded to the Women's Institute Hall in Cowl Lane for the jubilee tea and presentation of the souvenir mugs by Mrs. J. H. Dent-Brocklehurst and Mrs. G. N. Reynolds of Corndean Hall. The town's elderly people were welcomed to a meat tea in the town hall by Major Dent-Brocklehurst.

The evening's main event was a fancy dress dance organised by Winchcombe tennis club at the Old Tanneries dance hall, the proceeds of which were used to provide an ambulance trolley for the extension to Winchcombe hospital, as a permanent reminder of the jubilee. Dancing continued until 2 am in the morning, thanks to

Syd Tonge and his 'Cedros Mexican Band'. A beacon was lit on Langley hill and on the hill above Postlip warren.[18]

As something of an afterthought, in 1936, the playing fields to the south-west of Mill Lane were named king George's field, in honour of the king who died in that year. The gateposts at the entrance to the fields commemorate the king's reign from 1910 to 1936.

Fears of another world war

From 1935 onwards Britain's successive National governments were increasingly preoccupied with how to restrain the territorial ambitions of Adolf Hitler's Germany and Benito Mussolini's Italy. To over-simplify, public opinion was broadly divided between those who preferred to rely on the League of Nations (which Germany had abandoned in October 1933) as a means of international peace-keeping and those who believed that rearmament was essential in preparation for a seemingly inevitable European, or more widespread, war.

In Winchcombe these opposing views were represented at a meeting of the Winchcombe literary and debating society at the town hall, on 18 March 1935, to debate the question 'whether or not the League of Nations had justified its existence'. The opening speaker in support of relying on the League's peace-keeping efforts was Ernest Edmund Smith-Wood (still practising as a solicitor and living in St Kenelm's, Abbey Terrace). His views were supported by Father Wilfrid Palmer. The contrary view was maintained by George Arthurs (then practising as a land agent from Jacobean House) who pointed out that Germany had introduced conscription, France had extended the duration of national service and Soviet Russia was re-arming. He argued that the League of Nations had brought the world 'to the brink of another war, far worse than that of 1914-1918'. In the vote following the debate, ten of the society's members supported the proposition that the League had justified its existence while thirteen were against it.[19] George Arthurs and his supporters had the dubious satisfaction of being proved right in just over four years' time.

1   J. A. Oakey: 'Reminiscences', page 21
2   Kelly's Directory for Gloucestershire, 1927, page 384
3   Michael Cardew: 'A Pioneer Potter – An Autobiography', Collins, 1988, pages 56-59
4   H. J. Massingham: 'Shepherd's Country', Chapman & Hall, 1938, page 170
5   E. R. Delderfield: 'The Cotswold Countryside and its Characters', The Raleigh Press, 1967, page 63; and Carolyn Mason: 'Snowshill – A Gloucestershire Village', Thornhill Press, 1987, pages 50-51
6   F. C. Adey: 'A Cotswold Methodist Heritage', page 66
7   Eleanor Adlard: 'A Short History of the Postlip Mill, Winchcombe', 1949, page 19
8   *Cheltenham Chronicle and Gloucestershire Graphic*, 30 December 1933
9   A. J. P. Taylor: 'English History, 1914-1945', The Oxford History of England, 1965, page 181
10   D. Verey and A. Brooks: 'The Buildings of England – Gloucestershire I: The

Cotswolds', page 730

11   A. J. P. Taylor, op cit, pages 256-257

12   *The Evesham Journal*, 30 March 1935; archived on microfilm in Evesham Library

13   *The Evesham Journal*, 6 April 1935

14   *The Evesham Journal*, 13 April 1935

15   *The Evesham Journal*, 16 March 1935

16   *The Evesham Journal*, 23 March 1935

17   *The Evesham Journal*, 6 April 1935

18   *The Evesham Journal*, 11 May 1935

19   *The Evesham Journal*, 23 March 1935

CHAPTER 29

WORLD WAR TWO

O n 31 August 1939 German forces invaded Poland. It was finally clear that no hope remained of negotiating a secure future for smaller European nations. On 3 September the British government issued an ultimatum for the withdrawal of German forces from Poland, with a reply required by 11am. When no reply was received by this time-limit, Britain declared war on Germany, followed later in the day by the French government's war declaration.[1]

From the outset, the Second World War differed from the Great War in involving the entire population. Partial conscription had already been introduced, earlier in 1939, anticipating that the conscripts would be called-up for service at some time in 1941 or 1942. The immediate practical result of the war declaration was taking precautions against expected air attacks, including imposition of a blackout on homes, factories and meeting places; prohibition of headlights on motor vehicles; and the issue of gas masks to the whole population, including children.

Providing homes for evacuees

Although the war declaration was followed in the remaining months of 1939 and early-1940 by the period of 'phoney war', a large-scale evacuation of primary school-children and mothers with children aged under five, from the cities to rural areas, began almost immediately. In Winchcombe Mrs. A. Lishman, the town's billeting officer, and her assistants were responsible for finding accommodation for evacuees. Some of the first evacuees came from Birmingham and were allocated to local families on a necessarily makeshift basis, since neither the evacuees nor the families accommodating them knew how long the arrangement would last.

The experience of evacuation was often difficult for everyone involved in it. The most obvious result was overcrowding in houses which were often not intended to accommodate more than one family with reasonable privacy. City children had to adapt to Winchcombe's rural ways. The gentle Gloucestershire brogue must have appeared almost like a foreign language to some of them. Even their clothes were sometimes unsuitable, so that the accommodating families found it necessary to help with provision of better clothing and stouter footwear.[2]

It was also necessary to evacuate some city hospitals. Since accommodation was not available in rural cottage hospitals, emergency arrangements were required. In

Winchcombe, captain David Mitchell made Postlip Hall available for patients from Birmingham eye hospital; and, later, expectant and nursing mothers from the Birmingham area were accommodated there.[3] Some mothers moved on to accommodation in the house known as Martens, at Postlip, the home of Eleanor Adlard, who was in charge of the local branch of Women's Voluntary Service (the W.V.S. – not yet the W.R.V.S.).

When the phoney war lasted into the early months of 1940 some evacuees returned to their homes, in the belief that aerial attacks were less likely. However, with the start of persistent aerial bombing, especially of southern England and industrial targets in many cities, from April 1940 onwards, a further wave of evacuees arrived. How the evacuated families were allocated to a particular destination is unclear. One example illustrates how the process operated in Winchcombe. In the summer of 1940 the town of Eastbourne in Sussex experienced more than one hundred air raids, resulting in evacuation of mothers and children, by train, to the Cheltenham area in mid-September. On arrival in Cheltenham some two hundred of the evacuees were brought by bus to Winchcombe. They were then accommodated either in Winchcombe families' homes or in the Women's Institute hall in Cowl Lane, which was equipped with bunk beds to cater for larger family groups for whom rooms could not be found in the town.[4]

Depending upon their age, evacuee children went to the appropriate school in Winchcombe; and some mothers started work in the town, including manual jobs left vacant by men who had joined the armed forces. Eventually, some evacuees grew so accustomed to their new lives that they remained in the town, or the Cheltenham area, after the war ended.

Home defences

In anticipation of possible invasion a platoon of the Home Guard was formed, as No. 11 Platoon of the first Cheltenham battalion, with lieutenant S. C. Watson, who worked at the town mill in Mill Lane, as commanding officer. The Congregational Union church in Gretton Road became a temporary drill hall. As in the 1914-1918 war, some thirty special constables were sworn in and sergeant C. Francis, at Winchcombe police station, was put in charge of them. To provide civil defence services, twenty-six wardens were appointed, with lieutenant-colonel Davis as head warden. The town was divided into seven administrative areas for civil defence purposes, with a section leader for each area: the boys' school headmaster, C. P. G. Lewis, was section leader for North area and Arthur Shekell of West End Stores was leader for Central West area.

To deal with the threat of possible fire-bombing, Winchcombe fire brigade in what was then the National Fire Service, under its captain Arthur Hall, was strengthened and its equipment improved. In 1940 the previous fire station in Chandos Street (opposite what is now the public car park entrance) was given up and the land comprising the present site at the southern end of Gretton Road, including a shed for the fire appliances, was acquired. An adapted thirty horsepower Ford 'V8 Pilot' vehicle was provided for towing a new trailer pump.[5] There were eight regular fire-fighters, fourteen auxiliaries and two drivers. During the war the Winchcombe brigade was required to help deal with the aftermath of bombing raids as far afield as Coventry, Bristol, Bath and Weston-super-Mare.[6]

Practical steps were taken to hinder any invader's progress. Signposts, milestones and notices giving vital information were removed or obliterated; stone-built pillboxes (some of which survive), for directing weapon fire against an enemy, were erected in some of the fields around the town; and defence posts were built on all the approach roads, including Corndean Lane.

Accommodation for the armed forces

Evacuees were not the only people for whom accommodation had to be found in Winchcombe. Various army units underwent training in the district. Among the first to arrive, in October 1939, was a territorial artillery unit from Northumberland.[7] They were billeted in several places, including the malthouse at the Corner Cupboard inn, the workhouse hospital, and the Congregational Union schoolroom and manse at the southern end of Gretton Road. Eventually, a purpose-built military camp was established in the Sudeley castle grounds for various army units in training between 1940 and 1942.

Much later in the war, during the months leading to D-day in June 1944, United States troops were accommodated at Toddington manor, as part of the huge invasion and supply forces being assembled for the Normandy landings.[8]

Accommodation for prisoners of war

As the Allied forces captured prisoners of war, or accepted their surrender, accommodation had to be found for them. From about 1942 onwards, a prisoner of war camp capable of accommodating up to 400 prisoners was established in the Sudeley castle grounds, commanded by major Bromley, a serving army officer. Among the first to arrive were Italians captured in North Africa who are remembered for their beautiful decoration of a nissen hut's interior to provide a chapel.[9] Later arrivals included Austrians and Germans. The prisoners of war were guarded by a British army company who also had to organise working parties for them. The main source of work was on agricultural land throughout the district, where farmers urgently needed every able-bodied person to help increase food production. Some prisoners of war were sufficiently trustworthy to be accommodated with farming families.[10] One German prisoner was so reliable that he was allowed to help Arthur Barnes (who had evacuated his family to Winchcombe from West Bromwich) with showing films at the Old Tanneries cinema.[11] And the German prisoners were sufficiently enthusiastic to form an association football team that was permitted to play against local teams on king George's field.[12]

Winchcombe district invasion committee

The War Office was responsible for establishing invasion committees throughout the country whose job was to co-ordinate all the resources of people and equipment that could be provided locally to deal with an enemy invasion. In the north Cotswolds separate invasion committees were set up for Southam, Hawling, Alderton and the Washbournes, Toddington, and Stanway, Didbrook and Hailes, as well as Winchcombe.

The Winchcombe district invasion committee comprised eight regular members, with Dr. J. Spiridion (living at Irwell, Abbey Terrace – now Lloyds-TSB premises) as chairman and Amos Hall (of 23 Gloucester Street) as vice-chairman. The other regular members were police sergeant C. Francis, lieutenant S. C. Watson of the Home Guard, major Bromley, A. Leslie-Smith from the special constabulary (living at Wadfield House), and the town's two food officers, Charles Bentley and Alfred Gilbert (who had a grocery business in North Street). The committee could also call on some fifteen co-opted members, including Mrs. A. Lishman as billeting officer, Eleanor Adlard as W.V.S. representative, and Arthur Hall as fire service captain.

The committee's main administrative task was to prepare an extremely detailed, eighteen-page 'war book' stating the nature of the anticipated emergency and the resources available to deal with it. This war book gives the committee's purpose as 'maintenance of normal life and communications as far as possible, in view of the large number of factory workers who live in the district'. A possible attack was envisaged by way of airborne invasion or bombing; and, in either event, the prisoner of war camp at Sudeley was identified as a 'vulnerable point'. As already mentioned, the town was divided into seven administrative areas, each with its own civil defence warden, fire guard street captain and 'senior housewife'. Mrs. W. White, wife of the Wesleyan Methodist minister, Wilfred White, was appointed Winchcombe's 'head housewife'. Effective communications were to be maintained by means of motor cyclists, cyclists, two police patrol cars and some six horse riders who were thought likely to be very useful 'over the rough hilly country'. Seven members of the Girls Training Corps, including Dorothy Shekell (as she then was) of West End Stores, are listed as having been trained for carrying messages. Public information would be given on official notice boards, under the committee's control, at six separate places in the town; and the town crier was 'one means of conveying various instructions to the public'.

A serious deficiency the committee identified was any effective shelter from air raids. They inspected various cellars in the town but concluded that none was suitable as an air raid shelter. Slit trenches were therefore considered the only suitable form of shelter for Winchcombe's population and it was left to major Bromley and lieu-tenant Watson to identify sites for this purpose. Emergency food supplies were highly organised by Charles Bentley and Alfred Gilbert, with a food dump located behind Charles Greening's house in Gretton Road containing twenty tons of tinned foods in fifteen-pound packages. Emergency cooking facilities were to be available at five sites, including the workhouse and the town's flour mill (which continued to operate throughout the war) in Mill Lane; and Eleanor Adlard was put in charge of thirteen emergency cooks. Water supplies did not especially concern the committee because 'Winchcombe is particularly well supplied with sources of additional water and it is difficult to visualise circumstances in which the whole town would be without a water supply'. Nevertheless, arrangements were included for nineteen local owners of various lorries, vans and farm trailers to make them available for hauling emergency water supplies in fifty-gallon cisterns from springs at Sudeley, Postlip and Greet.

The available casualty services were severely limited, comprising thirty beds at Winchcombe hospital, thirty more at the boys' home and thirty-five at Postlip Hall, with first-aid posts in Chandos Street, Wesley Cafe (as it then was) in High Street, and the nursery school in Back Lane. The war book ended with an unavoidably macabre section entitled 'burial of the dead'. Common graves would be provided in the existing cemetery in Greet Road and on land on the opposite side of the road 'already earmarked for extension of the present cemetery'. Presuming that the Home Guard would deal effectively with any invaders, this section includes the statement: 'These sites are sufficient to cope with large quantities of enemy dead.'[13]

Mercifully, although Cheltenham experienced a serious air raid on the night of 11 December 1940 and members of the Royal Observer Corps' local unit on Cleeve hill could watch enemy aircraft flying on bombing missions to Birmingham, Coventry and other targets in the Midlands, Winchcombe was spared this experience. The invasion committee's thoroughly prepared plans were not tested in the heat of action, although they were probably tried out in mock raids. By autumn 1944 the War Office decided that invasion committees were no longer needed; and the Winchcombe war book became an historical record of the town's resources of people and equipment in the early 1940s.

Digging for victory

Unlike the 1914-1918 war, food rationing was introduced early in the Second World War, although the system that took effect in January 1940 relied at first as much on administration by retailers as on ration books with coupons. Arthur Shekell's memoirs provide some insight into the ingenious expedients used at West End Stores, and no doubt elsewhere, in attempts to overcome scarcity of grocery items without breaching the regulations.

The inevitable reduction in imported food supplies meant that all available agricultural land had to be brought quickly under cultivation. The Gloucestershire war agricultural executive committee was set up to organise farming activity throughout the county. As the majority of able-bodied men were needed in the armed forces, or for essential work in munitions and engineering factories, women had to be recruited urgently as farm workers. This need was met by forming the Women's Land Army, which consisted mainly of young women from towns and cities without previous experience of agricultural work. It was left mainly to local farmers to train them in what for many was a harsh regime of manual toil in all weathers. The women, in their distinctive uniform of green pullover and khaki breeches, soon became familiar figures at work on farms in the district.

The war's casualties

The Second World War did not involve the mass slaughter of young men in trench warfare for which the 1914-1918 war will always be remembered. And death also came randomly to civilians. Nevertheless, the suffering experienced by the families of members of the armed forces who were killed, or reported missing and presumed dead, was no less hard to bear than in the earlier conflict. The first person from Winchcombe to be killed on active service, in the Royal Air Force, was M. R. Forty, son of the prominent Methodist and Greet farmer Charles Forty.[14] By the end of the war nineteen men from Winchcombe, whose names were subsequently inscribed on the town's war memorial, had given their lives.

The war ends

Germany surrendered unconditionally to the Allies on all fronts in Europe on 7 May 1945. VE-day (Victory in Europe) was celebrated in Britain on 8 May. The war in the Far East continued until the Japanese surrender on 2 September 1945.

Demobilisation took place more slowly than after the 1914-1918 war, particularly of forces serving in Germany, some of whom became part of an army of occupation. In Winchcombe Charles Forty had taken the lead in establishing the Winchcombe Fighting Forces Home-coming Gift Fund and was chairman of the Fund's committee. It was not until 27 July 1946 that arrangements could be made for distribution of the Fund's proceeds to 122 men and women who had by then returned to Winchcombe. (Another 100 or so were still on duty.) The ceremony was held at the assembly rooms in Abbey Terrace where Charles Forty himself spoke with understandable emotion of those who would not return, but would be remembered with love, grief, pride and gratitude; and a cheque was presented individually to each recipient as he read out their names. In response, Sharman Mason proposed a vote of thanks to the Fund's committee, saying: 'We cannot say or think enough for what Winchcombe has done for us'. After the ceremony a concert was held in the evening, with entertainment provided mainly by returning members of the armed forces, during which Sharman Mason recited a stirring poem he had composed entitled 'England stood alone'.[15]

Post-war reconstruction

Although Winchcombe did not have to undertake the immense task of post-war reconstruction many British towns and cities faced, total concentration on the war effort during the previous six years had left many routine tasks of repair or rebuilding undone. In an atmosphere of continuing austerity some of these arrears were tackled by public authorities and private individuals. During 1946 Cheltenham rural district council began to develop municipal housing in Barnmeadow Road, on what was then a green field site. The first occupiers were able to move into the newly built houses late in 1946 and early in 1947; and housebuilding continued on this estate during 1947.

August bank holiday in 1946 (then held on the first Monday in August) saw an attempt to forget post-war austerity, for one day, with a fete in the grounds of Sudeley castle relying on contributions from many of Winchcombe's numerous organisations. The fete's aim was to raise money for two purposes. The first was to make a contribution to the fund of £1 million then being set up by the Soldiers', Sailors' and Airmen's Families' Association. The second was a familiar Winchcombe cause: to contribute to the sum of £3,000 then required to repair the parish church's roof. The fete began with a fancy dress parade from Abbey Terrace to the castle's grounds in what *The Evesham Journal's* reporter described as 'real garden party weather'. The fete was opened by the Duchess of Beaufort, who was thanked by the local Member of Parliament, W. S. Morrison (many years later to become Speaker of the House of Commons). The occasion was a great success: it was estimated that about 3,000 people attended and the ladies of the parochial church council accomplished the difficult task of serving teas for about 2,500 of them. The fancy dress competitions were judged by Lady Victoria Forester and Lady Hambro.[16]

As well as expressing a desire to help service families and to maintain the town's most important building, the fete's organisers were perhaps looking back nostalgically to the hierarchical society characteristic of Winchcombe at the outbreak of the 1914-1918 war and hoping to sustain it. But one result of the Second World War was that temporary incomers and returning servicemen helped to change the traditional hierarchy and to question some of its values. Winchcombe's old order was passing away.

1   A. J. P. Taylor: 'English History, 1914-1945', The Oxford History of England, 1965, pages 451-452

2   F. C. Adey: 'A Cotswold Methodist Heritage', 1979, page 73

3   F. C. Adey, op cit, page 73

4   Eugene Likeman in *The Gloucestershire Echo*, 16 November 1999

5   *Cheltenham Chronicle and Gloucestershire Graphic*, 9 August 1941

6   F. C. Adey, op cit, page 77

7   The Memoirs of Arthur Shekell, 1903-1980

8   F. C. Adey, op cit, page 78

9   D. H. Aldred: 'Around Bishop's Cleeve and Winchcombe in Old Photographs', Budding Books, 2000, page 152

10   F. C. Adey, op cit, page 78

11   Peter Gill: 'North Gloucestershire at War', Alan Sutton, 1995, page 30

12   Peter Gill, op cit, page 66

13   Winchcombe District Invasion Committee War Book, archived in Winchcombe Museum (GRO, P368a PC4)

14   F. C. Adey, op cit, page 77

15   *The Evesham Journal*, 3 August 1946

16   *The Evesham Journal*, 10 August 1946

CHAPTER 30

WINCHCOMBE'S PAST FIFTY YEARS

This concluding chapter attempts to give some account of Winchcombe's recent history, from about 1950 to the close of the twentieth century. To avoid a chronological recital of events some people living in the town can readily recall, the account selects themes intended to bring the immediate past into sharper focus. And, to ensure that possibly invidious references to individuals are excluded, no living person is mentioned.

The spreading common culture

Perhaps the most obvious contrast between the modern age and Winchcombe's experience before 1950 is the increasing dominance of a common culture. Two main factors combine to produce this effect.

First, the rapid growth in means of communication and personal mobility has meant that what is distinctive to Winchcombe, or the north Cotswold district, is now harder to identify. The information media and the entertainment business cater for a mass audience, so that what informs and amuses people in Wigan or Wimborne differs little from Winchcombe. These influences are so pervasive that even the local dialect which so enriched the speech of earlier generations is no longer used by most children born and brought up in the town. The common culture's dominance has been hastened by the arrival of a substantial proportion of the current population who are not native to Winchcombe. The morris dancers make a brave effort on May Day to keep alive their tradition, but the future belongs to the Winchcombe 'twirlers'. And a Winchcombe family's day out is quite likely to involve a car journey to some event or place elsewhere.

Secondly, the development of the welfare state since the post-war foundations were laid in 1948 has resulted in hitherto unimagined centralisation in providing services from which everyone wishes to benefit. Unrelenting pressure for access to equal standards of provision in social security benefits, medical care and education for all citizens has led central government (of whatever political persuasion) to introduce legislative and administrative systems which inevitably remove many previously local and traditional differences. Consequently, people nation-wide expect to pay largely equalised levels of taxation and, in return, obtain universally applicable benefits. This expectation is now so commonplace that it is easy to overlook how recent it is.

Population increase

The population of Winchcombe and Sudeley parishes in 1951 was 3,026. There was a small increase to 3,187 by 1961. However, by 1971, the population had reached 4,190; and the increase continued more slowly, to 4,780 in 1991. The present total is probably about 5,000 (not including Gretton).

Much of this population increase was made possible by speculative residential development permitted on both sides of Greet Road, between Greet Road and Gretton Road, on the Kyderminster and Rathmore estates on the western side of Gretton Road, and at The Hyde on the north-western side of Cheltenham Road. As well as enabling newcomers to live in Winchcombe, this housing has considerably altered the town's character and appearance.

A significant feature of the current population is that about forty per cent is over retirement pension age. Some retired people have specifically chosen the town as their retirement home, which has clearly influenced the type of housing built on some of the residential estates.

Probably about one-third of the working population earn their living in the town and its immediate vicinity. Another one-third work in and around Cheltenham; and the rest are in work elsewhere in the county or further afield. In summary, for about two-thirds of Winchcombe's currently employed population, the town is a dormitory for daily commuters.

Vehicles and highways

Perhaps the greatest environmental change, in comparison with the pre-war years, is the availability of personal transport. The ability to travel at will from home to virtually any destination by car, provided it can be afforded, has transformed most people's lives and changed the town's character. The sense of rural remoteness has disappeared almost entirely. Instead, the traffic congestion experienced in the comparatively narrow medieval streets in the town's core is sometimes overwhelming.

Various suggested remedies for the town's traffic problems have been canvassed during the last forty years, including the construction of a by-pass (for which a possible line was identified from near the foot of Corndean Lane to north of Footbridge in the 1960s), the imposition of a partial one-way system, more restricted on-street vehicle parking, additional traffic-calming measures, and stricter or better enforced speed limits. However, no compromise which would enable private and commercial vehicle use to be reasonably limited in the interests of those who live and work in the town's core area has yet proved acceptable.

The highway authority's approach has seemingly concentrated on ways to improve the flow of traffic. An example is the bridge over the river Isbourne, at Footbridge, completed in April 1984, to replace the narrower, humped bridge built in 1899. One result of widening the carriageway is to increase the traffic speed at this potentially hazardous point.

Public transport

The railway's late arrival in Winchcombe was followed by its early departure. On 7 March 1960 the local passenger service between Honeybourne and Cheltenham ceased. The line through Winchcombe remained in use for some freight and parcel services. When a coal train's derailment damaged the track near Greet in August 1976 the cost of repairs was considered excessive and the Cheltenham to Honeybourne line was officially closed on 1 November 1976.[1] The Gloucestershire Warwickshire Railway Society was formed in 1976, becoming a company in 1981. Its long-term objective is to restore the rail link between Cheltenham and Stratford-upon-Avon. By August 1987 passenger-carrying steam trains were operating between Toddington and Winchcombe stations; and the line was subsequently reopened as far as Gotherington. At the end of 2000, volunteers had succeeded in laying track as far as Cheltenham's racecourse station, creating a ten-mile stretch of railway from Toddington. Although the declared aim is to open this line to passengers by March 2003, it seems unlikely to progress from a very successful tourist attraction to a passenger-carrying service.

Winchcombe has a reliable bus service to Broadway and Cheltenham during normal working hours, provided by a company operating comfortable and well-maintained vehicles from its base in Greet Road. But, because personal convenience is usually the decisive factor in people's choice of travel and there is insufficient demand for a late-evening service to and from Cheltenham or any other destination, the bus is unlikely to displace the private car as the usual means of transport for those who can afford it.

Formal education

The post-war development of publicly provided education in Winchcombe followed from the Education Act of 1944, although it was some time before the Act's provisions were fully implemented.

In 1952 infants' education in the school at the western end of Back Lane, which had been established there in 1911, ceased and Winchcombe's infants were moved to the girls' school in Dent's national school building (immediately to the west of the parish church). The girls' school moved simultaneously to the premises in Back Lane vacated by the infants. The re-organised infants' school was known as Winchcombe Church of England infants' school. By the early-1960s the condition of the school buildings and facilities seriously concerned teachers and parents. The local education authority proposed that either the infants' and junior schools should be merged on one site, or the infants should be transferred to the boys' school at the southern end of Gretton Road (the building now used by Winchcombe youth club). As neither proposal proved acceptable to parents, the decision was taken to continue infants' education in Dent's national school building and improve its facilities. Some modernisation and provision of additional prefabricated classrooms took place in 1963, 1967, 1973 and 1974. The centenary of the original building's use as a school was celebrated in 1968, when some 300 parents and visitors were able to see a recreation of school life in the Victorian age. During the 1970s the school catered for some 160 infants.[2]

By the mid-1980s it had become clear that the infants' school building and facilities no longer met current expectations and modernisation would have been too costly. It was therefore decided to provide an entirely new, purpose-built infants' school on the site towards the eastern end of Back Lane, adjacent to Winchcombe library. Despite the use of reconstituted stone, the new school building is attractively designed and generally regarded as an asset to the town's building stock. When it was opened in 1988, Dent's national school ceased educational use and was subsequently converted to a number of residential units without appreciable harm to the building's structure or appearance.

To fulfil one of the purposes of the Education Act 1944, the removal of the girls' school from Dent's national school building in April 1952 was accompanied by a division by age between secondary and primary pupils, at both the girls' school and the boys' school in Gretton Road. This division enabled the former infants' school at the western end of Back Lane to become a secondary school and the building in Gretton road to be used as a junior school, both catering for girls and boys. At its inception in April 1952, 118 pupils attended this reorganised junior school; and by 1958 it was teaching over 170 children.[3]

The mixed secondary school in the Back Lane premises opened with 120 pupils in 1952, but the numbers increased before long to about 200. For a time the school's staff coped heroically with overcrowded premises and comparatively poor facilities, despite the addition of temporary classrooms.[4]

1962 saw a further reorganisation of Winchcombe's junior and secondary education, following the local education authority's decision to provide a new, purpose-built county secondary school, designed by the county architect, on what was then a green field site on the eastern side of Greet Road. The opening of this school enabled children of secondary age (up to fifteen, which was then the school-leaving age) to be transferred to it; and the building they vacated in Back Lane was occupied from October 1962 by the junior school pupils, who moved from the original boys' school premises in Gretton Road. By the mid-1970s some 300 pupils were attending the new secondary school. Both the secondary and junior schools were strongly supported by parents, whose efforts – with those of the teaching staff – enabled the facilities to be improved. In 1974, following an important archaeological investigation of the town's Saxon defences in what was then the junior school's playground, the education authority completed a new building on the site to provide two further classrooms, a library and cloakrooms.

By the late-1970s the reduction in the number of children of secondary school age in the Winchcombe district prompted the education authority to canvass proposals for the reorganisation of secondary education which seemed likely to result in closing Winchcombe's secondary school. These proposals caused immense concern, on account both of the school's prospective closure (which would have resulted in most children of secondary school age travelling daily to schools in Cheltenham) and the loss of an important facility. Concerned parents sought to persuade the education authority that secondary education should continue in the town. Eventually, this view prevailed and the secondary school was re-constituted on comprehensive lines as Winchcombe school and community centre in October 1981.

By the late-1990s it became clear that, with more than a hundred unfilled places in the two separate schools, Winchcombe's junior and infants' schools were under-subscribed. The education authority's proposal, in conjunction with Gloucester diocesan education board, was to merge the two schools in extended buildings on the infants' school site. After some initial misgivings, this proposal gained support in the town and a building programme, costing some £660,000, was approved to provide additional buildings and facilities, including five new classrooms for the merged school, capable of accommodating 259 pupils. Winchcombe Abbey Church of England junior school opened in September 2000, with about 220 children. The long-term future of the former junior school building, on the archaeologically important site at the western end of Back Lane, remains to be settled.

Winchcombe's fabric

Excepting a handful of properties (for example, Great House and The Follies), most privately owned dwellings in the town's core are not architecturally notable. Nevertheless, when groups of houses are viewed as an ensemble, they are often seen to possess a harmonious relationship in which stone-built facades (sometimes added to a considerably older structure) play a major part. In Gloucester Street and Hailes Street in particular, the comparatively narrow carriageway and pavements strengthen the sense of enclosure resulting from continuously terraced properties on either side. This harmonious relationship relies heavily on every occupier's good residential manners.

During the last fifty years remarkably few important buildings have been demolished. The most serious loss was undoubtedly the town's flour mill at the foot of Mill Lane. Described in 1933 as 'one of England's oldest working flour mills, still grinding corn by the old stone method', some of the structure was probably medieval.[5] Unhappily, the rot appears to have set in during the Second World War when the urgent need to increase production meant that a prefabricated upper storey was added. Although flour production continued throughout the war, alongside a flourishing bakery, the building was used as a warehouse during the 1960s when its condition gradually deteriorated. It was eventually demolished in 1973. This was not simply the loss of a treasured building: with it went the mill pond and mill race which had for centuries harnessed the river Isbourne's power to useful industry in tranquil surroundings. The mill building and its setting are illustrated in the photographs at Plates 19 and 20. The other serious loss was the demolition, in the 1960s, of the former Chandos grammar school, otherwise known as The Presbytery, which seems to have become uneconomic to refurbish.

Winchcombe's main public buildings have fared reasonably well in the recent past. As already mentioned in Chapter 22, some £148,000 was spent on refurbishing the

Plate 19

town hall in 1999; the parish church's roof was substantially repaired, between July 1999 and February 2000, at a cost of £189,000; and the Methodist church's interior was completely refurbished in late-1999 for some £160,000.

A change in the use of a treasured building may also seriously threaten its integrity. An example of what may happen, unless extreme care is taken, is provided by the George inn (as it was until May 1988) at The Cross. When the property was acquired, in December 1988, by a residential development company based in Cork, Republic of Ireland, there was concern about possible harm from any scheme for converting the former pilgrims' hostel and the adjacent building on this site at the town's heart. In the event, collaboration between an architectural partnership in Cheltenham, the City of Hereford Archaeology Unit, and a representative of English Heritage produced an analytical survey of the building, leading into a proposal for one shop and fourteen housing units (seven of which were to be virtually new buildings on the steeply sloping site at the back of The George). Tewkesbury borough council (as local planning authority) granted planning permission for this scheme in June 1989.[6] While the architectural purist may regret the developer's choice of rendered elevations, rather than building stone, for the new, three-storey dwellings at the back of the site, the general reaction to the whole scheme was probably relief that much of the inn's historic fabric had been retained and the High Street facade and inner courtyard (especially the rebuilt pilgrims' gallery of 1884) were largely unaltered.

The survival of well-built, Victorian public buildings no longer needed for their original purpose has created a dilemma in many towns during the past fifty years. While nobody would regret that Winchcombe's workhouse ceased to fulfil its original

Plate 20

purpose and became, first, a boys' home administered by Gloucestershire county council's public assistance department and, subsequently, premises for a youth centre, the demolition in the 1950s of what was still externally a solid, stone-built structure may have been over-hasty. However, a compensating factor was that municipal ownership of the former workhouse site enabled purpose-built dwellings for elderly people to be provided on part of it, commonly called Barksdale. These dwellings at Langley Close have now been transferred to Severn Vale Housing Society Limited.

Numerous buildings in the town's core have been statutorily listed as buildings 'of special architectural or historic interest'. This procedure is inevitably imperfect. The omission of some treasured buildings is questionable: the parish hall in Cowl Lane is perhaps one example. Although the regime of listed building control is intended to prevent unsympathetic or harmful development of buildings to which it applies, whether that intention is realised in practice depends principally on two factors, namely an owner's sensibility to the effects of modifying or altering a building's struc-ture (including the interior) and the local planning authority's vigilance in administering the regime. And, even when an owner wishes to ensure that a building's architectural integrity is maintained, the cost and availability of suitable materials (for example, Stonesfield slates) and skilled craftsmen may compel the adop-tion of a second-best scheme.

Virtually the whole of what can justifiably be regarded as the town's historic core was statutorily designated, by Gloucestershire county council, on 19 March 1971, as a conservation area. Since the major reorganisation of local government on 1 April

1974 it has been Tewkesbury borough council's responsibility to pursue the aims of this designation, namely to preserve or enhance the character or appearance of the area. The south-eastern boundary of the conservation area may seem unusual, and even arbitrarily chosen, in following the line of the previously proposed Winchcombe by-pass from the foot of Corndean Lane in the west to Footbridge on the Broadway Road in the east. But, although the construction of any by-pass for the town now seems improbable, the choice of this line is persuasively (if somewhat bureaucratically) explained in the county council's original statement of planning policies for the conservation area, as follows:

'Proposals to develop open areas and significant natural features forming an essential part of the character of an area will not normally be permitted. This applies particularly to the fields lying between the river Isbourne and the line of the proposed by-pass to the south of the town, which should remain open in order to preserve the setting of the ancient town. From these fields, and in the future from the by-pass, the town appears to be set on a platform which stands out from the gently sloping sides of the valley with the high ground of Langley hill beyond forming the background.'[7]

With the advantage of hindsight, the statement's author might now add that the experience of numerous towns, during the last forty years, has been that the line of a by-pass, when built, effectively becomes the boundary of residential development, thus creating inexorable pressure to permit such development over much of the intervening (often green-field) area.

An undervalued component of Winchcombe's fabric is its shop-fronts. As numerous shops and ground-floor business premises are in former houses, the potential for spoiling the original building's architectural unity is considerable. Serious disruption of an existing facade can also result from ripping out a carefully proportioned shop-front and substituting an excessively large area of glass or synthetic materials. Shop owners and customers can together achieve worthwhile compromise. Shops, restaurants, cafés and public houses contribute significantly to the sense of vitality in the town's core. The hackneyed phrase 'use it or lose it' contains a salutary warning. Shopkeepers and other commercial providers need regular customers in order to survive; and reliance on a strong customer base generally lessens the need for aggressive external advertisement and loud self-promotion. By regularly shopping elsewhere for items readily obtainable in the town, Winchcombe's residents effectively threaten part of the community's well-being.

Winchcombe's surroundings

Residents and visitors admire Winchcombe as a Cotswold borough in its scenically exquisite setting. H. J. Massingham described it memorably in 1938 when he wrote: ' ... Langley [Hill] to the west, Corndean on the south, Salter's Hill and Sudeley to the north and east. The arc of hills holds this most venerable of towns as in a cup of its hand ... '[8] This beauty is fragile. With the intention of helping to safeguard it, some 582 square miles of the Cotswolds were designated in August 1966 as an area of outstanding natural beauty. In Winchcombe's vicinity the designated area's boundary is the western side of Gretton Road, as far south as Delavale Road, and the eastern side of Broadway Road as far south as Footbridge, so that the town's historic core is included within the designation. By themselves, boundary lines drawn on a map may please a bureaucrat's tidy mind and no more. Of greater importance are the effectiveness of rural planning policies aimed at fulfilling a countryside designation's purpose and the local planning authority's decisions in dealing with proposals for development in the designated area. And, no matter how diligent the planning authority may be, the decisive factor is usually the individual landowner's commitment to conserving treasured landscape by sympathetic management.

It may seem unusual, possibly even unjustified, to include much of Winchcombe's historic core within the Cotswolds area of outstanding natural beauty. But the justification is evident. As John Leland recognised in the mid-sixteenth century, the town's roots are in the Cotswolds, not in the Vale. Despite the late-twentieth-century residential development, agricultural land still impinges closely on the urbanised area and farming enterprise continues vigorously to its edge in some places. Winchcombe is thus indissolubly linked to its surroundings, so that landscape and townscape can be experienced as an organic whole.

Local government

During almost thirty years following the end of the Second World War, Winchcombe relied on Gloucestershire county council and Cheltenham rural district council for local government services. Winchcombe parish council remained in being with a reduced role. On 1 April 1974, major local government reorganisation took effect throughout England, in accordance with complex provisions in the Local Government Act 1972. One result of the revised scheme was the abolition of the previous urban district and rural district councils. The administrative fashion of the time favoured larger 'units of government' which were claimed to provide 'economies of scale' in delivering local government services.

The result of this reorganisation in the north-east Cotswolds was to transfer the parish of Winchcombe and some neighbouring parishes into the administrative area of the newly-created Tewkesbury borough council. Although it has since been slightly reduced, this new council's territory was initially very extensive and situated mainly in the Severn Vale. The reorganisation of 1974 also provided for Gloucestershire county council to continue in being for county-wide services, such as highways, education, social services, libraries and, within the planning system, a new feature known as the structure plan for the entire county. In Winchcombe the parish council continued to provide the same local services, but now re-titled Winchcombe town council.

The rationale for Winchcombe's inclusion in Tewkesbury borough council's area remains debatable. Tewkesbury itself is awkwardly situated in the north-western corner of the council's administrative area, in a direction to which the majority of Winchcombe's inhabitants do not naturally look for work, schools or colleges, and entertainment. And, however resolutely Winchcombe's representatives may strive to pursue the town's interests within the borough council's decision-making processes, they are in a minority of three. One especially notable result of Winchcombe's inclusion in Tewkesbury's administrative area is to be seen in the housing allocations (that is, new housebuilding provision) derived from the structure and local plan processes. Because the structure plan places the emphasis upon new housebuilding in the Severn Vale, where much of the borough council's area is, Winchcombe is consequently expected to bear some proportion of the total housing allocation in the local plan, although the town has no natural affinity with settlements in the Vale. Winchcombe is thus subjected to what some residents regard as excessive pressure, through the local planning process, to meet externally generated housing targets, usually involving new housebuilding on green-field sites.

While Winchcombe town council works hard to uphold and further the town's best interests, its role is advisory in many issues. Although not unique to Winchcombe, the lack of decision-making responsibility for vital matters affecting the community's well-being has compelled this tier of local government to function at times as a pressure group. Nevertheless, in comparatively minor environmental matters, for example tree-planting and improving footpaths, the town council has made a worthwhile contribution. Another example is the recent installation in Abbey Terrace of attractively designed and well-proportioned lamp standards and lamps.

Perhaps the greatest irony in Winchcombe's local government arrangements as the twentieth century closes is that, although the town's residents are better educated, wealthier and more concerned about their community's well-being than ever before, the individual's scope for participating in, and directly influencing, local government decision-making is less than at any time during the last hundred years.

A community of many talents

For centuries Winchcombe's geographical isolation helped to make its inhabitants self-reliant and compelled them to seek their own pastimes. Despite widespread access to ready-made entertainment, one of the most striking features of Winchcombe's past fifty years is the development of an enormous range of clubs, societies, associations and groups which enable individuals to participate actively in community activities and provide opportunities for personal creativity. To list these organisations would be tedious and, worse still, risk omitting one of them. It suffices to say that they cater for all manner of cultural, social, spiritual, charitable and sports activities which help to enrich the community's life.

There is also a healthy, but not overbearing, sense of self-esteem in Winchcombe. It shows itself in public recognition that the town is a place to treasure as well as to inhabit. Two examples demonstrate the practical result. In 1928, Eleanor Adlard was a guiding spirit in setting up a small collection illustrating various aspects of Winchcombe's past, painstakingly assembled in what was then known as the church porch room museum (because the priest's room above the parish church's south porch was used to accommodate the museum). The collection subsequently fell into disuse and some of it was unfortunately dispersed. Happily, the 1990s saw a welcome revival with the development of the Winchcombe folk and police museum in the town hall's upper rooms. The museum now gives residents and visitors some historical insight into the town's past; and artefacts, photographs and documents are being left in its safe keeping for the benefit of future generations. And finally, at the close of the second millennium, the Winchcombe Project Group (2000) produced the celebratory volume entitled 'Winchcombe, our home – our heritage', enabling numerous people in the town to show their heartfelt appreciation of its place in their lives.

1   Colin Maggs and Peter Nicholson: 'The Honeybourne Line', Line One Publishing Ltd., 1985, pages 18-19
2   Winchcombe silver jubilee souvenir booklet 1977, pages 55-57
3   Winchcombe silver jubilee souvenir booklet 1977, page 59
4   Winchcombe silver jubilee souvenir booklet 1977, page 80
5   *Cheltenham Chronicle and Gloucestershire Graphic*, 1 April 1933
6   James Ayres: 'More Room at the Inn', Architects' Journal, 23 October 1991, pages 34-43
7   Tewkesbury borough council (as successor authority): statement entitled 'Winchcombe Conservation Area', August 1979
8   H. J. Massingham: 'Shepherd's Country', page 170

Plans

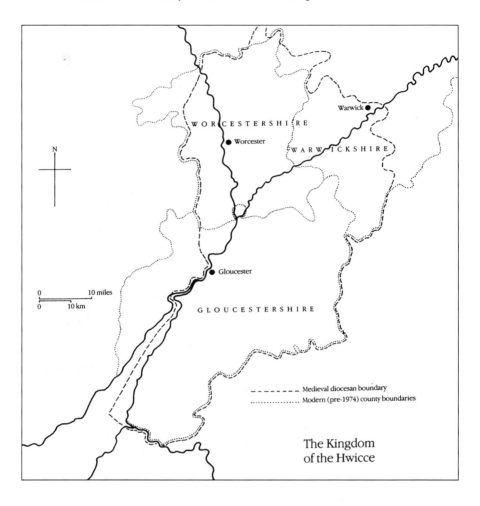

Warwick ●

W O R C E S T E R S H I R E

● Worcester

W A R W I C K S H I R E

N

0   10 miles

0   10 km

● Gloucester

G L O U C E S T E R S H I R E

– – – – – – – Medieval diocesan boundary
. . . . Modern (pre-1974) county boundaries

The Kingdom
of the Hwicce

Plan 1

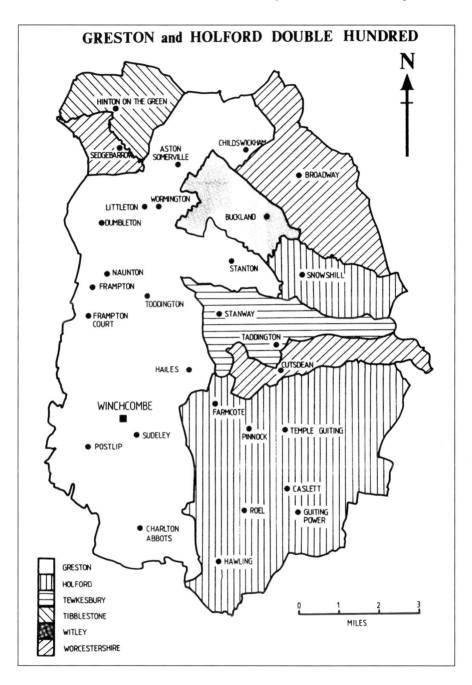

GRESTON and HOLFORD DOUBLE HUNDRED

N

HINTON ON THE GREEN

CHILDSWICKHAM

SEDGEBARROW

ASTON SOMERVILLE

BROADWAY

WORMINGTON

LITTLETON

BUCKLAND

DUMBLETON

NAUNTON

STANTON

SNOWSHILL

FRAMPTON

TODDINGTON

FRAMPTON COURT

STANWAY

TADDINGTON

CUTSDEAN

HAILES

WINCHCOMBE

FARMCOTE

PINNOCK

TEMPLE GUITING

SUDELEY

POSTLIP

CASLETT

ROEL

GUITING POWER

CHARLTON ABBOTS

HAWLING

GRESTON
HOLFORD
TEWKESBURY
TIBBLESTONE
WITLEY
WORCESTERSHIRE

0   1   2   3
MILES

Plan 2

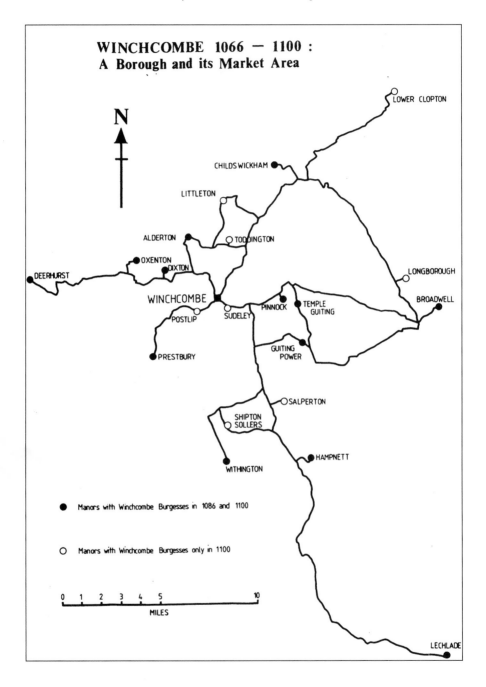

WINCHCOMBE 1066 — 1100 :
A Borough and its Market Area

N

LOWER CLOPTON

CHILDS WICKHAM

LITTLETON

ALDERTON

TODDINGTON

OXENTON

DIXTON

DEERHURST

LONGBOROUGH

WINCHCOMBE

BROADWELL

POSTLIP

SUDELEY

PINNOCK

TEMPLE
GUITING

PRESTBURY

GUITING
POWER

SALPERTON

SHIPTON
SOLLERS

HAMPNETT

WITHINGTON

● Manors with Winchcombe Burgesses in 1086 and 1100

○ Manors with Winchcombe Burgesses only in 1100

0 1 2 3 4 5   10

MILES

LECHLADE

Plan 3

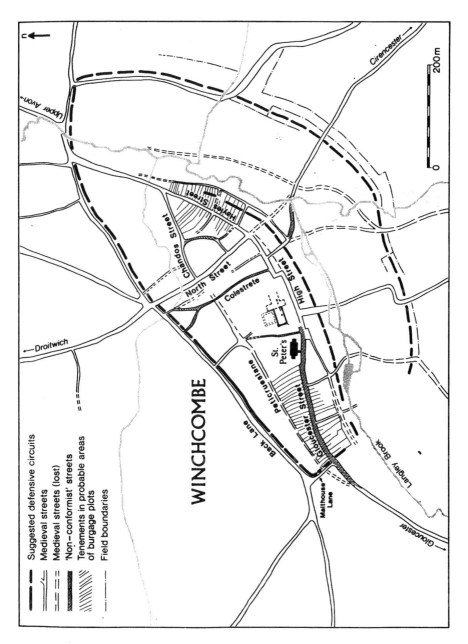

Late medieval Winchcombe, on the basis of archaeological, topographical and written evidence. Lengths of street (including Gloucester Street) which are shown as 'non-conformist' are those which appear to be secondary developments, running counter to a predominant, loosely rectilinear, street pattern

Plan 4

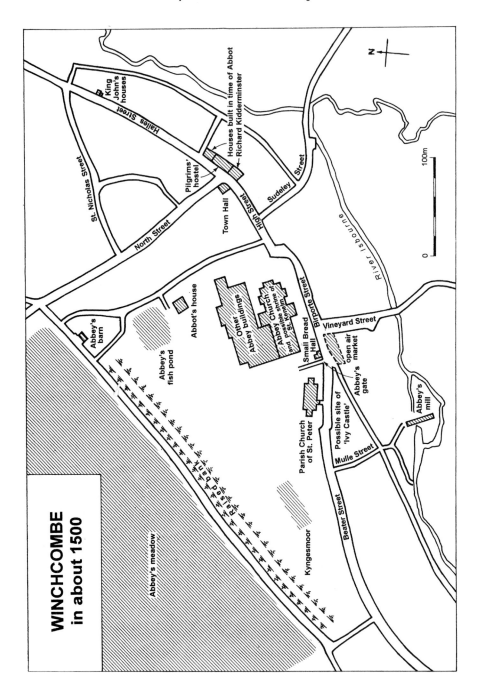

WINCHCOMBE in about 1500

King John's houses
Hailes Street
Houses built in time of Abbot Richard Kidderminster
Pilgrims' hostel
St. Nicholas Street
North Street
Town Hall
High Street
Sudeley Street
River Isbourne
100m
0
Abbey's barn
Abbot's house
Abbey's fish pond
Other Abbey buildings
Abbey Church of St. Kenelm and possible shrine of
Small Bread Hall
Birporte Street
Vineyard Street
open air market
Abbey's gate
Abbey's mill
Parish Church of St. Peter
Possible site of 'Ivy Castle'
Mulle Street
Beater Street
Abbey's meadow
River Isbourne
Kyngesmoor

Plan 5

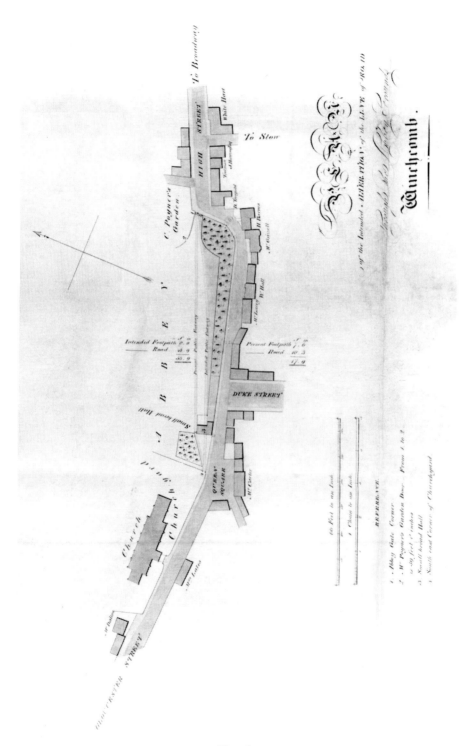

Plan 6

SELECT BIBLIOGRAPHY

Frank C. Adey: '*A Cotswold Methodist Heritage*', Winchcombe Methodist Church, 1979

Eleanor Adlard: '*Winchcombe Cavalcade*', E. J. Burrow, 1939

Eleanor Adlard: '*A Short History of the Postlip Mill*', Frederick Muller Ltd., 1949

David H. Aldred: '*Around Bishop's Cleeve and Winchcombe*', Alan Sutton, 1989

David H. Aldred: '*Bishop's Cleeve to Winchcombe in Old Photographs*', Alan Sutton, 1987

David H. Aldred: '*Cleeve Hill: The History of the Common and its People*', Alan Sutton, 1990

Alecto Historical Editions (editor-in-chief Dr. Ann Williams): '*The Gloucestershire Domesday*', 1989

J. T. Appleby: '*The Troubled Reign of King Stephen*', Bell, 1969

Sir Robert Atkyns: '*The Ancient and Present State of Gloucestershire*', 1712

W. St. Clair Baddeley: '*A Cotteswold Shrine*', John Bellows, 1908

S. R. Bassett: '*The administrative landscape of the diocese of Worcester in the tenth century*' in '*St Oswald of Worcester*', edited by Nicholas Brooks and Catherine Cubitt, Leicester University Press, 1996

S. R. Bassett: '*The origins and early development of Winchcombe and its district*', unpublished B. A. dissertation, University of Birmingham, January 1977

S. R. Bassett: '*In search of the origins of Anglo-Saxon kingdoms*' in '*The origins of Anglo-Saxon kingdoms*', edited by S. R. Bassett, Leicester University Press, 1989

S. R. Bassett: '*A Probable Mercian Royal Mausoleum at Winchcombe, Gloucestershire*', The Antiquaries Journal, Volume LXV, Part I, 1985

S. R. Bassett: '*Church and diocese in the West Midlands: the transition from British to Anglo-Saxon control*' in '*Pastoral Care Before the Parish*', edited by John Blair and Richard Sharpe, Leicester University Press, 1992

Ralph Bigland: '*Historical, Monumental and Genealogical Collections relative to the County of Gloucester*', edited by Brian Frith, BGAS, Part 4 (U-Y), 1995

Jean Bray: '*The Lady of Sudeley*', Long Barn Books, 2000

Edith Brill: '*Old Cotswold*', David & Charles, 1968

James Campbell (editor): '*The Anglo-Saxons*', Phaidon, 1982

O. G. S. Crawford: '*The Long Barrows of the Cotswolds*', John Bellows, 1925

R. R. Darlington: '*Winchcombe Annals 1049-1181*' in '*A Medieval Miscellany for D. M. Stenton*', edited by P. M. Barnes and C. F. Slade, The Pipe Roll Society, 1962

Timothy Darvill: '*Prehistoric Gloucestershire*', Alan Sutton, 1987 (County Library Series)

Emma Dent: '*Annals of Winchcombe and Sudeley*', John Murray, 1877

D. N. Donaldson: '*The Parish Church of St Peter, Winchcombe: a historical guide*', 1979

William Dreghorn: '*Geology Explained in the Severn Vale and Cotswolds*', David & Charles, 1967

C. C. Dyer: '*Lords and Peasants in a Changing Society: the Estates of the bishopric of Worcester, 680-1540*', Cambridge, 1980

H. P. R. Finberg: '*The Gloucestershire Landscape*', Hodder & Stoughton, 1955

H. P. R. Finberg (editor): '*Gloucestershire Studies*', Leicester University Press, 1957

Josceline Finberg: '*The Cotswolds*', Eyre Methuen, 1977

Peter Gill: '*North Gloucestershire at War*', Alan Sutton, 1995

L. V. Grinsell, C. E. Blunt and Michael Dolley: '*Sylloge of Coins of the British Isles – 19: Bristol and Gloucester Museums*', British Academy (Oxford), 1973

Gordon Haigh: '*The History of Winchcombe Abbey*', Skeffington and Son Ltd, 1947

Carolyn Heighway: '*Anglo-Saxon Gloucestershire*', Alan Sutton, 1987 (County Library Series)

Martin Henig: '*Roman Sculpture from the Cotswold Region*', British Academy (Oxford), 1993

R. H. Hilton: '*A Medieval Society*', Weidenfeld and Nicolson, 1966

Della Hooke: '*The Anglo-Saxon Landscape, the Kingdom of the Hwicce*', Manchester University Press, 1985

R. W. Hoyle (editor): '*The Military Survey of Gloucestershire, 1522*', BGAS, 1993

John Leland: '*Itinerary*', edited by Thomas Hearne, Oxford, 1769

W. Levison: '*England and the Continent in the Eighth Century*', Oxford, 1946

E. P. Loftus Brock: '*The Excavation of a Roman Villa in the Wadfield*', British Archaeological Association, 1895

C. M. MacInnes: '*The Early English Tobacco Trade*', Kegan Paul, 1926

Alan McWhirr: '*Roman Gloucestershire*', Alan Sutton, 1981 (County Library Series)

H. J. Massingham: '*Shepherd's Country*', Chapman and Hall, 1938

T. E. Meurig-Davies: '*A Handbook to Winchcombe Parish Church*', 1939

Celia Miller (editor): '*The Account Books of Thomas Smith, Ireley Farm, Hailes, Gloucestershire, 1865-71*', BGAS, 1985

J. S. Moore (editor and translator): '*Domesday Book: Gloucestershire*', Phillimore, 1982

J. S. Moore: '*The Sudeley and Toddington Area in Domesday Book*' in '*The Sudeleys – Lords of Toddington*', proceedings edited by Lord Sudeley, The Manorial Society of Great Britain, 1985

John Oakey: '*Reminiscences of Winchcombe, 1935*', privately printed, 1936

Nicholas Orme: '*Education in the West of England, 1066-1548*', University of Exeter Press, 1976

F. W. Potto Hicks: '*The Story of Winchcomb Abbey, Gloucestershire*', 1945

A. L. F. Rivet: '*Town and Country in Roman Britain*', Hutchinson, 1964

Royal Commission on Historical Monuments: '*Iron Age and Romano-British Monuments in the Gloucestershire Cotswolds*', HMSO, 1976

Samuel Rudder: '*A New History of Gloucestershire, 1779*', reprinted with introduction by N. M. Herbert, Alan Sutton, 1977

A. H. Smith: '*The Place-Names of Gloucestershire*', English Place-Name Society, especially Volume xxxix, Part Two, '*The North and West Cotswolds*', Cambridge, 1964

John Smith: '*Men & Armour for Gloucestershire in 1608*', republished by Alan Sutton, 1980

W. E. Tate: '*The Parish Chest*', Cambridge, 1946

Joan Thirsk: '*Projects for Gentlemen, Jobs for the Poor: Mutual Aid in the Vale of Tewkesbury, 1600-1630*' in '*Essays in Bristol and Gloucestershire History*', edited by P. McGrath and J. Cannon, BGAS, 1976

David Verey: '*Cotswold Churches*', Batsford, 1976

David Verey and Alan Brooks: '*The Buildings of England – Gloucestershire I: The Cotswolds*', Penguin Books, 1999

Victoria History of Gloucestershire, Volume II, edited by William Page, Oxford, 1907

A. R. Warmington: '*Civil War, Interregnum and Restoration in Gloucestershire, 1640-1672*', The Boydell Press, 1997

Ron Wheeler: '*Winchcombe Pottery: the Cardew-Finch tradition*', White Cockade Publishing, 1998

J. R. S. Whiting: '*Prison Reform in Gloucestershire, 1776-1820*', Phillimore, 1975

Julian Whybra: '*A Lost English County, Winchcombeshire in the Tenth and Eleventh Centuries*', The Boydell Press, 1990

The Winchcombe and Sudeley Record, January 1890 to December 1896, published by W. C. Belcher, Winchcombe

Doreen Winkless: '*Hailes: The Story of a Gloucestershire Abbey*', The Spredden Press, 1990

INDEX